Exchange Rates, Currency Crisis and Monetary Cooperation in Asia

Also by Ramkishen S. Rajan:

Authored / Co-authored:

SINGAPORE'S TRADE AND INVESTMENT PERFORMANCE AND POLICIES (with Shandre Thangavelu), 2009.

EXCHANGE RATE REGIMES, AND MACROECONOMIC MANAGEMENT IN ASIA (with Tony Cavoli), 2009.

ASIA IN THE GLOBAL ECONOMY: FINANCE, TRADE AND INVESTMENT (with Sunil Rongala), 2007.

ECONOMIC GLOBALIZATION AND ASIA: ESSAYS ON FINANCE, TRADE AND TAXATION, 2003.

SINGAPORE'S ATTRACTION TO FREE TRADE AREAS: BILATERAL TRADE RELATIONS WITH JAPAN AND THE US (with Rahul Sen and Reza Siregar), 2001.

Edited / Co-edited:

PRINCETON ENCYCLOPEDIA OF THE WORLD ECONOMY (with Kenneth Reinert as co-editor and Lewis Davis and Amy Glass as associate editors), 2008

MONETARY, EXCHANGE RATE AND FINANCIAL ISSUES AND POLICIES IN ASIA (with Shandre Thangavelu and Rasyad Parinduri), 2008.

INTRA ASIAN FDI FLOWS: MAGNITUDE, TRENDS, PROSPECTS AND POLICY IMPLICATIONS (with Rajiv Kumar and Nicola Virgill), 2008.

MANAGING GLOBALISATION: LESSONS FROM CHINA AND INDIA (with David Kelly and Gillian Goh), 2006.

SUSTAINING COMPETITIVENESS IN THE NEW GLOBAL ECONOMY: THE EXPERIENCE OF SINGAPORE, 2003.

Exchange Rates, Currency Crisis and Monetary Cooperation in Asia

Written and Edited by

Ramkishen S. Rajan
Associate Professor, School of Public Policy, George Mason University, USA

palgrave
macmillan

First published 2009 by
PALGRAVE MACMILLAN

Palgrave Macmillan in the UK is an imprint of Macmillan Publishers Limited, registered in England, company number 785998, of Houndmills, Basingstoke, Hampshire RG21 6XS.

Palgrave Macmillan in the US is a division of St Martin's Press LLC, 175 Fifth Avenue, New York, NY 10010.

Palgrave Macmillan is the global academic imprint of the above companies and has companies and representatives throughout the world.

Palgrave® and Macmillan® are registered trademarks in the United States, the United Kingdom, Europe and other countries.

ISBN-13: 978–0–230–57705–3 hardback
ISBN-10: 0–230–57705–9 hardback

This book is printed on paper suitable for recycling and made from fully managed and sustained forest sources. Logging, pulping and manufacturing processes are expected to conform to the environmental regulations of the country of origin.

A catalogue record for this book is available from the British Library.

Library of Congress Cataloging-in-Publication Data

Exchange rates, currency crisis and monetary cooperation in Asia / edited by Ramkishen S. Rajan.
p. cm.
Includes bibliographical references and index.
ISBN 978–0–230–57705–3
1. Foreign exchange rates—Asia. 2. Currency crises—Asia. 3. Monetary policy—Asia. 4. Finance—Asia. I. Rajan, Ramkishen S.

HG3968.E946 2009
332.4'95—dc22 2008052859

10 9 8 7 6 5 4 3 2 1
18 17 16 15 14 13 12 11 10 09

Printed and bound in Great Britain by
CPI Antony Rowe, Chippenham and Eastbourne

Dedicated to my team:

Harminder and Shreyas Rajan

Contents

Figures and Box

Box

Tables

Acknowledgments

Many of the chapters in this book are based on co-authored papers with my colleagues in different parts of the world. I have learned a great deal from collaborating with them and am grateful for their inputs and cooperation. In particular, I would like to thank the following individuals: Alice Ouyang and Tom Willett (Chapter 1), Amit Ghosh (Chapters 2 and 3), Shen Chung-Hua (Chapter 4), Makarand Paraulkar (Chapter 6), Jie Li (Chapter 8), Graham Bird and Reza Siregar (Chapter 9) and Victor Pointines (Chapter 11). Many of the chapters were completed while I visited various institutes and universities in the Asia-Pacific, most notably the Asian Development Bank in Manila, the Asian Development Bank Institute in Tokyo, the Hong Kong Institute for Monetary Research, the National University of Singapore (NUS), and the University of Adelaide in Australia. I would like to acknowledge with gratitude but without attribution the support and resources provided to me at these institutions. I would also like to place on record the support of my colleagues and resources provided in my current place of employment, the School of Public Policy at George Mason University (SPP-GMU) in Virginia, USA. Needless to say, the views expressed in this volume are personal, and in particular I am solely responsible for any errors.

I would like to thank the various journal editors and publishers who kindly allowed my articles to be reprinted in this book.

Lastly, but most importantly, my family members have remained unstinting in their support of my career and provided me the stability necessary to remain focused on my writings.

RAMKISHEN S. RAJAN
School of Public Policy
George Mason University
Arlington, Virginia
USA
October 2008

Contributors

Graham Bird is Professor at the Department of Economics and Director of the Surrey Centre for International Economics Studies (SCIES) of the University of Surrey, Guildford, UK.

Amit Ghosh is Assistant Professor at the Department of Economics of Illinois Wesleyan University, Bloomington, Illinois, USA.

Jie Li is Assistant Professor at the Central University of Finance and Economics and Director of the CUFE Research Center for Foreign Reserves, Beijing, China.

Alice Y. Ouyang is Assistant Professor at the China Academy of Public Finance and Public Policy of the Central University of Finance and Economics, Beijing, China.

Makarand Parulkar is Deputy Chief Operating Officer at Bradford College of the University of Adelaide, Adelaide, Australia.

Victor Pontines is Lecturer of Economics and Public Policy at Carnegie Mellon University H. John Heinz III School of Public Policy and Management, Adelaide, Australia.

Chung-Hua Shen is a Professor at the Department of Finance of National Taiwan University, Taipei, Taiwan.

Reza Siregar is International Economic Consultant at the International Monetary Fund—Singapore Regional Training Institute, Singapore.

Thomas D. Willett is Director of the Claremont Institute for Economic Policy Studies and Horton Professor at the School of Politics and Economics of Claremont Graduate University, Claremont, California, USA.

Introduction

Prior to the Asian financial crisis of 1997–1998, scant attention was paid by policymakers to monetary and financial issues. The predominant focus then was on the real side of the economy (trade and development). The crisis and its aftermath quickly shifted attention to and interest in concerns about currency crises and exchange rate movements in an era of rapid global capital flows. Given the high degree of economic openness in the region and its consequent heavy dependence on trade and investment, the Asian economies are especially susceptible to shifts in global capital flows and sharp exchange rate movements. While many Asian economies have taken a number of steps individually to fortify themselves against future external shocks, they have, as a group, simultaneously initiated a slow but steady process of enhancing monetary and financial cooperation. Since the region holds the largest reserves in the world and consequently plays a significant role in the global macroeconomic imbalances, Asian monetary and financial issues have clearly taken on global importance. The collection of chapters in this volume therefore attempts to explore various aspects of monetary, exchange rate and financial issues in Asia.[1]

The book is truly pan-Asia-focused with chapters on China, Japan, Korea, India and Southeast Asia. The chapters are focused on important policy issues of contemporary relevance, but are informed by analytical frameworks, data and empirics. While the chapters have been written in a manner that is able to stand up to academic scrutiny,[2] they are also meant to be accessible to policymakers, researchers and financial journalists who might be interested in Asian monetary, exchange rate and financial issues, concerns and policies.

The book concentrates on three broad themes, viz. exchange rates and their macroeconomic consequences in Asia; analytical and empirical issues relating to currency crises and policy responses with reference to Asia; and monetary and financial cooperation in Asia. Below is a summary of each of the eleven chapters.

The first three chapters in Part I deal with the inflationary consequences of exchange rate movements and exchange rate interventions in Asia.

Chapter 1 is entitled "Managing the Liquidity Effects of Reserve Stockpiling in Emerging Asia." The huge increase in international reserve holdings by Asian countries since the 1997 crisis has been one of the most important recent developments on the international financial scene. These buildups have contributed substantially to concerns about the creation of excessive global liquidity. How justified these concerns are would depend considerably on the extent to which the reserve accumulating countries have been able to mop up or sterilize its effects on their domestic monetary aggregates. This chapter uses a unified theoretical framework to undertake dynamic estimations of the magnitude of sterilization and offset coefficients (which measure the degree of capital mobility) for a large set of Asian economies. Empirical findings suggest that, despite substantial capital mobility, there has been a high degree of effective sterilization to date.

Chapter 2 is entitled "What is the Impact of Exchange Rate Changes on Inflation in Asia?" An important but age-old transmission channel of global factors into domestic prices is via exchange rate movements, so-called exchange rate pass-through (ERPT). It is generally believed that Asian economies are potentially susceptible to the inflationary effects of exchange rate changes since they are highly trade-dependent. This chapter explores this issue, paying particular attention to production sharing—a key characteristic of Asian trade—and its implications for the inflationary consequences of exchange rate movements.

Chapter 3 is entitled "A Closer Examination of Exchange Rate Pass-through in Korea and Thailand." This chapter examines the extent and evolution of ERPT into Korea's and Thailand's consumer and import prices at the aggregate level for the period over the last two decades. Results suggest that ERPT is consistently higher for Thailand as compared with Korea; while for both nations the ERPT of their respective bilateral rates with respect to the US dollar is higher than with respect to the Japanese yen. The chapter also investigates whether and how ERPT has changed in these two economies over time, especially during and after the currency crisis period of 1997–1998.

The next five chapters in Part II deal with analytical and policy issues relating to financial crises in emerging economies, with particular reference to Asia.

Chapter 4 is entitled "Are Crisis-Induced Devaluations Contractionary? If so, Why?" Why are some currency crises followed by economic contractions while others are not? This chapter is an attempt at answering this query. In particular, the chapter investigates two closely-related questions. First, is there is a difference in the output effects of a devaluation during "normal" periods as against those during crisis periods? After all, during non-crisis periods, real exchange devaluation is seen as an important policy option for promoting exports and output growth. Yet, the literature has not made a distinction between crisis and non-crisis periods. To preview the main conclusion, results indicate that the contractionary effects tend to exist only during the crisis period. Building on this, the chapter goes on to explore the factors that cause a crisis-induced devaluation to be contractionary.

Chapter 5 is entitled "Financial Crisis, Capital Outflows and Monetary Policy Responses: Simple Analytics with Reference to East Asia." Financial crises seem to have become the norm rather than the exception since 1992. This chapter examines the impact of a crisis of confidence and resultant capital outflows from a small and open economy, and the possible policy options in response to such outflows using simple tools and definitions that will be familiar to any money and banking or intermediate macroeconomics student. To facilitate the discussion, examples are drawn from the East Asian crisis of 1997–1998 (Indonesia, Korea, Malaysia and Thailand), although the analysis remains pertinent to emerging economies in general.

Chapter 6 is entitled "Understanding Currency Crises and Monetary Policy Responses in Emerging Economies." When analyzing the appropriate response for monetary policy during a currency crisis, it is important to keep in mind two distinct channels: the effect of raising interest rates on exchange rates and the direct effect of exchange rate changes on output. The first pertains to the monetary side of the economy as given by the interest parity condition. The second deals with the real side of the economy. The interaction between these two parts of the economy derives the equilibrium output and exchange rate in the economy. This chapter expands the Aghion et al. (2000) monetary model with nominal rigidities and foreign currency debt to examine the interaction between the real and monetary sides of the economy and to analyze the effect of monetary policy on the real economy. We find that the effect of monetary policy on exchange rate and output is theoretically ambiguous. This in turn suggests that the appropriate monetary policy response could vary among countries at any point in time, or for a particular country between two different periods.

Chapter 7 is entitled "How Best to Manage New Style Currency Crises?" The new-style currency crises that have affected a number of developing and emerging economies of late are characterized by "sudden stops" in capital inflows and adverse balance sheet effects. Given the potential high costs of these crises, there is an ongoing debate on how best they might be managed when they do arise. This chapter argues that the time-honored Swan diagram, appropriately modified, is able to provide useful insights into how a country might manage a new-style crisis through a combination of adjustment (which involves expenditure switching and reducing polices) and financing.

Chapter 8 is entitled "Can High Reserves Offset Weak Fundamentals?" While the previous chapter focused on crisis management, this chapter concentrates on crisis prevention and the role of international reserves in staving off a future crisis. In particular it develops a simple optimizing model to determine the optimal reserve holdings by a country looking to minimize the net costs of holding reserves. In so doing it attempts to determine the validity of the assertion that is sometimes made that sufficiently high levels of reserves can compensate for weak fundamentals.

Ever since the currency crisis of 1997–1998, there has been a great deal of interest in enhancing regional economic cooperation in Asia. The last three chapters in Part III tackle selected issues on Asian monetary and financial cooperation.

Chapter 9 is entitled "Examining the Case for an Asian Reserve Pool." As noted previously, many Asian economies are stockpiling reserves as a means of self-insurance against future crises. Holding such large volumes of reserves is costly but it also suggests that the regional economies have the capacity to develop a common reserve pool arrangement. This chapter investigates the gains, if any, to be reaped if East Asian economies were to pool their reserves. It also briefly discusses how the proposed reserve pool would fit into the larger context of evolving East Asian monetary regionalism.

Chapter 10 is entitled "Taking Stock of Monetary and Financial Cooperation in Asia." It is important to keep in mind that economic regionalism is multidimensional in nature. The focus of this chapter is on policy initiatives underway in Asia to enhance monetary and financial regionalism and the analytical bases for these initiatives, rather than on examining the *de facto* level of financial and monetary links that already exist (which may or may not have been facilitated via regional policy mechanisms). This chapter focuses more narrowly on "medium forms" of monetary and financial regionalism, broadly defined as the development of regional liquidity arrangements and regional financial markets.

Chapter 11 is entitled "Is there a Role for an Asian Currency Unit?" While most observers agree that the time is not yet ripe for Asia to consider a common currency, there has been some discussion about the possible creation of an Asian Currency Unit (ACU). This chapter examines the specific issue of the ACU which, in a general sense, is a weighted average of regional currencies *a la* the European Currency Unit (ECU).

The chapter critically examines the rationale for the ACU proposal and offers an initial attempt at computing optimal currency composition of the ACU. The optimal basket weights computed are aimed at ensuring a regional currency basket that has minimal variance. Hence it should deliver stability in intraregional exchange rates for alternative configurations of currency baskets in the Asian and Pacific region.

Notes

1. Issues that might be missing from this book such as the choice of exchange rate regimes, inflation targeting, and dynamics of capital flows have been explored in a companion volume (Cavoli and Rajan, 2009).
2. Indeed, a number of the chapters draw on and build upon papers published in refereed journals.

References

Aghion, P., P. Bacchetta, and A. Banerjee (2000). "A Simple Model of Monetary Policy and Currency Crises," *European Economic Review,* 44, 728–738.

Cavoli, T. and R.S. Rajan (2009). *Exchange Rate Regimes and Macroeconomic Management in Asia*, Hong Kong: Hong Kong University Press.

Part I

Exchange Rates and Macroeconomic Consequences

1

Managing the Liquidity Effects of Reserve Stockpiling in Emerging Asia[1]

(Co-authored with Alice Y. Ouyang and Thomas D. Willett)

1.1 Introduction

Asia accounted for over half of global international reserve holdings during the period 1999–2005, up from one-third in the period 1990–1995 (Kharas et al. 2006).[2] While China and Japan have been the main drivers of the massive stockpiling of reserves in the region, India, Hong Kong, Korea, Singapore and Taiwan, and some middle-income Southeast Asian economies have also experienced significant swelling of their reserves since the crises (Figure 1.1).

For Korea and other regional economies that were hit by the regional crisis, policymakers appear to have deliberately chosen to amass high levels of reserves for precautionary or self-insurance motives against future financial crises (Aizenman and Marion 2003; Bird and Rajan 2003; also see Chapter 8 of this volume).[3] Reserve accretion as a financial safeguard is consistent with modern second generation (escape clause-based) currency crises models *a la* Obstfeld (1986, 1994).[4] However, many Asian countries have continued accumulating reserves well beyond plausible precautionary levels (also see Chapter 9 of this volume).

Some have argued that the reserve growth in emerging Asia more recently is a by-product of a desire by central banks to smooth exchange rate movements, but smoothing behavior by central banks should, in general, have no net impact on reserves over time. The continued build-up of reserves suggests that intervention is largely asymmetric and that it stems largely from a desire to maintain relatively stable and/or "ultra-competitive" exchange rates.[5] A number of commentators have expressed concerns that such large-scale intervention runs a serious risk of generating increases in inflation in the intervening countries, and some have even suggested that such reserve accumulations have played a major role in the creation of excessive global liquidity. Key to such issues is the extent to which monetary authorities can successfully sterilize the

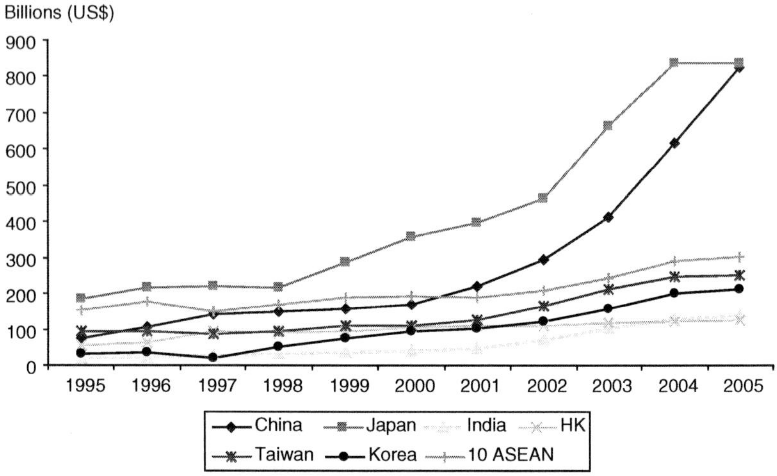

Figure 1.1 International reserve holdings in emerging Asia (including gold), 1990–2005 (US$ Billions)

Source: Based on data from International Financial Statistics (IFS), except Taiwan. The data from 1995–2004 for Taiwan is from AREMOS dataset which is published by Taiwan Economic Data Center. The 2005 data for Taiwan is updated from Taiwan's central bank website.

domestic monetary effects of reserve accumulation. Most monetary models of the exchange rate and balance of payments assume no sterilization so that large reserve accumulations would automatically lead to rapid growth in domestic money and credit. Sufficiently high levels of international capital mobility would make effective sterilization impossible, no matter the intensity of efforts of the domestic monetary authorities. In recent research Ouyang, Rajan, and Willett (2007) analyzed these issues for China and found that it had been able to effectively sterilize a high proportion of its recent reserve increases. China has substantial capital controls, however, so the People's Bank of China's ability to sterilize would not necessarily carry over to the other Asian economies.

The aim of this chapter is to investigate the extent of monetary sterilization and the degree of capital mobility to eight Asian economies: ASEAN-4 (Indonesia, Malaysia, Philippines, Thailand), India, Korea, Singapore, and Taiwan.[6] All these economies were impacted by the Asian crises of 1997–1998. While Indonesia, Korea, Philippines and Thailand have all implemented open economy inflation targeting regimes (open economy in the sense of there being a role for exchange rate management as well), India, Singapore and Taiwan operate managed floating regimes, a policy also adopted by Malaysia since July 2005 (Table 1.1 and Rajan 2006).[7]

Table 1.1 *De facto* IMF exchange rate classifications, 1998–2004

	As of July 1998	As of July 1999	As of July 2000	As of July 2001	As of July 2002	As of July 2003	As of July 2004	As of December 2004
Indonesia	Independently floating	Independently floating	Independently floating	Independently floating	Managed floating with no predetermined path	Managed floating with no predetermined path	Managed floating with no predetermined path	Managed floating with no predetermined path
India	Managed floating with no predetermined path	Managed floating with no predetermined path	Managed floating with no predetermined path	Managed floating with no predetermined path	Managed floating with no predetermined path	Managed floating with no predetermined path	Managed floating with no predetermined path	Managed floating with no predetermined path
Korea	Independently floating	Independently floating	Independently floating	Independently floating	Independently floating	Independently floating	Independently floating	
Malaysia	Conventional pegged arrangement	Conventional pegged arrangement	Conventional pegged arrangement	Conventional pegged arrangement	Conventional pegged arrangement	Conventional pegged arrangement	Conventional pegged arrangement	Conventional pegged arrangement
Philippines	Independently floating	Independently floating	Independently floating	Independently floating	Independently floating	Independently floating	Independently floating	
Singapore	Managed floating with no predetermined path	Managed floating with no predetermined path	Managed floating with no predetermined path	Managed floating with no predetermined path	Managed floating with no predetermined path	Managed floating with no predetermined path	Managed floating with no predetermined path	Managed floating with no predetermined path
Thailand	Managed floating with no predetermined path	Managed floating with no predetermined path	Managed floating with no predetermined path	Managed floating with no predetermined path	Managed floating with no predetermined path	Managed floating with no predetermined path	Managed floating with no predetermined path	Managed floating with no predetermined path

Note: Taiwan is excluded from IMF reports.

Source: Authors.

The remainder of the chapter is organized as follows. Section 1.2 offers a brief overview of the evolution of the balance of payments in the eight emerging Asian economies and a first look at the extent of monetary sterilization. Section 1.3 outlines a set of simultaneous equations to examine the feedback effects between net domestic assets (NDA) and net foreign assets (NFA) as a means of estimating the extent of *de facto* sterilization (sterilization coefficient) and capital mobility (offset coefficient) concurrently. The theoretical foundations of the equations to be estimated are based on a modified version of a model originally outlined by Brissimis-Gibson-Tsakalotos (2002). Section 1.4 offers an overview of the data and definitions of variables to be used in the empirics. This section also discusses the empirical results of the sterilization and offset coefficients based on quarterly data for the period 1990:q1 to 2005:q3. We divide the whole sample period into two subsamples: the pre-crises period (defined as 1990:q1 to 1997:q1), and the post-crises period (defined as 1998:q3 to 2005:q3).[8] By comparing the different values of offset and sterilization coefficients in these two subsamples we are able to ascertain how the extent of sterilization and degree of capital mobility have changed in the two periods for the emerging Asian economies under consideration. We also conduct a recursive estimation to investigate the dynamic change of estimated offset and sterilization coefficients. Given the limited observations for each country, our estimations are based on a panel. Section 1.5 concludes the chapter.

1.2 Balance of payments dynamics and sterilization in emerging Asia: A first look

The sharp switch from current account deficit to surplus for emerging Asia as a group has been well documented and is apparent from Table 1.2. An aggregate current account deficit which averaged US$ 40 billion in 1995–1996 turned into a surplus of over US$ 100 billion in 1998–1999 and more than doubled by 2005.[9] While this abrupt turnaround in the current account has been the main reason for the reserve accretion in emerging Asia immediately after the 1997–1998 crises, there has also been a resurgence in net private capital flows to the emerging Asian region.[10] The combination of current account surplus and renewed private capital inflows, along with active exchange rate management by the regional central banks, has contributed to the rapid and significant reserve build-up in emerging Asia in recent years.

What are the monetary consequences of this reserve accretion? Referring to Figure 1.2, it appears that central banks in the eight

Table 1.2 Sources of reserve accumulation in emerging Asia, 1995–2005 (US$ Billions)

	1995	1996	1997	1998	1999	2000	2001	2002	2003	2004	2005
Change in reserves	−42.6	−46.8	−35.8	−53.1	−88.2	−53.7	−90.2	−148.8	−226.5	−340.1	−281.9
Current account balance	−40.0	−40.1	14.0	114.0	106.0	85.0	88.4	127.5	166.3	183.5	240.8
Private capital flows, net	101.5	121.1	47.6	−53.8	3.1	6.5	19.6	20.8	63.5	120.3	53.8
Official capital flows, net	−4.7	−16.1	14.0	19.6	1.8	−11.7	−11.7	4.6	−17.6	1.8	5.0

Notes: Capital flows to "emerging Asia" are dominated by ten economies, viz. the eight economies in this chapter (India, Indonesia, Korea, Malaysia, Philippines, Singapore, Taiwan, Thailand), as well as China and Hong Kong. It also includes a number of other countries categorized as "developing Asia" by the IMF.

Source: IMF, *World Economic Outlook Database*, April 2006.

emerging Asian economies under consideration have been actively neutralizing the impact of the reserve build-up in the sense that the NDA (which is broadly a proxy for domestic credit) has been moving in the opposite direction to NFA (which is broadly a proxy for foreign reserves).[11] The two most commonly used instruments for monetary sterilization are open market operations (OMOs) and changes in legal reserve requirements (see Mohanty and Turner 2005, for details). However, the emerging Asian central banks have also employed a number of other tools such as shifting public sector or pension funds from commercial banks to the central banks, adjusting discount rates, setting the restricted lending policy, or capital controls.[12]

Since the foreign exchange and the domestic monetary markets are tightly interrelated, it is important to recognize the contemporaneous relationship between net NDA and NFA, failing which there will be a "simultaneity bias". In other words, both the "sterilization coefficient" (i.e. how much domestic credit changes in response to a change in international reserves) and the "offset coefficient" (i.e. how much the balance of payments changes in response to a change in domestic credit) need to be estimated simultaneously (Argy and Kouri 1974 and

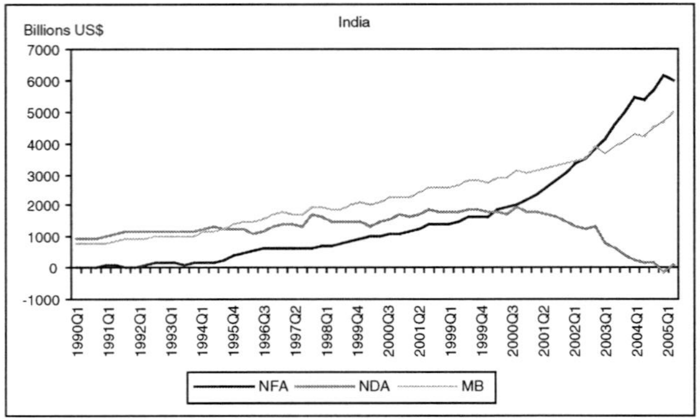
India
Billions US$
7000
6000
5000
4000
3000
2000
1000
0
-1000
1990Q1
1991Q1
1992Q1
1993Q1
1994Q1
1995Q4
1996Q3
1997Q2
1998Q1
1999Q4
2000Q3
2001Q2
1999Q1
1999Q4
2000Q3
2001Q2
2002Q1
2003Q1
2004Q1
2005Q1
NFA
NDA
MB

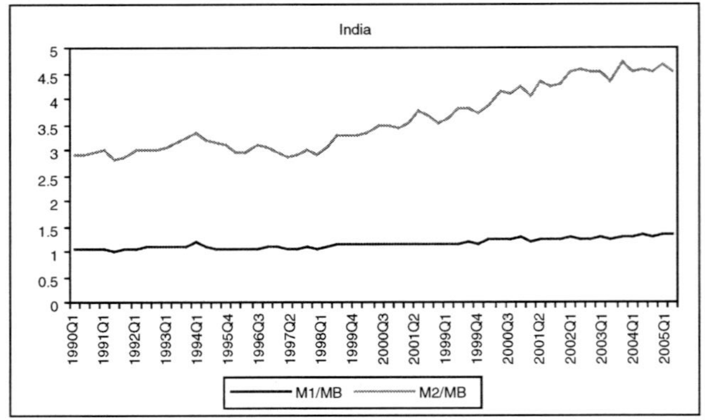
India
5
4.5
4
3.5
3
2.5
2
1.5
1
0.5
0
1990Q1
1991Q1
1992Q1
1993Q1
1994Q1
1995Q4
1996Q3
1997Q2
1998Q1
1999Q4
2000Q3
2001Q2
1999Q1
1999Q4
2000Q3
2001Q2
2002Q1
2003Q1
2004Q1
2005Q1
M1/MB
M2/MB

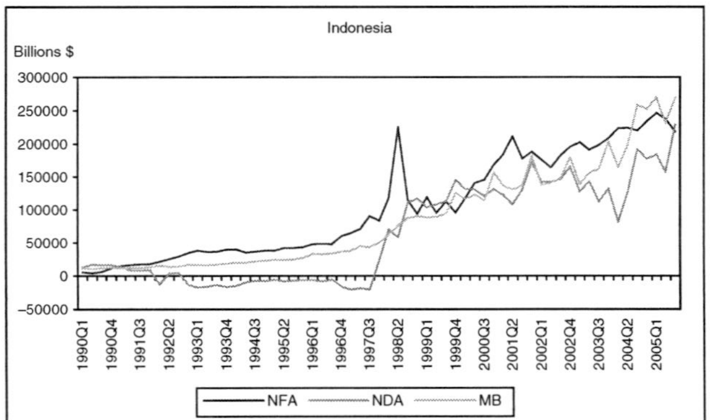
Indonesia
Billions $
300000
250000
200000
150000
100000
50000
0
–50000
1990Q1
1990Q4
1991Q3
1992Q2
1993Q1
1993Q4
1994Q3
1995Q2
1996Q1
1996Q4
1997Q3
1998Q2
1999Q1
1999Q4
2000Q3
2001Q2
2002Q1
2002Q4
2003Q3
2004Q2
2005Q1
NFA
NDA
MB

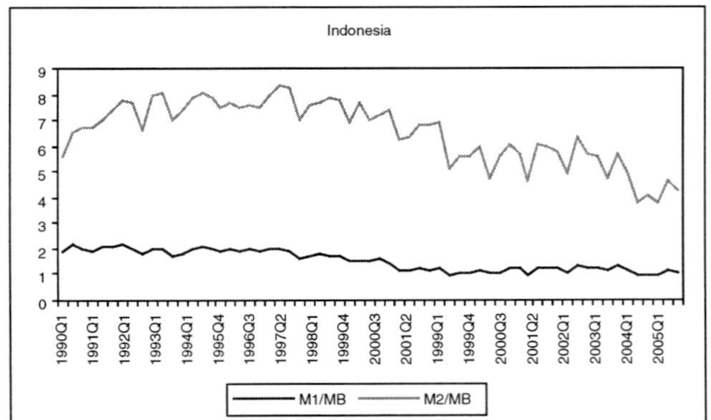
Indonesia
9
8
7
6
5
4
3
2
1
0
1990Q1
1991Q1
1992Q1
1993Q1
1994Q1
1995Q4
1996Q3
1997Q2
1998Q1
1999Q4
2000Q3
2001Q2
1999Q1
1999Q4
2000Q3
2001Q2
2002Q1
2003Q1
2004Q1
2005Q1
M1/MB
M2/MB

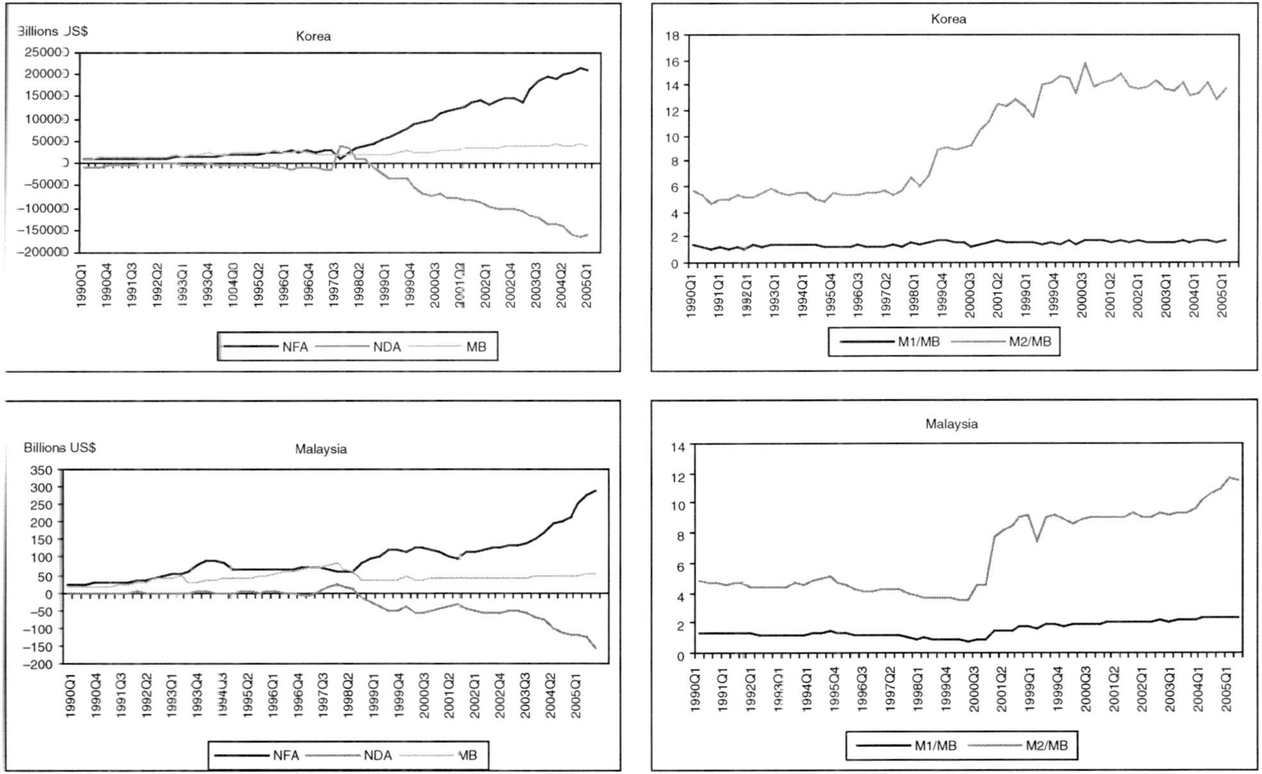

Figure 1.2 Continued

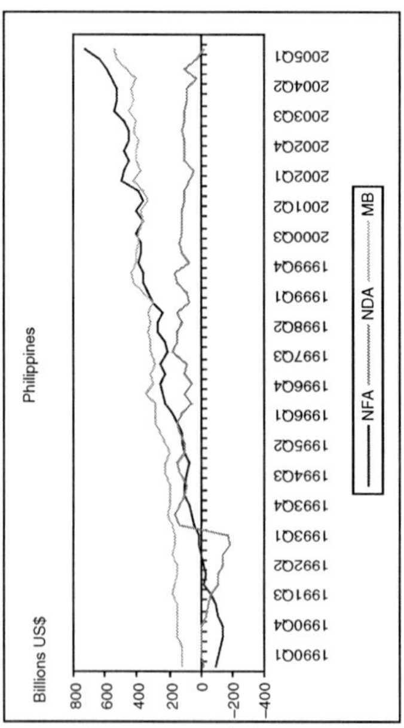
Philippines
Billions US$
NFA
NDA
MB

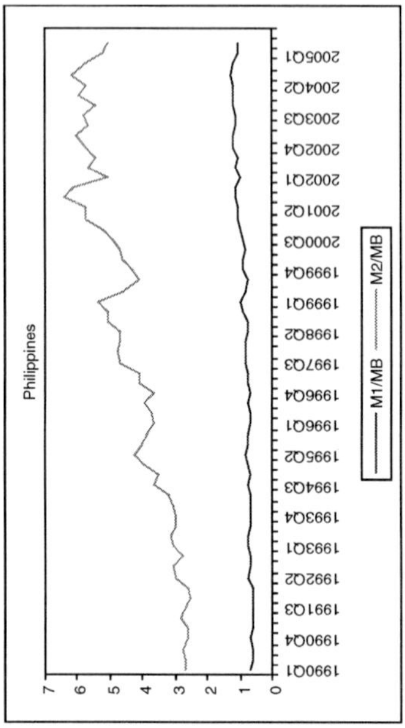
Philippines
M1/MB
M2/MB

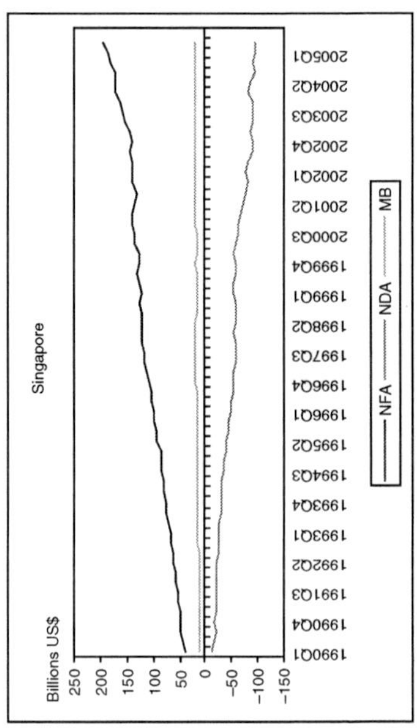
Singapore
Billions US$
NFA
NDA
MB

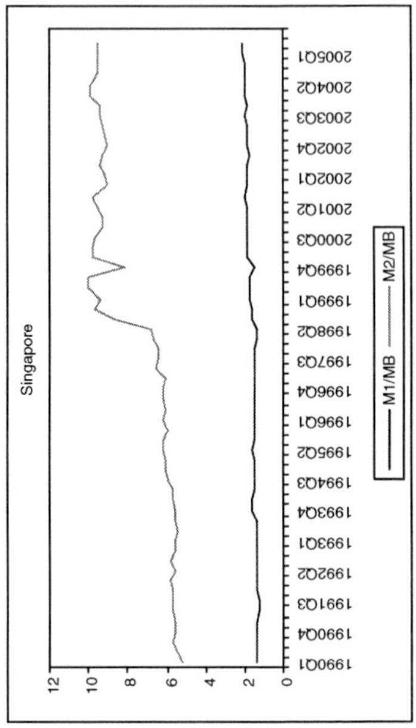
Singapore
M1/MB
M2/MB

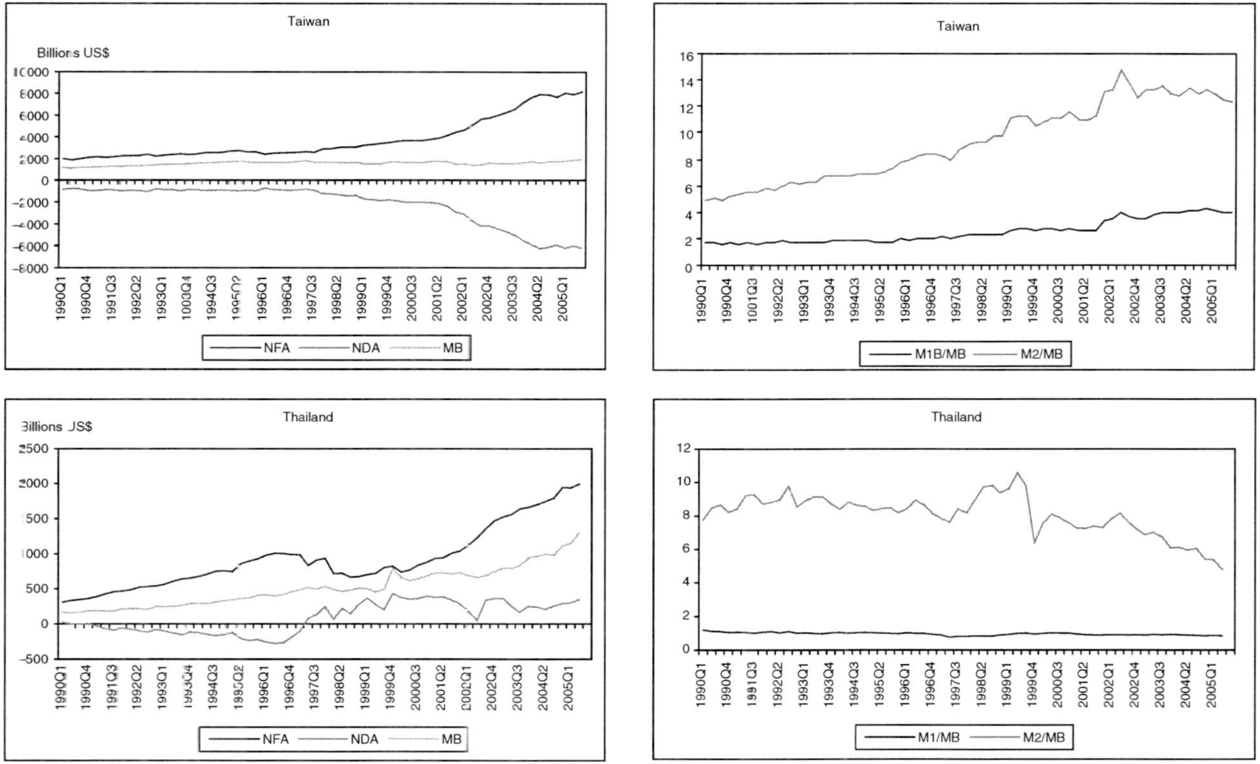

Figure 1.2 NDA, NFA, Monetary base and money multipliers in emerging Asia, 1990:q1–2005:q1 (US$ Billions)

Source: Based on data from IFS, except Taiwan. The data from 1995–2004 for Taiwan is from AREMOS dataset which is published by Taiwan Economic Data Center. The 2005 data for Taiwan is updated from Taiwan's central bank website.

Obstfeld 1982). The typical model specification for a set of simultaneous equations is:

$$\Delta NFA_t = \alpha_0 + \alpha_1 \Delta NDA_t + X_1'\delta_1 + u_{1t} \quad (1a)$$
$$\Delta NDA_t = \beta_0 + \beta_1 \Delta NFA_t + X_2'\delta_2 + u_{2t} \quad (1b)$$

where: X_1 and X_2 are the vector of controls in the balance of payments function and monetary reaction function, respectively.[13] The coefficient α_1 in eq. 1a is the "offset coefficient", i.e. impact of a change in domestic liquidity conditions on capital flows. The expected value of the offset coefficient is bound by 0 in the event of no capital mobility, and –1 in the event of perfect capital mobility. The coefficient β_1 in eq. 1b is the "sterilization coefficient". The expected value of the sterilization coefficient is –1 if reserve build-up is perfectly sterilized and 0 if the central bank does not sterilize at all. In general, the greater the degree of capital mobility the less effective is monetary sterilization; a small offset coefficient and large sterilization coefficient are usually viewed as the central bank having a fairly high degree of monetary policy independence to neutralize the impact of capital flows effectively on a sustained basis.

1.3 Theoretical basis for the simultaneous equations

An obvious concern with estimating eqs. 1a and 1b is the choice of control variables. Most existing empirical studies have chosen control variables based on informal theorizing. One exception is the paper by Brissimis-Gibson-Tsakalotos (BGT) (2002), which develops a formal theoretical model from which the foregoing set of simultaneous equations are derived from explicit minimization of a simple loss function of the monetary authority, subject to a number of constraints that reflect the workings of the economy. We modify the BGT in four important ways. One, unlike the original BGT model, which assumes that the central bank is concerned about the deviation of the exchange rate from a target *level* and therefore incorporates the exchange rate in the loss function directly, we assume instead that the central bank is primarily concerned with exchange rate *volatility*.[14] Undoubtedly most central banks are concerned with both, but it is much less difficult to operationalize exchange-rate volatility than the target exchange rate. Two, unlike the original BGT model, we assume that the exchange rate impacts inflation directly via pass-through. In other words, the monetary authority is not concerned about the exchange rate for its own sake, but rather because of its impact on inflation and trade. Three, we endogenize the current account by assuming it is affected by both income and price (exchange rate) effects. Four, we also incorporate the role of government spending on cyclical output. These modifications are broadly consistent with the managing floating regimes operated by many emerging Asian economies.[15]

1.3.1 A simple model

In our modified version of the BGT model the loss function of the monetary authority is:

$$L_t = \beta(\Delta p_t)^2 + \gamma(Y_{c,t})^2 + \delta(\sigma_{r,t})^2 + \epsilon(\sigma_{s,t})^2 \tag{2}$$

The monetary authority's loss function is determined by the change in the logarithm of the price level (i.e. the difference in p_t and p_{t-1}); cyclical income ($Y_{c,t}$); and the volatilities of the interest rate ($\sigma_{r,t}$) and the exchange rate ($\sigma_{s,t}$). All the parameters are assumed to be positive.

The evolution of key variables including inflation and cyclical income is discussed below.

a) Inflation

The evolution of inflation can be written as follows:

$$\Delta p_t = \pi_1[(\Delta \mathrm{NFA}_t + \Delta \mathrm{NDA}_t)mm_t + \mathrm{MB}_t \Delta mm_t] + \pi_2 \Delta p_{t-1} + \pi_3 \Delta s_t \text{ [16,17]} \tag{3}$$

where: $\pi_1 > 0$, $0 < \pi_2 < 1$, $\pi_3 > 0$, MB_t is the monetary base and mm_t is the money multiplier. Equation 3 states that inflation is a monetary phenomenon with a lagged effect. In addition, depreciation of the nominal exchange rate (rise in s_t) could increase inflationary pressures due to increased prices of tradable goods.

b) Cyclical income

The evolution of cyclical income can be written as follows:

$$Y_{c,t} = \phi_1[(\Delta \mathrm{NFA}_t + \Delta \mathrm{NDA}_t)mm_t + \mathrm{MB}_t \Delta mm_t] + \phi_2 Y_{c,t-1} + \phi_3 \Delta G_t \tag{4}$$
$$\phi_1 > 0,\ 0 < \phi_2 < 1,\ \phi_3 > 0.$$

where: G_t is the government expenditure.[18] We assume that both expansionary fiscal and monetary policies can boost cyclical output.

c) Balance of payments

The balance of payments is defined as usual (ignoring errors and omissions):

$$\Delta \mathrm{NFA}_t = \mathrm{CA}_t + \Delta \mathrm{NK}_t \tag{5}$$

where: CA is the current account balance and ΔNK_t is the net capital inflow in time t.[19]

The current account in turn is assumed to depend simply on both cyclical output and the lagged real effective exchange rate (REER) (to capture inertial effects) in a linear manner[20]:

$$CA_t = \alpha_0 + \alpha_1 Y_{c,t} + \alpha_2 \Delta REER_{t-1}, \qquad \alpha_1 < 0,\ \alpha_2 < 0 \tag{6}$$

where: *REER* is the real effective exchange rate (rise implies a currency appreciation).

The net capital inflow is assumed to depend imperfectly on the uncovered interest differentials:

$$\Delta NK_t = (1/c)\Delta(s_t - E_t s_{t+1} + r_t - r_t^*) \tag{7}$$

where: s_t is the current exchange rate (logarithm); $E_t s_{t+1}$ is the current expectation of the exchange rate at time t+1; r_t is the domestic interest rate; r_t^* is the foreign interest rate; and c represents the degree of substitutability between domestic and foreign assets, i.e. the degree of international capital mobility. This in turn is affected by the extent of capital controls.

The interest rate is determined by the change in money supply:

$$\Delta r_t = \psi_1[(\Delta NDA_t + \Delta NFA_t)mm_t + MB_t \Delta mm_t] \qquad \psi_1 > 0 \tag{8}$$

After substituting eqs. 6 to 10 into 9 we derive:

$$\begin{aligned}\Delta p_t = {} & (\pi_1 mm_t + c\pi_3 + \pi_3 c\alpha_1\phi_1 mm_t + \pi_3\psi_1 mm_t)\Delta NFA_t \\ & + (\pi_1 mm_t + \pi_3 c\alpha_1\phi_1 mm_t + \pi_3\psi_1 mm_t)\Delta NDA_t \\ & + (\pi_1 MB_t + \pi_3 c\alpha_1\phi_1 MB_t + \pi_3\psi_1 MB_t)\Delta mm_t \\ & + (\pi_3 c\alpha_1\phi_2)Y_{c,t-1} + (\pi_2)\Delta p_{t-1} + (\pi_3 c\alpha_1\phi_3)\Delta G_t \\ & + (\pi_3 c\alpha_2)\Delta REER_{t-1} + (\pi_3)\Delta(r_t^* + E_t s_{t+1})\end{aligned} \tag{9}$$

d) Interest rate volatility

Interest rate volatility follows the original BGT model:

$$\sigma_{r,t} = \eta\sigma_{r,t-1} - \theta|\Delta NDA_t| \qquad \eta,\theta > 0 \tag{10}$$

Interest rate volatility is assumed to depend negatively on the absolute amount of intervention undertaken by the central bank in the domestic money market. For estimation purposes eq. 10 is transformed into non-absolute terms. For example, the original BGT model assumes that the central bank injects liquidity ($\Delta NDA_t > 0$) to prevent an interest rate rise while the money market is in deficit. The same logic can be applied to the case when the money market is in surplus. When the money market is in surplus the central bank withdraws money to prevent interest rates from falling so that ($\Delta NDA_t < 0$). Therefore, if the money market is in deficit, $\Delta NDA_t > 0$ and eq. 10 can be rewritten as follows:

$$\sigma_{r,t} = \eta\sigma_{r,t-1} - \theta(\Delta NDA_t - d_1\Delta NDA_t) \tag{10a}$$

where: d_1 is the dummy which takes on a value of 0 when the money market is in deficit and a value of 2 when it is in surplus.

e) Exchange rate volatility

Exchange rate volatility follows the original BGT model:

$$\sigma_{s,t} = \eta\sigma_{s,t-1} - \theta|\Delta NFA_t| \qquad \eta,\theta > 0 \tag{11}$$

Exchange rate volatility depends negatively on the absolute amount of intervention undertaken by the central bank in the foreign exchange market.[21] Using the same logic as in the case of interest rate volatility we can redefine eq. 11 as follows:

$$\sigma_{s,t} = \kappa\sigma_{s,t-1} - \varsigma(\Delta NFA_t - d_2\Delta NFA_t) \qquad \kappa,\varsigma > 0. \tag{11a}$$

where: d_2 is a dummy variable which takes on a value of 2 when there is an excess demand for foreign currency (and the central bank is losing reserves) and a value of 0 when foreign currency is in excess supply (and the central bank is stockpiling reserves).

As is typical of a managed floater, we assume that the central bank consciously attempts to alter domestic credit (and thus interest rates) and undertakes foreign exchange rate intervention (i.e. managed float) with the aim of minimizing its loss function (eq. 2). It is important to keep in mind that since we are not attempting to specify a policy rule for the monetary authority it is reasonable to derive an equation for ΔNDA_t as opposed to interest rates (as in Cavoli and Rajan 2009, chapter 6 for instance) despite most of the regional central banks having adopted the interest rate as the policy instrument. Estimating a set of simultaneous equations with ΔNDA_t and ΔNFA_t as dependent variables is more consistent with the literature.

Given this we can solve for $\partial L_t/\partial \Delta NDA_t = 0$ and $\partial L_t/\partial \Delta NFA_t = 0$, and, after substituting the constraints into the loss function, we derive two reduced-form equations:

$$
\begin{aligned}
\Delta \mathrm{NFA}_t = &-\{[\beta c\pi_3(\pi_1+\pi_3\psi_1+c\alpha_1\varphi_1\pi_3)mm_t+\beta(\pi_1+\pi_3\psi_1+c\alpha_1\varphi_1\pi_3)^2 mm_t^2+r\varphi_1^2 mm_t^2]/u_1\}\Delta \mathrm{NDA}_t \\
&-\{[\beta c\pi_3(\pi_1+\pi_3\psi_1+c\alpha_1\varphi_1\pi_3)\mathrm{MB}_t+\beta(\pi_1+\pi_3\psi_1+c\alpha_1\varphi_1\pi_3)^2 mm_t \mathrm{MB}_t+r\varphi_1^2 mm_t \mathrm{MB}_t]/u_1\}\Delta mm_t \\
&-\{[\beta\pi_2(\pi_3 c+(\pi_1+\pi_3\psi_1+c\alpha_1\varphi_1\pi_3)mm_t)]/u_1\}\Delta p_{t-1} \\
&-\{[\beta c\alpha_1\varphi_2\pi_3(\pi_3 c+(\pi_1+\pi_3\psi_1+c\alpha_1\varphi_1\pi_3)mm_t)+r\varphi_1\varphi_2 mm_t]/u_1\}Y_{c,t-1} \\
&-\{[\beta c\alpha_1\varphi_3\pi_3(\pi_3 c+(\pi_1+\pi_3\psi_1+c\alpha_1\varphi_1\pi_3)mm_t)+r\varphi_1\varphi_3 mm_t]/u_1\}\Delta G_t \\
&-\{[\beta c\alpha_2\pi_3(\pi_3 c+(\pi_1+\pi_3\psi_1+c\alpha_1\varphi_1\pi_3)mm_t)]/u_1\}\Delta \mathrm{REER}_{t-1} \\
&-\{[\beta\pi_3(\pi_3 c+(\pi_1+\pi_3\psi_1+c\alpha_1\varphi_1\pi_3)mm_t)]/u_1\}\Delta(r_t^*+E_t s_{t+1})-\{[\varepsilon\varsigma\kappa(d_2-1)]/u_1\}\sigma_{s,t-1}
\end{aligned}
\qquad (12a)
$$

where: $u_1 = \beta[\pi_3 c + (\pi_1 + \pi_3\psi_1 + c\alpha_1\varphi_1\pi_3)mm_t]^2 + r\varphi_1^2 mm_t^2 + \epsilon\varsigma^2(d_{2-1})^2 > 0.$

$$
\begin{aligned}
\Delta \mathrm{NDA}_t = &-\{[\beta c\pi_3(\pi_1+\pi_3\psi_1+c\alpha_1\varphi_1\pi_3)mm_t+\beta(\pi_1+\pi_3\psi_1+c\alpha_1\varphi_1\pi_3)^2 mm_t^2+r\varphi_1^2 mm_t^2]/u_2\}\Delta \mathrm{NFA}_t \\
&-\{[\beta(\pi_1+\pi_3\psi_1+c\alpha_1\varphi_1\pi_3)^2 mm_t \mathrm{MB}_t+r\varphi_1^2 mm_t \mathrm{MB}_t]/u_2\}\Delta mm_t \\
&-\{[\beta\pi_2(\pi_1+\pi_3\psi_1+c\alpha_1\varphi_1\pi_3)mm_t]/u_2\}\Delta p_{t-1} \\
&-\{[\beta c\alpha_1\varphi_2\pi_3(\pi_1+\pi_3\psi_1+c\alpha_1\varphi_1\pi_3)mm_t+r\varphi_1\varphi_2 mm_t]/u_2\}Y_{c,t-1} \\
&-\{[\beta c\alpha_1\varphi_3\pi_3(\pi_1+\pi_3\psi_1+c\alpha_1\varphi_1\pi_3)mm_t+r\varphi_1\varphi_3 mm_t]/u_2\}\Delta G_t \\
&-\{[\beta c\alpha_2\pi_3(\pi_1+\pi_3\psi_1+c\alpha_1\varphi_1\pi_3)mm_t]/u_2\}\Delta \mathrm{REER}_{t-1} \\
&-\{[\beta\pi_3(\pi_1+\pi_3\psi_1+c\alpha_1\varphi_1\pi_3)mm_t]/u_2\}\Delta(r_t^*+E_t s_{t+1}) \\
&-\{[\delta\theta\eta(d_1-1)]/u_2\}\sigma_{r,t-1}
\end{aligned}
\qquad (12b)
$$

where: $u_2 = \beta[\pi_1 + \pi_3\psi_1 + c\alpha_1\varphi_1\pi_3)mm_t]^2 + r\varphi_1^2 mm_t^2 + \delta\theta^2(d_{2-1})^2 > 0.$

1.3.2 Interpreting the simultaneous equations

Eqs. 12a and 12b can be generalized as follows:

$$
\begin{aligned}
\Delta \mathrm{NFA}_t^* = \alpha_0 &- \sum_{i=0}^{n}\alpha_{1i}\Delta \mathrm{NDA}_{t-i}^* + \sum_{i=0}^{n}\alpha_{2i}\Delta mm_{t-i} + \sum_{i=1}^{n}\alpha_{3i}(\Delta p_{t-i}) + \sum_{i=1}^{n}\alpha_{4i}Y_{c,t-i} + \sum_{i=0}^{n}\alpha_{5i}\Delta G_{t-i} \\
&+ \sum_{i=1}^{n}\alpha_{6i}\Delta \mathrm{REER}_{t-i} + \sum_{i=0}^{n}\alpha_{7i}\Delta(r_{t-i}^* + E_t s_{t+1-i}) + \sum_{i=1}^{n}\alpha_{8i}(d_2-1)\sigma_{s,t-i} + \varepsilon_t
\end{aligned}
\qquad (13a)
$$

$$
\begin{aligned}
\Delta \mathrm{NDA}_t^* = \beta_0 &- \sum_{i=0}^{n}\beta_{1i}\Delta \mathrm{NFA}_{t-i}^* + \sum_{i=0}^{n}\beta_{2i}\Delta mm_{t-i} + \sum_{i=1}^{n}\beta_{3i}\Delta p_{t-i} + \sum_{i=1}^{n}\beta_{4i}Y_{c,t-i} + \sum_{i=0}^{n}\beta_{5i}\Delta G_{t-i} \\
&+ \sum_{i=1}^{n}\beta_{6i}\Delta \mathrm{REER}_{t-i} + \sum_{i=0}^{n}\beta_{7i}\Delta(r_{t-i}^* + E_t s_{t+1-i}) + \sum_{i=1}^{n}\beta_{8i}(d_1-1)\sigma_{r,t-i} + \nu_t
\end{aligned}
\qquad (13b)
$$

where:

$\Delta \mathrm{NFA}_t^*$ = The change in the adjusted net foreign assets scaled by the GDP (adjustments to be discussed in Section 1.4.2).

$\Delta \mathrm{NDA}_t^*$ = The change in the adjusted net domestic asset scaled by the GDP.

Δmm_t = The change in money multiplier for M2.[22]

Δp_t = The change in consumer price index.

$Y_{c,t}$ = Cyclical income.[23]

ΔG_t	= The change in government expenditure scaled by the GDP.
ΔREER_t	= The change in the REER.
$\Delta(r_t^* + s_{t+1}^e)$	= The change in foreign interest rate plus the expected nominal exchange rate (foreign currency per US$).[24]
σ_s	= The standard deviation of the within quarter change in the bilateral US$ exchange rate.
σ_r	= The standard deviation of the within quarter change in the monthly domestic interest rate (bank rate).
d_1	= A dummy which takes a value of 0 when the domestic money market is in deficit and a value of 2 when it is in surplus.
d_2	= A dummy which takes a value of 2 when there is an excess demand for foreign currency (and the central bank is losing reserves) and a value of 0 when foreign currency is in excess supply (and the central bank is stockpiling reserves).

The balance of payments function (Eq. 13a) is essentially a combination of monetary and portfolio balance models and consists of seven control variables. One, a rise in the M2 money multiplier, increases the domestic money supply and pushes interest rates down, thus reducing the extent of capital inflows and reserve build-up. More generally a rising multiplier might also be capturing overall tightening of credit policy, including a more restrictive policy towards capital inflows. The monetary multiplier changed substantially for some of our sample, so its inclusion is important. Two, higher inflation generates concerns about exchange rate depreciation, interest rate hikes and capital losses thereof, hence causing a reduction in reserve accumulation.[25] Three, higher lagged real output could worsen the current account (due to the income effect), reducing foreign reserve accumulation. While not explicitly captured in the model, we should note that this variable is a double-edged sword in the sense that a cyclical upturn may act as a pull factor causing more capital to flow into the economy. As such the prior expected sign of this variable is ambiguous. Four, an expansionary fiscal policy (higher government expenditure) will raise cyclical income and once again worsen the current account as discussed above. Five, foreign reserves will be decumulated due to a decrease in the current account if the lagged real effective exchange rate rises (price effect). The use of one period lags in REER, cyclical output, and inflation also reduce the possible endogeneity problems.[26] For instance, it could be argued that greater capital inflows and reserve build-up could lead to a domestic economic boom and an exchange rate appreciation (for instance, see Athukorala and Rajapatirana 2003). Similarly, we use a one period lag of the government expenditure variable to account for the possibility that a contractionary fiscal policy may be a consequence of capital inflows (i.e. fiscal tightening as an instrument of indirect sterilization) rather than the other way around.[27] Six, higher exchange rate expectations adjusted foreign interest rates can also lead to capital outflows from the country, hence reducing reserve build-up.[28] Finally, to reduce exchange rate volatility, the central bank tends to buy or sell foreign reserves (i.e. foreign exchange market intervention) when there is an excess supply or demand for foreign currency, respectively. The more volatile the exchange rates the heavier the degree of central bank intervention. Therefore, the expected sign for the interaction term should be negative.

The monetary policy function (Eq. 13b) also consists of seven control variables in the monetary reaction function in addition to the change of NFA. These control variables are considered as being important factors influencing monetary policy actions. The monetary authority generally implements a contractionary monetary policy in response to a rise in inflation, an increase in the money multiplier (to curb overall money supply growth) or to an expected exchange rate depreciation (either for its own sake or because of pass-through concerns). Thus, the expected coefficients should be negative. In addition the monetary authority tends to adopt a tighter monetary policy stance when there is a cyclical rise in income or a more expansionary fiscal deficit, implying negative expected coefficients again.[29] Both a rise in the REER and higher exchange rate expectations adjusted foreign interest rates can lead to a worsening of the balance of payments, causing the monetary authority to implement a contractionary monetary policy to attract capital inflows. Finally, to reduce interest rate volatility the central bank injects or withdraws funds from the market when the domestic money market is in deficit or in surplus, respectively, and the more volatile the domestic interest rate the greater is the extent of central bank intervention.

1.4 Empirics

1.4.1 Data and definitions

The estimation is based on quarterly data over the sample period from 1990:q1 to 2005:q3. We divide the whole sample period into two subsamples: the pre-crises period defined as 1990:q1 to 1997:q1, and the post-crises period defined as 1998:q3 to 2005:q3. By comparing the different values of offset and sterilization coefficients in these two subsamples we can ascertain how the extent of sterilization and degree of capital mobility have changed in the two periods for the emerging Asian economies under consideration. We supplemented the country-specific regressions with a set of pooled time series and cross-section regressions (with fixed effects) for both the pre and post-crises periods. With regard to the exchange rate expectations, we assume that economic agents have perfect foresight of future exchange rates. So, the actual nominal exchange rate at the next period is used to proxy the expected exchange rate for the next period. In addition, static expectations of future exchange rate are also used to check the robustness. If this is the case, then the current nominal exchange rate is used to proxy the expected exchange rate for the next period.

Table 1.3 summarizes the definitions and sources of the various data used in the estimating equations. The relevant variables, such as the change in the "adjusted" ΔNFA_t^* and ΔNDA_t (where * denotes

Table 1.3 Definitions and measurement of the variables used in empirical study

Variables	Definitions	Measured as	Data (Source)
NFA_t^*	Foreign reserves denominated in domestic currency minus foreign liabilities.	*Reserve($)* × S_t – *Foreign Liabilities.*	IFS
ΔNFA_t^*	The change in NFA_t^* without revaluation effect scaled by the GDP.	$[NFA_t - NFA_{t-1}\left(\frac{S_t}{S_{t-1}}\right)]/GDP_t$	
ΔNDA_t^*	The change in (net domestic assets + net other assets) scaled by the GDP.	$[\Delta NDA_t + \Delta NOA_t - \Delta K_t + NFA_{t-1}^*\left(\frac{S_t}{S_{t-1}}-1\right)]/GDP_t$.	IFS
mm_t	Money Multiplier for M2.	*M2*/Reserve Money.	IFS
Δmm_t	The change in money multiplier for M2.	$\ln(mm_t) - \ln(mm_{t-1})$	

Continued

Table 1.3 Continued

Variables	Definitions	Measured as	Data (Source)
ΔREER_t	The change in Real Effective Exchange Rate.	$\ln(\text{REER}_t) - \ln(\text{REER}_{t-1})$	IFS
$Y_{c,t}$	Cyclical Income. The real output deviated from its trend scaled by the trend. The trend is measured by HP filter.	*[ln(Real GDP)—HP filter trend]/HP filter trend.*	*IFS and TEJ Great China Database*
Δp_t	Inflation Rate.	$\ln(cpi_t) - \ln(cpi_{t-1})$*	IFS
$\Delta(r_t^* + E_t s_{t+1})$	The change in exchanged adjusted foreign interest rate. The foreign interest rate is the interest rate for US 3-month treasury bill.	$\Delta(r_t^* + \ln s_{t+1})$ *if perfect foresight.* $\Delta(r_t^* + \ln s_t)$ *if static expectations.*	IFS
ΔG_t	The change in government fiscal deficit scaled GDP.	$\Delta G_t / GDP_{t^*}$	IFS
σ_s	Volatility of exchange rate.	*The standard deviation of the within quarter change in the daily bilateral US$ exchange rate.*	*Bloomberg , Board of Governors of Federal Reserve and Reserve Bank of Australia*
σ_r	Volatility of domestic short-term interest rate.	*The standard deviation of the within quarter change in the monthly domestic interest rate (bank rate).*	IFS
D_1	Dummy variable for $\Delta \text{NFA}_t < 0$.	$d_1 = 2$ *if* $\Delta \text{NDA} < 0$; *0 otherwise.*	
D_2	Dummy variable for $\Delta \text{NFA}_t < 0$.	$d_2 = 2$ *if* $\Delta \text{NFA}_t < 0$; *0 otherwise.*	
$q2$–$q4$	Seasonal dummies.	*q2 = 1 if the second quarter; q3 = 1 if the third quarter; q4 = 1 if the fourth quarter; otherwise 0.*	

Source: Authors.

adjustments which are discussed in section 1.4.2) and ΔG_t, are scaled by GDP. To check for stationarity we applied the standard unit root test using the Augmented Dickey Fuller (ADF) to each of the variables and found them all to be stationary at the 10 per cent level of significance (see Tables 1.4a and 1.4b).[30] We used the Hodrick-Prescott (HP) method to measure the trend of real output. In addition we used the standard deviation of the within quarter change in the daily US$ bilateral exchange rate and short-term bank rates to proxy the volatility of exchange rate and volatility of domestic interest rate, respectively.[31] Since we do not have consistent quarterly data on forward rates we assumed that economic agents had either perfect foresight or static expectations to proxy the expected exchange rates for the next period. We also included three quarterly dummies in the model to account for any possible seasonality effects.

1.4.2 Adjusting the net foreign asset and net domestic asset figures

Since both the NDA_t and NFA_t are based on the monetary authorities' balance sheet, care must be taken in accounting for non-policy related changes in the variables such as the revaluation effects due to gold value and exchange rate fluctuations.[32] To exclude monetary gold from the foreign assets we use the product of foreign reserves denominated in US dollar and the bilateral exchange rate (domestic currency/US$) to proxy foreign assets. The NFA without the revaluation effect can be stated as follows:

$$\text{NFA}_t = (R_t \times s_t) - \text{FL}_t \tag{14}$$

where: R_t is the foreign exchange reserves denominated in US$, s_t is the exchange rate against US$, and FL_t refer to the central bank foreign liabilities.

We use the $(R_t \times s_t)$ rather than FA_t as there are some differences between the two in the case of many of the emerging Asian economies, and, from an analytical perspective, monetary sterilization pertains specifically to international reserves.[33] However, the problem with using $(R_t \times s_t)$ is that reserve values could change because of currency fluctuations, but these valuation effects will be captured in the bank capital and will not alter the domestic currency value of the banking system's holding of high powered money.[34] As such we need to exclude these effects before estimation. Ideally if we had the currency composition of reserves we could adjust for the valuation changes. Given that such data

Table 1.4a Unit-root test (ADF test): Pre-crises period (1990:q1–1997:q1)

	India	Indonesia	Korea	Malaysia	Philippines	Singapore	Taiwan	Thailand
ΔNFA_t^*	–2.980**	–3.493**	–3.046**	–3.562**	–3.909***	–5.220***	–4.006***	–3.521**
ΔNDA_t^*	–4.936***	–3.188**	–7.033***	–3.265**	–4.273***	–4.613***	–4.452***	–5.284***
Δmm_t	–5.000***	–7.101***	–6.316***	–3.046**	–5.182***	–3.712***	–3.332**	–6.542***
Δp_t	–7.454***	–5.704***	–4.361***	–4.958***	–3.173**	–3.594**	–5.846***	–4.198***
$Y_{c,t}$	–5.808***	–3.232**	–4.916***	–4.718***	–6.007***	–4.357***	–3.627**	–2.711*
ΔG_t	–3.904***	–8.091***	–6.999***	–6.662***	–6.577***	–7.038***	–5.499***	–8.538***
$\Delta(r_t^* + E_t s_{t+1})$	–3.714***	–3.476**	–3.268**	–4.649***	–2.639*	–2.809*	–2.648*	–5.195***
$\Delta REER_t$	–4.331***	–5.659***	–4.375***	–3.897***	–3.896***	–5.592***	–4.977***	–3.575**
$(d_2 - 1)\,\sigma_{s,t}$	–4.233***	–5.606***	–1.885*	–3.689**	–4.861***	–4.341***	–4.167***	–1.656*
$(d_1 - 1)\,\sigma_{r,t}$	–4.606***	–4.273***	–4.967***	–2.308**	–3.553**	–4.633***	–7.284***	–4.029***

Table 1.4b Unit-root test (ADF test): Post-crises period (1998:q3–2005:q3)

	India	Indonesia	Korea	Malaysia	Philippines	Singapore	Taiwan	Thailand
ΔNFA_t^*	–3.690**	–6.022***	–4.517***	–2.667*	–3.765***	–3.784***	–2.968*	–3.282**
ΔNDA_t^*	–2.831*	–6.191***	–4.082***	–2.898*	–6.754***	–3.362**	–3.338**	–3.045**
Δmm_t	–5.466***	–6.056***	–4.333***	–3.011**	–3.724***	–4.064***	–3.431**	–5.576***
Δp_t	–4.854***	–4.032***	–5.089***	–5.381***	–2.672*	–2.945*	–3.601**	–3.426**
$Y_{c,t}$	–6.611***	–3.256**	–2.753*	–4.045***	–8.266***	–2.896*	–4.064***	–3.597**
ΔG_t	–4.132***	–3.729***	–4.664***	–5.483***	–5.807***	–10.80***	–6.973***	–8.095***
$\Delta(r_t^* + E_t s_{t+1})$	–4.050***	–4.715***	–2.799*	–5.330***	–4.264***	–4.493***	–4.033***	–2.637*
$\Delta REER_t$	–3.416**	–3.725**	–4.111***	–3.079**	–4.010***	–3.103**	–3.219**	–4.179***
$(d_2 - 1)\,\sigma_{s,t}$	–3.560**	–4.728***	–3.424**	–26.76***	–3.941***	–5.260***	–3.494**	–3.784***
$(d_1 - 1)\,\sigma_{r,t}$	–5.672***	–2.630*	–4.792***	–2.779*	–2.944*	–4.726***	–3.948***	–4.478***

Note: (*) Significant at more than 10 per cent; (**) significant at more than 5 per cent; (***) significant at more than 1 per cent.

Source: Authors.

are not available, the best we can do is assume that all the reserves are held in US dollar and adjust the reserves for changes in the bilateral US dollar rate.[35] Since the revaluation effect is the change in the NFA due to exchange rate fluctuation, it can be measured as follows:

$$\text{Revaluation effect} = \text{NFA}_{t-1}\left(\frac{s_t}{s_{t-1}} - 1\right) \quad (15)$$

Therefore, the revised change of net foreign assets $\Delta\text{NFA}_t^* = \text{NFA}_t - \text{NFA}_{t-1}(s_t/s_{t-1})$. The adjusted variable excludes the price or valuation effect, which, as noted, should have no direct impact on liquidity.

ΔNDA_t^* is defined as $\Delta\text{NDA}_t + \Delta\text{NOA}_t - \Delta K_t$ + Revaluation effect. Since revaluation effect is realized in the equity account of balance sheet, the revaluation effect has to be excluded (plus back) from NDA at the same time when we exclude revaluation effect from ΔNFA_t^*.[36] While the ΔNOA_t usually reflects the increase in interbank borrowing and the decline in the capital accounts and other domestic liabilities of the banking system and capital accounts, in some cases it is quite important, as central bank bills and notes which are used to sterilize inflows are sometimes included under this category.[37] To illustrate the importance of ensuring that the central bank-based variables are appropriately adjusted, Table 1.5 shows simple correlations between ΔNFA_t and ΔNFA_t^* as well as between ΔNDA_t and ΔNDA_t^*. The correlations regarding the former are positive in all countries and are fairly high (i.e. over 0.8) in India and Malaysia, and moderate in Korea, the

Table 1.5 Simple correlations between actual and adjusted ΔNFA and ΔNDA

	Corr (ΔNFA_t^*, ΔNFA_t)	Corr (ΔNDA_t^*, ΔNDA_t)
India	0.949	0.968
Indonesia	0.189	0.907
Korea	0.632	0.933
Malaysia	0.913	0.969
Philippines	0.791	0.964
Singapore	0.636	0.775
Taiwan	0.771	0.925
Thailand	0.309	0.820

Note: Actual change in NDAs can be measured by deducting actual change in NFAs from change in monetary base. Therefore, $\Delta\text{NDA}_t = \Delta\text{MB} - \Delta\text{NFA}_t$. The definition of adjusted ΔNFA and ΔNDA can be found in Section 1.4.2.

Source: Authors.

Philippines, Singapore, and Taiwan (0.6–0.7), but rather low in the cases of Thailand (0.33) and Indonesia in particular (0.18). In the case of the latter (ΔNDA_t and ΔNDA_t^*) correlations are positive and high in all economies. Overall, the important point is that the correlations between the adjusted and unadjusted figures are not perfect, which suggests that failure to make the appropriate adjustments when estimating the offset and sterilization coefficients can lead to misleading results.

1.4.3 Empirical results

We use the two-stage least square (2SLS) method to estimate the simultaneous eqs. 15a and 15b. We ran the regressions based on both perfect foresight and static exchange rate expectations. Since the Hausman test (Table 1.6) shows that there is no significant difference in the estimations using fixed and random effects, we only report the empirical results estimated by random effects. The empirical results for panel data are reported in Table 1.7. For ease of interpretation we discuss the absolute values of the sterilization and offset coefficients.

The pre-crises offset coefficients in both the perfect foresight and static exchange rate expectations models are around 0.8, while the sterilization coefficients are about 1. Post-crises, while the offset coefficients fell to between 0.5 and 0.6 in both models, it is somewhat harder to draw a conclusion regarding the sterilization coefficient. In the case

Table 1.6 Hausman test

	Balance of payments function	Monetary reaction function
Perfect foresight		
Pre-crises period	5.53 (0.903)	–6.82
Post-crises period	4.10 (0.943)	2.34 (0.997)
Static expectation		
Pre-crises period	6.82 (0.814)	–6.87
Post-crises period	6.21 (0.797)	–6.03

Notes: 1) The number in parentheses is the P-value. All tests failed to reject the null hypothesis that the coefficients estimated by the efficient random effects estimator are the same as the ones estimated by the consistent fixed effects estimator.
2) Monetary Reaction Function fitted on data fails to meet the asymptotic assumption of Hausman test during post-crises period.

Source: Authors.

Table 1.7 Panel data with random effects estimation, 1990:q1–1997:q1 and 1998:q3–2005:q3

Random effects model	1990:q1–1997:q1		1998:q3–2005:q3	
	ΔNFA_t^*	ΔNDA_t^*	ΔNFA_t^*	ΔNDA_t
Perfect foresight				
Intercept	**0.015***	0.008	**0.018****	0.007
	(0.007)	(0.008)	(0.007)	(0.010)
ΔNDA_t^*	**–0.796*****	–	**–0.601*****	–
	(0.074)		(0.065)	
ΔNFA_t^*	–	**–1.046*****	–	**–1.265*****
		(0.083)		(0.118)
Δmm_t	**–0.338*****	**–0.419*****	**–0.289*****	**–0.519*****
	(0.057)	(0.044)	(0.053)	(0.043)
Δp_{t-1}	–0.035	0.092	–0.312	0.058
	(0.263)	(0.268)	(0.201)	(0.216)
$Y_{c,t-1}$	0.006	–0.038	0.025	0.021
	(0.093)	(0.091)	(0.016)	(0.020)
ΔG_{t-1}	0.083	**0.106***	**–0.173*****	**–0.168****
	(0.064)	(0.063)	(0.055)	(0.075)
$\Delta(r_t^* + E_t s_{t+1})$	**–0.352*****	**–0.310****	**–0.440*****	**–0.640*****
	(0.119)	(0.133)	(0.082)	(0.098)
$\Delta REER_{t-1}$	0.163	0.147	**–0.117***	**–0.247*****
	(0.110)	(0.116)	(0.068)	(0.091)
$(d_2 - 1)\,\sigma_{s,t-1}$	0.001	–	0.00003	–
	(0.001)		(0.00002)	
$(d_1 - 1)\,\sigma_{r,\,t-1}$	–	0.0001	–	**0.005****
		(0.001)		(0.002)
q1	**0.020****	**0.023****	0.012	**0.022****
	(0.010)	(0.010)	(0.009)	(0.011)
q2	**0.016***	**0.016***	–0.007	–0.001
	(0.009)	(0.009)	(0.009)	(0.012)
q3	0.004	0.005	**0.020****	**0.021***
	(0.009)	(0.009)	(0.009)	(0.012)
Adj. R^2	0.699	0.741	0.700	0.774
Static expectation				
Intercept	**0.013***	0.006	**0.019****	**–0.015***
	(0.008)	(0.008)	(0.009)	(0.009)
ΔNDA_t^*	**–0.838*****	–	**–0.514*****	–
	(0.080)		(0.090)	
ΔNFA_t^*	–	**–0.966*****	–	**–0.846*****
		(0.079)		(0.130)
Δmm_t	**–0.364*****	**–0.428*****	**–0.230*****	**–0.545*****
	(0.060)	(0.042)	(0.067)	(0.041)

Continued

Table 1.7 Continued

Random effects model	1990:q1–1997:q1		1998:q3–2005:q3	
	ΔNFA_t^*	ΔNDA_t^*	ΔNFA_t^*	ΔNDA_t
Δp_{t-1}	−0.087	0.032	−0.176	**0.606****
	(0.267)	(0.257)	(0.262)	(0.237)
$Y_{c,t-1}$	−0.032	−0.067	0.027	0.001
	(0.093)	(0.086)	(0.018)	(0.019)
ΔG_{t-1}	0.095	**0.105***	**−0.165*****	−0.056
	(0.065)	(0.060)	(0.062)	(0.070)
$\Delta(r_t^* + E_t s_{t+1})$	−0.052	0.078	−0.159	**0.618*****
	(0.130)	(0.129)	(0.185)	(0.181)
$\Delta REER_{t-1}$	0.148	0.138	−0.247	**0.355***
	(0.114)	(0.112)	(0.192)	(0.196)
$(d_2 - 1)\,\sigma_{s,t-1}$	0.001	–	**0.0001*****	–
	(0.001)		(0.00002)	
$(d_1 - 1)\,\sigma_{r,t-1}$	–	0.001	–	0.003
		(0.001)		(0.002)
q1	**0.020****	**0.022****	0.014	**0.019***
	(0.010)	(0.010)	(0.010)	(0.011)
q2	**0.016***	0.014	−0.004	0.005
	(0.009)	(0.009)	(0.010)	(0.011)
q3	0.002	0.003	**0.022****	**0.019***
	(0.009)	(0.009)	(0.011)	(0.011)
Adj. R^2	0.687	0.746	0.638	0.769

Notes: (*) Significant at more than 10 per cent; (**) significant at more than 5 per cent; (***) significant at more than 1 per cent.
There are 232 observations for each sub-period.

Source: Authors.

of the perfect foresight model the coefficient rose to above 1, while in the case of the static expectations model the coefficient declined to around 0.8. So all that can be said with certainty is that the regional economies as a whole have experienced lower *de facto* capital mobility post-crises, while the extent of sterilization has remained fairly high after the crises.

This fall in estimated capital mobility may strike some as surprising in the light of all the discussion of growing financial globalization, but we find it quite plausible. One of the major contributing factors to the development of the Asian crisis was the insufficient recognition of exchange risk by many international lenders and borrowers.[38] This resulted in the large unhedged foreign debt positions that made currency depreciation so costly. Recognition of such exchange risk not only led to large initial capital outflows but could also be expected to reduce the interest sensitivity of post-crisis capital flows.[39]

The coefficients for the money multiplier terms are statistically significant and negative in both periods in all regressions. Interestingly, while the coefficient has risen in the case of the monetary reaction function, it has declined in the case of the balance of payments function. The lagged inflation and cyclical output terms are generally insignificant across both regressions and have inconsistent signs. These findings of either lack of statistical significance or incorrect signs of the inflation and output coefficients may be due to the fact that, while the dependent variables are fairly volatile, the inflation and detrended output series are quite stable. The lagged change in the REER is statistically significant post-crises with the correct sign under the assumption of perfect-foresight expectations, as is the lagged government expenditure variable.

Arguably of most interest when trying to differentiate between the two regressions is the coefficient for the exchange rate expectations adjusted foreign interest rate term. This term is negative and significant for both functions in both regressions pre- and post-crises under the assumption of perfect foresight. However, it is statistically significant only in the monetary reaction function post-crises and insignificant in other cases in the case of static expectations. Based on this it appears that the perfect foresight model seems to work somewhat better for the pooled sample.

We ran a simple Chow breakpoint test with a null hypothesis of no structural change between the pre and post-crises periods for all the regressions (country and pooled). The null hypothesis can be rejected in all cases, suggesting there was a structural break post-crises (Table 1.8). We also undertook a number of robustness checks on the pooled regression. Among the more important checks are the following. One, we replaced the lagged cyclical income and lagged change in REER with trade balance (akin to the original BGT model). Two, we replaced $\Delta REER_t$ with deviation of REER from trend (as ideally one needs to use a measure of real exchange rate misalignment rather than change). Three, to account for the possibility of structural changes affecting the trend output, we replaced $Y_{c,t-1}$ with ΔY_{t-1}. In all the cases the regression results (goodness of fit and

Table 1.8 Chow breakpoint test (H_0: No Structural change), pre- and post-crises periods

	Balance of payment function		Monetary reaction function	
	Perfect foresight	Static expectations	Perfect foresight	Static expectations
Pooled sample	2.335*	2.551*	59.217***	24.925***

Note: (*) Significant at more than 10 per cent; (**) significant at more than 5 per cent; (***) significant at more than 1 per cent.

Source: Authors.

statistical significance of key variables) were either unchanged or inferior to the base cases.

1.4.4 Recursive estimates

We also applied recursive estimates to investigate the dynamic changes in the offset and sterilization coefficients using the perfect foresight model which appears to be a better fit for reasons discussed above.[40] The estimated recursive offset coefficients indicate that the emerging Asian economies considered here had a relatively high degree of *de facto* capital mobility before the Asian currency crises (Figure 1.3). The estimated offset coefficients remained high and constant at around 0.8 to 0.9. However, the degree of capital mobility declined significantly during the crises period and then remained as low as 0.25 to 0.4 until mid-2003. Since then the degree of *de facto* capital mobility in Asia increased rapidly to 0.7 in 2005. This may reflect the reduced volatility of exchange rates and increasing confidence that large changes are unlikely.

The recursive estimated sterilization coefficients reveal that most monetary authorities in Asian economies sterilized quite heavily in the pre-crises period (Figure 1.4). The extent of sterilization remained high after the crises occurred in mid-1997 but declined to around 0.6 when most Asian economies implemented expansionary monetary policies to stimulate weak economies during the early 2000s. However, the marked increase in the recursively estimated sterilization coefficients after 2003 suggests that the monetary authorities in Asian economies have once again aggressively mopped up excess liquidity as the region experienced new surges in net capital inflows.[41]

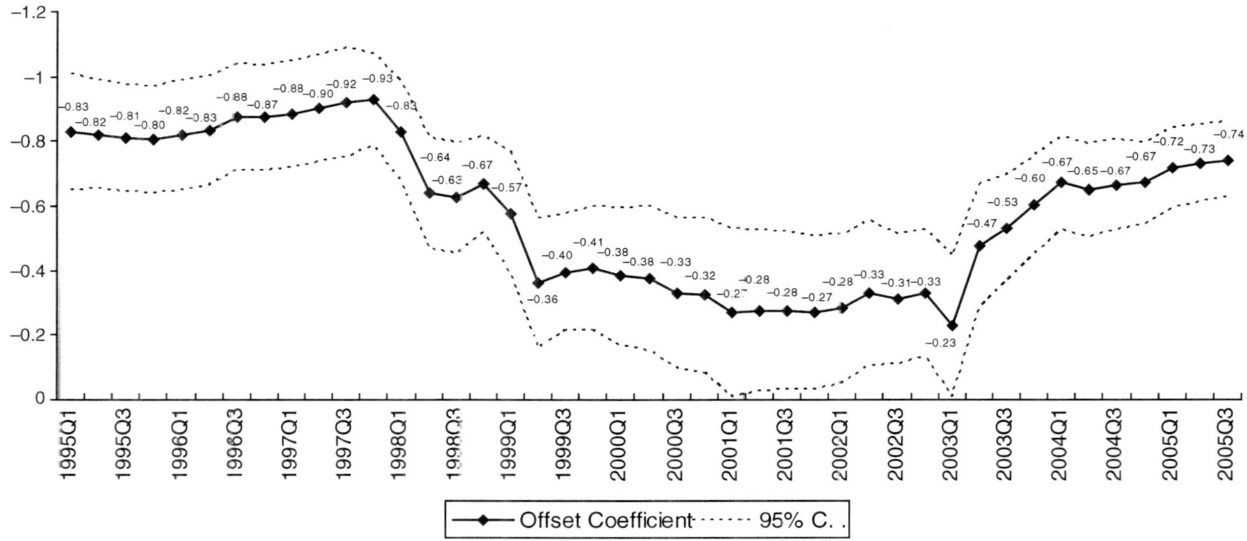

Figure 1.3 Recursive estimated offset coefficients (Based on perfect foresight model with random effects)

Source: Authors.

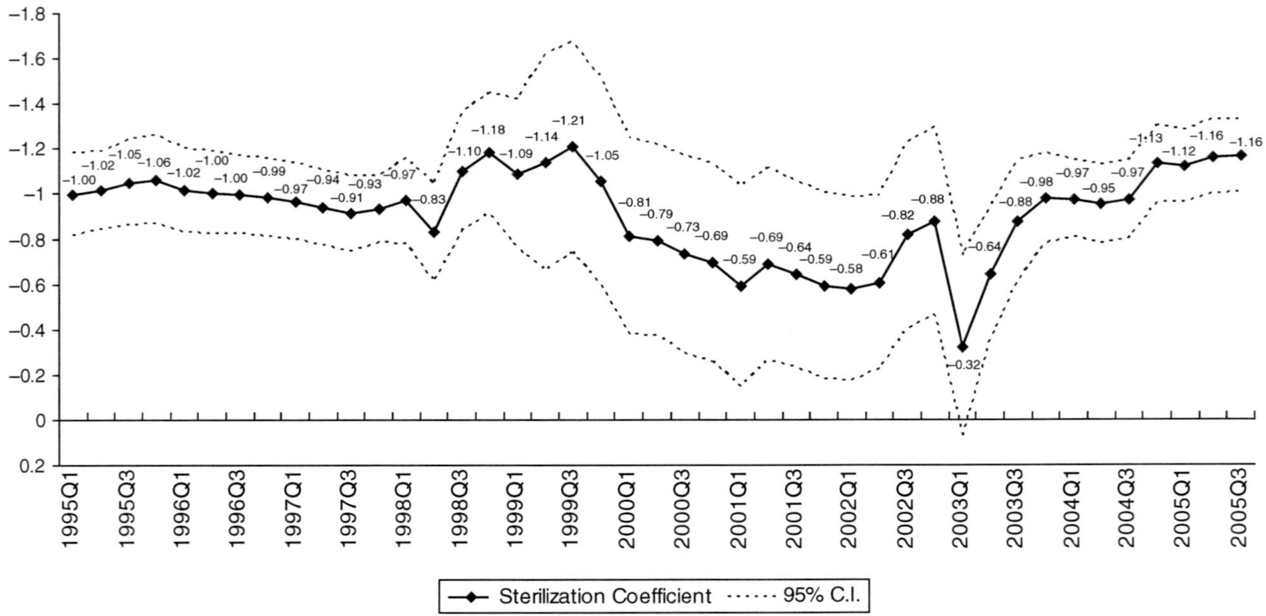

Figure 1.4 Recursive estimated sterilization coefficients (Based on perfect foresight model with random effects)

Source: Authors.

1.5 Conclusion

This chapter has used a unifying framework and common methodology to estimate the degree of *de facto* capital mobility and sterilization in emerging Asian economies (India, Indonesia, Malaysia, Philippines, Thailand, Singapore, Korea and Taiwan) in the pre-crises and post-crises periods. For the eight economies as a group, the estimated offset coefficient decreased from around 0.8–0.9 to 0.5–0.6 post-crises, indicating that the degree of *de facto* capital mobility dropped after the crises. However, there is evidence that capital mobility has picked up between 2003 and 2005 as the region has seen a resurgence in net capital inflows. There is evidence that the sterilization coefficient remained close to 1 between 1995 and 1999 and between 2003 and 2005, suggesting full sterilization of reserve accumulations. If, however, the reserve build-up persists unabated and the fiscal costs of sterilization begin to escalate (Calvo 1991) it is unlikely that the regional monetary authorities can persist with aggressive sterilization on such a huge scale.[42] In such a situation domestic macroeconomic stability could be compromised. Our conclusion that past reserve accumulations have not been a major source of excessive liquidity creation should not be taken as suggesting that there is nothing to worry about.

Notes

1. This chapter draws on an article originally published in *Global Economic Review*, 37 (2), 2008, 171–199 (Taylor & Francis Ltd). Reprinted with permission.
2. See Genberg et al. (2005) for more detailed descriptive data of reserve stockpiling in Asia.
3. There has been a growing body of literature exploring various aspects of the precautionary motive for reserve hoarding. See Aizenman et al. (2007), Garcia and Soto (2004), Jeanne and Ranciere (2006), Kim et al. (2005) and Chapter 7 of this volume.
4. As noted by the BOT (2005):

   > For a while after the 1997 crisis, accumulating foreign exchange reserve was another important consideration for exchange rate management. A strong stock of reserve helps to minimize external vulnerability and increase confidence in the economy, especially among foreign investors. (p. 280)

   A similar point has been made regarding Korea:

   > Since adoption of the free floating exchange rate system, the Korean authorities have actively endeavoured to achieve stabilisation of the foreign exchange market. In the process of overcoming the currency crisis, the Korean authorities tried to expand the nation's international reserves. (Rhee and Lee 2005, p. 204)

The importance of intervention in order to accumulate reserves comes out clearly from the survey of selected central banks by Mihaljek (2005).

5. See, for example, Willett and Kim (2006). Of course, if an economy has been maintaining a fairly stable and rigid exchange rate peg like China and Hong Kong without there being opportunistic devaluations, it may be inappropriate to characterize that as being mercantilist. With regard to the supposed floaters in emerging Asia, there is evidence that they continue to actively manage their currencies vis-à-vis the US dollar even post-1998 (see Cavoli and Rajan 2009, chapter 1; Willett et al. 2005 and McKinnon and Schnabl 2004). In addition, part of the change in reserves in US dollar terms arises from "revaluation gains" due to the depreciation of the US dollar against the major currencies in which reserves might be held, especially the Euro.
6. Our focus is on emerging Asian economies. Japan was not considered since it stopped large-scale intervention in 2004.
7. We have excluded Hong Kong from the empirical analysis as the theoretical framework to be used as motivation for the empirics (Section 1.3) is somewhat more appropriate for quasi-flexible/managed exchange rate regimes. In any event, Hong Kong does not appear to use monetary instruments to sterilize reserve build-up, as one would expect with a currency board arrangement (Mohanty and Turner 2005 and Pang 2005).
8. We exclude the period 1997:q2–1998:q2 as this is broadly the period of crises and acute monetary, exchange rate and financial instability in the region. The dating corresponds to Khalid and Kawai (2003) who identify July 1997 to June 20, 1998 as the currency crises period in Asia. (Indonesia is the possible exception to this.)
9. Needless to say that one cannot generalize across all countries. For instance, in ASEAN and the NIEs, the current account switch has largely been due to a collapse in investment rates. While investment rates in China have remained high, the current account surplus in China is primarily fuelled by rising savings rates (especially corporate savings) (see Kharas et al. 2006 and references cited within).
10. See Kharas et al. (2006) and IMF (2006) for recent discussions of capital flows in emerging Asia.
11. We make adjustments for the NDA and NFA data later in the chapter.
12. Mohanty and Turner (2005) summarize the main monetary and fiscal instruments used by some of the emerging Asian economies.
13. For instance, see Celasun et al. (1999), Fry (1993), Kim (1995), Nyatepe and Coo (1995), Sarjito (1996), Rooskareni (1998) and Brissimis, Gibson, and Tsakalotos (2002).
14. For instance in the case of Thailand the central bank has noted:

    Since 2 July 1997, Thailand has adopted a managed-float exchange rate regime, replacing the basket-peg regime which had been in operation since 1984. The value of the baht has since then been largely determined by market forces. The Bank of Thailand manages the exchange rate by intervening in the foreign exchange market from time to time in order to prevent excessive volatilities in the markets, while fundamental trends are accommodated. In other words, movements in the exchange rates which are in line with the changes in economic fundamentals and financial development would only be smoothed and not resisted. (BOT 2005, p. 276)

A broadly similar point is noted in the case of Korea:

Considering Korea's thin foreign exchange market as a small open economy, and the vulnerability of the won exchange rate to diverse external shocks and the changing global environment, the Korean authorities' efforts to stabilise the exchange rate could be regarded as inevitable. (Rhee and Lee 2005, p. 205)

Also see the survey of selected central banks by Mihaljek (2005).

15. Even in the case of Singapore, which is a basket pegger, Cavoli and Rajan (2009, chapter 5) show that the central bank loss function can be modeled in terms of output and inflation, the only difference being that they use the nominal effective exchange rate (NEER) rather than the interest rate as the policy instrument (also see Khor et al. 2004).
16. While one should ideally use the nominal effective exchange rate (NEER), we use bilateral US dollar rates as it substantially eases model solution. In any event, insofar as the bulk of trade in Asia is US dollar denominated, we probably do not lose much in terms of generality by using nominal bilateral rather than effective rates.
17. It is possible that a change in capital flows will cause a change in the money multiplier (for instance, see Chapter 5 of this volume). More generally one might think about specifying a separate equation endogenizing the money multiplier (Jha and Rath 2001).
18. More precisely, one would want to use a measure of broader fiscal stance, viz. full employment primary fiscal balance. As Athukorala and Rajapatirana (2003) note:

    (A) measure widely used to represent a fiscal policy stance in this type of analyses is the budgetary balance (measured as a ratio of GDP). But we believe that government expenditure is a superior indicator because in the context of an economic boom a country could well experience a "revenue surplus", a reflection of a faster revenue growth compared to expenditure growth. Meaningful deficit comparison across countries should correct for such biases. Another problem with published data on budget deficits is that different definitions of taxation and borrowing can heavily skew the measured deficit.
19. In reality, the current account and capital account may not be completely independent. However, since the exact links are far from clear—for instance, high capital inflows could lead to trade liberalization to curb the inflationary effects or the domestic boom, or does greater trade liberalization lead to intensified capital inflows—the assumption of independence may not be entirely inappropriate.
20. There are, of course, many other ways one could model the current account (see Edwards 2002 for a review). Given that our focus is on sterilization as opposed to the current account *per se*, a parsimonious modeling approach to the current account seems reasonable.
21. Given that we need daily data to compute a reliable within-the-quarter volatility measure, we use bilateral US dollar rates.
22. We also tried the *M1* money multiplier but the results did not change much.

23. Cyclical is defined as deviations from trend, where trend is based on the entire sample (i.e. pre and post-crises). For a more careful analysis of output gaps in the East Asian economies in our sample (i.e. excluding India) as well as Hong Kong, see Gerlach and Yiu (2004), who discuss various ways of measuring the output gap in emerging Asian economies that are undergoing significant structural changes. They find that various output gap measures, including estimates derived from the HP-filter rule, are quite highly correlated.
24. The exchange rate is in logarithm term.
25. Additionally, higher inflation could in practice engender greater uncertainty, leading to reduced capital flows, though using forward looking inflation and cyclical income in the estimations leads to concerns about causality as discussed above.
26. We tried more than one period lags but they were not significant.
27. This said, as highlighted in Table 1.3, most regional economies did not use fiscal consolidation as a means of curbing the inflationary consequences of capital inflows. The IMF (2005) makes a similar point when it notes of emerging Asia "(f)iscal policy was not used extensively to counter the aggregate demand impact of capital inflows" (p. 61).
28. Three caveats should be noted. One, we use only foreign interest rates rather than interest rate differentials as the domestic interest rates are already captured in the ΔNDA_t term (see eq. 8). Two, the "c" term in eq. 7 is a measure of risk aversion. As discussed in Section 1.2, declining risk aversion is often cited as a reason for capital inflows to Asia. Since we lack good proxies for this variable, the term is kept constant and embedded within coefficients of the structural model. Three, the other oft-noted push factor, viz. industrial country growth, is likely to be highly correlated with domestic country cyclical growth, which is already included in the equation. Dasgupta and Ratha (2000) and Montiel and Reinhart (2000) discuss the determinants of capital flows into developing economies.
29. Of course there are exceptions. For instance, during an economic downturn there could be simultaneous use of expansionary monetary and fiscal policies, and vice versa during an upturn in economic activity.
30. Siklos (2000) pointed out a similar problem with the Hungarian–German interest rate differential and has argued that interest rates should not be difference stationary. The ADF results were confirmed by the Kwiatkowski–Phillips–Schmidt–Shin (KPSS) test.
31. Specifically, for Korea, Philippines, Taiwan and Thailand we use the Money market rate. For Indonesia we use the Call money rate. For Malaysia we use the Interbank overnight money rate. For Singapore we use the 3-month Interbank rate.
32. Another factor includes interest earnings earned from foreign reserves accumulation. We ignore this issue.
33. Loosely speaking, this should correspond to the liquid part of foreign assets of the central bank. Ideally we should also be using only the liquid portion of central bank foreign liabilities. These data are not available.
34. In general, the monetary authority recognizes the end-year revaluation of foreign currency liabilities and assets in the Profit and Loss account of the income statement. Since the end-year income statement balance will be

included in the equity (K) account of balance sheet, the change of NFA due to the revaluation effect can be offset by the change of equity so that the domestic monetary base will be unchanged. In other words, if NFA rises because of an increase in s_t, MB = NFA ↑ + NDA + NOA – K ↑.

35. Of course, we could assume different scenarios such as Prasad and Wei (2005) do in the case of China. However, we have no basis of making such assumptions, and, given the number of other issues we deal with in this chapter, it seems wise to refrain from making such ad hoc adjustments.
36. Korea, Singapore, and Taiwan do not report data for equity (K) account on IFS, even though the balance sheet is in balance. Therefore, for these three economies, $\Delta NDA_t^* = \Delta NDA_t + \Delta NOA_t +$ revaluation effect.
37. For instance, see Hu (2004) in the case of China.
38. See the analysis and references in Willett et al. (2005).
39. While some countries tightened capital controls during the crisis, average levels of controls are not noticeably tighter after the crisis than before. See Li et al. (2006).
40. The coefficients are initially estimated for the period between 1990:q1 and 1995:q1. Then, whenever we add one more observation to estimate the following offset and sterilization coefficients, we drop the earliest observation at the same time so as to ensure uniform sample size. For example, the second coefficient is estimated by using the sample period from 1990:q2 to 1995:q2. So each coefficient is estimated by using five year observations. To capture the effect of the currency crises, we add a crises dummy (equals 1 between 1997:q2 and 1998:q2) in the model.
41. See Kharas et al. (2006) for a discussion of capital flows in East Asia.
42. The World Bank (2005) and Mohanty and Turner (2005) discuss the latter two costs and Rodrik (2006) discusses the issue of opportunity costs. These costs need to be balanced against the likelihood that higher reserve holdings reduce a country's perceived international credit standing, hence lowering the country's risk premium.

References

Aizenman, J. and N. Marion (2003). "The High Demand for International Reserves in the Far East: What's Going On?," *Journal of Japanese and International Economics*, 17, 370–400.

Aizenman, J., Y. Lee, and Y. Rhee (2007). "International Reserves Management and Capital Mobility in a Volatile World: Policy Considerations and a Case Study of Korea," *Journal of the Japanese and International Economics*, 21, 1–15.

Argy, V. and P.J.K. Kouri (1974). "Sterilization Policies and the Volatility of International Reserves," in R.Z. Aliber (eds), *National Monetary Policies and the International Financial System*, Chicago: University of Chicago.

Athukorala, P.C. and S. Rajapatirana (2003). "Capital Inflows and the Real Exchange Rate: a Comparative Study of Asia and Latin America," *The World Economy*, 26, 613–637.

Bank of Thailand (BOT) (2005). "Foreign Exchange Policy and Intervention in Thailand," in *Foreign Exchange Market Intervention in Emerging Markets: Motives, Techniques and Implications*, BIS Papers No. 24, 276–282.

Bird, G. and R.S. Rajan (2003). "Too Good to be True?: The Adequacy of International Reserve Holdings in an Era of Capital Account Crises," *The World Economy*, 26, 873–891.

Brissimis, S., H. Gibson, and E. Tsakalotos (2002). "A Unifying Framework for Analyzing Offsetting Capital Flows and Sterilization: Germany and the ERM," *International Journal of Finance and Economics*, 7, 63–78.

Calvo, G. (1991). "The Perils of Sterilization," *IMF Staff Papers*, 38, 921–936.

Cavoli, T. and R.S. Rajan (2009). *Exchange Rate Regimes and Macroeconomic Management in Asia*, Hong Kong: Hong Kong University Press (forthcoming).

Celasun, O., C. Denizer, and D. He (1999). "Capital Flows, Macroeconomic Management, and the Financial System: Turkey, 1989–97," Policy Research Working Paper No. 2141, The World Bank.

Dasgupta, D. and D. Ratha (2000). "What Factors Appear to Drive Private Capital Flows to Developing Countries? And How does Official Lending Respond?" Policy Research Working Paper No. 2392, The World Bank.

Edwards, S. (2002). "Does the Current Account Matter?," in S. Edwards and J.A. Frankel (eds), *Preventing Currency Crises in Emerging Markets*, Chicago and London: University of Chicago Press.

Fry, M.J. (1993). "Foreign Debt Accumulation: Financial and Fiscal Effects and Monetary Policy Reactions in Developing Countries," *Journal of International Money and Finance*, 12, 347–367.

Garcia P. and C.G. Soto (2004). "Large Hoarding of International Reserves: Are they Worth it?," in R. Caballero, C. Calderón and L.F. Céspedes, *External Vulnerability and Preventive Policies*, Central Bank of Chile.

Genberg, H., R.N. McCauley, Y.C. Park, and A. Persaud (2005). *Official Reserves and Currency Management in Asia: Myth, Reality and the Future*, Geneva Reports on the World Economy 7, International Center for Monetary and Banking Studies.

Gerlach, S. and M. Yiu (2004). "Estimating Output Gaps in Asia: A Cross-country Study," *Journal of Japanese and International Economics*, 18, 115–136.

Hu, F. (April 2004). "Capital Flows, Overheating, and Nominal Exchange Rate Regime in China," mimeo.

International Monetary Fund (IMF) (September 2005). *Regional Economic Outlook: Asia and Pacific*, IMF.

IMF (May 2006). *Regional Economic Outlook: Asia and Pacific*, IMF.

Jeanne, O. and R. Ranciere (2006). "The Optimal Level of International Reserves for Emerging Market Economies: Formulas and Applications," unpublished, IMF.

Jha, R. and D.P. Rath (2001). "On the Endogeneity of the Money Multiplier in India," Working Paper Series No. 2001–01, Australia National University.

Khalid, A.M. and M. Kawai (2003). "Was Financial Market Contagion the Source of Economic Crisis in Asia? Evidence using a Multivariate VAR Model," *Journal of Asian Economics*, 14, 131–156.

Kharas, H., R.S. Rajan, and E. Vostroknutova (2006). "Finance (In East Asia)," in H. Kharas and I. Gill (eds), *An East Asian Renaissance: Ideas for Competitive Growth*, Washington, DC: The World Bank.

Khor, H.E, E. Robinson, and J. Lee (2004). "Managed Floating and Intermediate Exchange Rate Systems: The Singapore Experience," *Staff Paper No. 37*, Monetary Authority of Singapore (MAS).

Kim, G. (1995). "Exchange Rate Constraints and Money Control in Korea," Working Paper No. 1995–011A, Federal Reserve Bank of San Francisco.

Kim, J.S., Jie Li, S. Ozon, R,. Rajan, and T.D. Willett (2005). "Reserve Adequacy in Asia Revisited: New Benchmarks Based on the Size and Composition of Capital Flows," *Monetary and Exchange Rate Arrangement in East Asia*, Seoul: Korea Institute for Economic Policy.

Li, J., O. Sula, and T.D. Willett (2006). "A New Framework for Analyzing Adequate and Excessive Reserve Levels Under High Capital Mobility," paper presented at the 2006 Annual Meeting of the Asia Pacific Economics Association, Seattle.

McKinnon, R. and G. Schnabl (2004). "The Return to Soft Dollar Pegging in East Asia: Mitigating Conflicted Virtue," *International Finance*, 7, 169–201.

Mihaljek, D. (2005). "Survey of Central Banks' Views on Effects of Intervention," in *Foreign Exchange Market Intervention in Emerging Markets: Motives, Techniques and Implications*, BIS Papers No. 24, 82–96.

Montiel, P. and C. Reinhart (2000). "The Dynamics of Capital Movements to Emerging Economies during the 1990s," in S. Griffith-Jones and M. Montes (eds), *Short-term Capital Movements and Balance of Payments Crises*, Oxford: Oxford University Press.

Mohanty, M.S. and P. Turner (2005). "Intervention: What are the Domestic Consequences?," in *Foreign Exchange Market Intervention in Emerging Markets: Motives, Techniques and Implications*, BIS Papers No. 24, 56–81.

Nyatepe-Coo, A.A. (1995). "Resource Shocks, Real Exchange Rate Appreciation and the Independence of Monetary Policy in Developing Oil-Exporting Countries," *International Economic Journal*, 9, 91–107.

Obstfeld, M. (1982). "Can We Sterilize? Theory and Evidence," *American Economic Review*, 72, 45–50.

Obstfeld, M. (1986). "Rational and Self-fulfilling Balance of Payments," *American Economic Review*, 76, 72–81.

Obstfeld, M. (1994). "The Logic of Currency Crises," *Cahiers Économiques et Monetaries*, 43, Banque De France, Paris, 189–213.

Ouyang, A.Y., R.S. Rajan, and T.D. Willett (2007). "China as a Reserve Sink: The Evidence from Offset and Sterilization Coefficients," WP No.10/2007, Hong Kong Institute for Monetary Research.

Pang, P. (2005). "Foreign Exchange Operations: The Recent Experience of Hong Kong," in *Foreign Exchange Market Intervention in Emerging Markets: Motives, Techniques and Implications*, BIS Papers No. 24, 162–170.

Prasad, E. and S.J. Wei (December 2005). "Understanding the Structure of Cross-border Capital Flows: The Case of China," mimeo, IMF.

Rhee, G.J. and E.M. Lee (2005). "Foreign Exchange Intervention and Foreign Exchange Market Development in Korea," in *Foreign Exchange Market Intervention in Emerging Markets: Motives, Techniques and Implications*, BIS Papers No. 24, 196–208.

Rodrik, D. (2006). "The Social Cost of Foreign Exchange Reserves," *International Economic Journal*, 20, 253–266.

Rooskareni, N. (1998). "The Effects of Monetary Policy in Indonesia," unpublished PhD dissertation, The Claremont Graduate University.

Sarjito, I. (1996). "The Short-Run Independence of Monetary Policy in Indonesia: Estimation of the Offset Coefficient and the Monetary Authority's Reaction Function," unpublished PhD dissertation, The Claremont Graduate School.

Siklos, P. (2000). "Capital Flows in a Transitional Economy and the Sterilization Dilemma: The Hungarian Experience, 1992–97," *Journal of Policy Reform*, 3, 413–438.

Willett, T.D., and Y. Kim (2006). "Assessing Korea's Post Crisis Managed Float," in *Korea's Economy*, Korea Economic Institute, Washington, DC.

Willett, T.D., Y. Kim, and I. Nitithanprapas (2005). "Some Methodological Issues on Classifying Exchange Rate Regimes," Working Paper, Claremont Graduate University.

World Bank (2005). Global Development Finance 2005, New York: Oxford University Press.

2
What is the Impact of Exchange Rate Changes on Inflation in Asia?[1]

(Co-authored with Amit Ghosh)

2.1 Introduction

Exchange rate pass-through (ERPT) refers to the transmission of exchange rate changes into import (export) prices of specific goods in the destination market currency price of goods. ERPT is said to be partial or incomplete if the import price rises by less than 1 percent, as the exporters absorb a portion of the exchange rate change. This may arise, for instance, because firms engage in pricing-to-market (PTM), which effectively implies that firms with market power in a segmented market are able to sell the same product at different prices in different markets (Dornbusch 1987; Krugman 1987; also see the surveys by Goldberg and Knetter 1997 and Menon 1995).

The issue of ERPT is particularly important in view of its policy implications for small and open economies. Specifically, if ERPT is low, use of any exchange rate based adjustments to improve the trade balance for these economies may be rendered less effective, an issue that has been of some concern in the case of the persistent US trade deficit despite secular declines in the US dollar.[2] Conversely, low ERPT implies that small and open economies may be less concerned about the potential inflationary consequences of exchange rate fluctuations.[3] The degree of ERPT has implications for the transmission of shocks for nations characterized by high levels of intraregional trade.

ERPT is commonly analyzed at two levels. One set of studies deals with the transmission of exchange rate changes into import and export prices. This is referred to as "first stage pass-through." Under this category the literature has examined ERPT both at the aggregate level (for total exports and import prices) and at disaggregated levels (using industry or product specific import/export price data). The second set of studies examines ERPT into overall domestic prices such as the CPI, PPI or WPI. This is referred to as "second stage pass-through." Second stage ERPT is typically lower than that of the first stage. This is because aggregate price indices may include non-tradable goods and may be impacted by domestic taxes, as well as the fact that wholesalers and retailers in the importing nation may absorb some of the exchange rate changes.

The bulk of the ERPT literature to date has been focused on the US and other industrial countries. However, given the extent of openness of Asian economies to international trade flows, the factors determining the extent of ERPT into import/export prices are naturally a key area of policy interest to the region. This chapter examines the recent analytical and empirical literature on ERPT with particular reference to Asia. The present analysis attempts to survey and synthesize the existing findings. We also outline some further areas of research in ERPT pertinent to Asia.

The remainder of the chapter is organized as follows. The next section develops a simple framework to analyze ERPT and offers an overview of the determinants of ERPT. Section 2.3 goes on to review some of the empirical literature on ERPT in Asia. Section 2.4 considers the issue of production sharing, which is a key characteristic of trade in Asia, and its consequent implications for ERPT. Section 2.5 offers a few concluding remarks on areas for future research.

2.2 What does the analytical literature on ERPT tell us?

2.2.1 A simple framework to understand ERPT

To aid in the discussion of the determinants of ERPT and the analysis of the empirical studies discussed in the remainder of this chapter, we develop a stylized framework of ERPT and PTM. We consider two countries trading a single good Y, with country A being the importing nation and country B the exporting one. Let E_B^A be the bilateral exchange rate defined as the number of units of A's currency per unit of B's.

Assuming law of one price (LOP) holds in relative terms:

$$\frac{\Delta \ln P_Y^A}{\Delta \ln E_B^A} = \frac{\Delta \ln P_Y^B}{\Delta \ln E_B^A} + 1 \qquad (1)$$

where P_Y^A = price of Y in local currency of A. P_Y^B = price of Y in the currency of B, with all variables being expressed in log form. So, ERPT into A's currency is given by eq. (1). ERPT for B in its own currency is given by the first term on the right hand side of eq. (1).

If $(\Delta \ln P_Y^B / \Delta \ln E_B^A) = 0$, this implies no PTM by exporters of B into their currency denominated prices and consequently full pass-through to A's imports. On the other hand, if $(\Delta \ln P_Y^B / \Delta \ln E_B^A) = -1$, this implies full PTM by exporters in country B, and consequently zero pass-through into A's imports.

Under imperfect competition we can write P_Y^B more generally as:

$$\ln P_Y^B = \ln MC_Y^B + \ln\left[MKP_Y^B\left(E_B^A\right)^{-}\right] \quad (2)$$

where MC = marginal costs and MKP = exporter's mark-up.

The literature generally assumes that MC is constant to a change in the exchange rate (though this assumption is too strong as will be noted below) and MKP varies with exchange rate. Specifically $-1 < (\Delta \ln MKP_Y^B / \Delta \ln E_B^A) < 0$. So the greater the PTM by exporters in country B, the more willing they are to raise mark-ups in response to a depreciation in their country's currency. In other words, as $(\Delta \ln MKP_Y^B / \Delta \ln E_B^A) \rightarrow -1$, $(\Delta \ln P_Y^B / \Delta \ln E_B^A) \rightarrow -1$ and therefore, $(\Delta \ln P_Y^B / \Delta \ln E_B^A) \rightarrow 0$.[4]

We now assume that country B imports intermediate goods from country A. In this situation we have $\ln MC_Y^B = \ln [MC_Y^B(E_B^A)]$ and $-1 < (\Delta \ln MC_Y^B / \Delta \ln E_B^A) < 0$, that is a depreciation of country B's currency increases the costs of procuring intermediate goods from country A. The more reliant is B on imported intermediate goods from A and the greater the import elasticity, the more likely that $(\Delta \ln MC_Y^B / \Delta \ln E_B^A) \rightarrow -1$. In this case, $(\Delta \ln P_Y^B / \Delta \ln E_B^A) \rightarrow -1$. This scenario, whereby country B is exporting the final good to its partner nation A while simultaneously importing intermediate goods, is referred to as the "production sharing." With this pattern of trade, production sharing reduces the extent of ERPT to the importing country. In the remainder of this section we survey some of the recent empirical literature on ERPT in Asia.

2.2.2 Determinants of ERPT

There is a voluminous body of literature which has helped rationalize the factors that affect the extent of ERPT into import (export) prices as well as into aggregate price indices such as CPI, PPI or WPI.

First, at the disaggregated level is the nature of the goods/industries under consideration. If exporters do not face much competition then mark-ups/prices of the exporters may be somewhat less responsive to fluctuations in the value of the exporter's currency against the buyers. In this situation exchange rate changes are fully passed through in terms of the buyers' currency. Conversely, if the destination market is highly competitive, firms may try to guard their market share by absorbing exchange rate changes by accepting lower mark-ups. The willingness to accept lower domestic unit prices in turn leads to lower levels of ERPT.

In a pioneering study Knetter (1993) found differences in industries to be critical in explaining different degrees of ERPT. For example, exports to certain US industries, such as automobiles and alcoholic beverages, showed higher PTM and correspondingly lower ERPT as exporters tried to maintain market share. More broadly, studies have consistently found that manufactured goods experience lower ERPT than agriculture products (Campa and Goldberg 2005; also see Marazzi et al. 2005).

Second is the duration of exchange rate changes. For instance, Meurers (2003) undertakes Blanchard–Quah decompositions to identify permanent and temporary exchange rate changes in the US, Japan, Germany, France and Italy. The author finds that ERPT tends to be almost complete in the long run with persistent exchange rate shocks. On the other hand, if the exchange rate change is temporary (depreciation in the importing country, for instance), an exporter may be more willing to accept a temporary cut in profit margins to maintain market share given the possibility of "hysteresis effects" *a la* Baldwin (1988), Baldwin and Krugman (1989), Dixit (1989) (also see Froot and Klemperer 1989).

Third is the direction of exchange rate changes, which could also be explained by the hysteresis effects. A commonly noted example is that in the mid-1980s the US dollar appreciation lowered import prices, but, when the US dollar subsequently depreciated, import prices in the US rose only partially. The existing literature suggests that the response of exporters to exchange rate changes is often asymmetric, depending on whether the exchange rate appreciates or depreciates. A weakening of the destination market's currency causes the exporter to reduce its export price and keep the importing nation's product price more or less stable, consequently implying lower ERPT. However, when the exporters' currency depreciates, exports become relatively cheaper in the destination market. This may create an incentive for exporters to maintain their export prices or, in some cases, even to reduce their own currency price and amplify the impact of their currency depreciation (so as to gain market share), leading to a higher ERPT (Pollard and Coughlin 2003 and Madhavi 2002).

Fourth is the size of the exchange rate changes. When the magnitude of the exchange rate change is small, firms are generally willing to absorb it and keep domestic prices unchanged due to the costs associated with changing prices. Apart from the actual menu costs of small and frequent price variations, according to Krugman (1987), when a firm announces a price it has to honor its announcements. Thus, the unexpected changes in costs caused by temporary fluctuations that are not "too large" may not be passed on in terms of higher prices as firms do not want to lose reputation.[5] The importance of the size of exchange rate changes ERPT into import prices in the US has been empirically confirmed by Pollard and Coughlin (2003) and others.

Fifth, the degree of ERPT into aggregate import prices may be affected by a country's various macroeconomic fundamentals (as outlined in Chapter 3 of this volume). Campa and Goldberg (2005) test the importance of changes in macroeconomic variables and the extent of ERPT into aggregate import prices for 25 OECD nations for the period 1975–1999. The authors find that the lower the average rate of inflation and the less variable the exchange rate, the lower is the corresponding extent of ERPT. However, these macro factors play a minor role in affecting ERPT compared with the changing composition of a nation's imports away from raw materials and energy imports towards manufacturing imports. Otani et al. (2003) also highlight the importance of changing product composition as being among the main factors in explaining differing rates of ERPT over time in Japan, while Marazzi et al. (2005) stress its importance in the case of the US.[6]

In addition to the foregoing, it is generally acknowledged that ERPT tends to be greater in lower income economies and relatively smaller and more open economies where there is a high share of traded goods, high import content,[7] limited domestic substitutes (thus limiting the extent of "flight from quality" *a la* Burnstein et al. 2007), and high degree of integration with the global trading system.[8] This inevitably makes much of developing Asia potentially more vulnerable to ERPT than other parts of the world, particularly vis-à-vis industrial countries.[9] Another important factor that might affect ERPT is the presence of non-tariff barriers (NTBs)—exchange rate changes are prevented from being fully passed through into import prices due to the import premium afforded to current exporters (Bhagwati 1991). There is some empirical confirmation of this. For instance, Menon (1996) found that quantitative restrictions lowered ERPT into import prices for Australia's manufacturing trade in the 1980s.

While many of the foregoing hypotheses have been tested in industrial country contexts, relatively sparse work has been undertaken for Asia. We turn to Asia specifically in the next section.

2.3 What does the empirical literature on ERPT in Asia tell us?

Menon (1995) provides a comprehensive survey of empirical studies on ERPT. This section further extends the analysis with specific focus on

Asia and examines some of the relatively recent empirical literature on ERPT in Asia. Special attention is paid to the implications of production sharing based trade—which is significant in Asia—for ERPT. We first discuss *multi-country* studies using aggregate prices then consider studies on disaggregated or industry-specific prices.[10] As will be apparent, the survey of studies includes both ERPT of imports as well as of exports. The latter is a measure of the extent—or lack thereof—of PTM. If a change in exchange rate is fully transmitted into export prices in the exporter's currency then there is full PTM and consequently no pass-through into the importer's prices.

2.3.1 Selected aggregate-level studies on ERPT in Asia

Ito et al. (2005) examine the extent of ERPT into both aggregate import prices and consumer prices (CPI) for eight East Asian countries during the period 1986:q1–2004:q2. The authors use a first differenced model with a lag of the effective exchange rate up to four periods. They find that the ERPT estimates into import prices to be high and significant for four economies, viz. Hong Kong (49 percent), Indonesia (100 percent), Japan (99 percent), and Thailand (166 percent, i.e. more than full ERPT). The estimates for the other three economies (Korea, Singapore and Taiwan) were insignificant. Inevitably, the ERPT into consumer prices was found to be relatively lower than import prices, but among the countries it was highest for Indonesia (57 percent), followed by Thailand (26 percent), Singapore (20 percent), the Philippines (15 percent) and Korea (13 percent).

From a methodological perspective, the above analysis uses single equation estimation technique. Under this framework the estimating equation uses the import prices as the dependent variable and the exchange rate as the independent variable, with the coefficient of exchange rate (either the nation's bilateral or effective) giving the extent of pass-through. Moreover, cost conditions in the exporter's market, the price of domestic substitute goods in the importing nation, as well as a proxy for demand shifters for imports, like the importing nation's Gross Domestic Product (GDP) or Industrial Production, are used as other control variables. The other methodology in the empirical literature uses a systems approach. Unlike a single equation specification, which assumes exchange rate changes to be exogenous, the VAR methodology does not *a priori* assume any exogenous variable and treats each variable as endogenous. VAR analysis is generally used for measuring pass-through into a nation's aggregate CPI, PPI or import price. This approach allows one to analyze the impact of macroeconomic shocks on import prices or CPI.

Using such a VAR analysis, Ito et al. (2005) also examine the effects of exchange rate changes, monetary policy, demand shocks (proxied by the output gap) and supply shocks (proxied by oil price change) on aggregate prices (CPI, PPI) and import prices for the period 1995:m1–2004:m8. The impulse response functions show the response of import prices to all four variables is highest, followed by the PPI and then the CPI.[11] The authors also conduct a variance decomposition analysis to determine the relative importance of these four variables on domestic prices. Exchange rate shocks account for 40 percent of the variation in CPI for both Indonesia and Korea, but less than 20 percent in the cases of Malaysia, Singapore and Thailand. As for import prices, exchange rate shocks account for 50 percent of variation in import prices in Korea, 20 percent in Indonesia and Thailand, and only 10 percent in Singapore's import prices. The relatively low ERPT in the case Singapore, which is a small and open economy, is somewhat of a puzzle in the first instance. Export and import price indices (i.e. import and export price indices that are constructed using prices obtained from traders) appear to be available only for Japan, Korea and Taiwan. For many of the other Asian countries all that are available is the "unit value" indices (indices based on unit values constructed by dividing reported export value by export volume). The data limitations should be kept in mind when considering ERPT studies at a product or industry level and could explain part of the puzzle noted above. Apart from data issues, part of this puzzle may be explained by the high level of production sharing in Singapore's trade and domestic production as highlighted in Section 2.3.1 (also see Section 2.4.1).[12]

Using a similar VAR methodology, Kang and Wang (2003) analyze the effect of exchange rate changes on both import prices and CPI for Japan, Singapore, Korea and Thailand during the period 1991m1 to 2001:m12. The impulse response functions show that, for all the four countries, the response of import prices to changes in exchange rates is higher than the corresponding response of CPI. Moreover, for the post-crisis period (1998–2001), import prices as well as consumer prices in Korea and Thailand appear to have responded more to exchange rate changes, while there was no difference pre and post-crisis for Japan and Singapore. This may be explained by the fact that Japan and Singapore were not as impacted by the crisis in a structural sense (i.e. directly) as were Korea and Thailand. In fact, a variance decomposition analysis shows that the contribution of exchange rate shocks in explaining variations in both import prices and CPI changes is higher for the post-crisis period in Korea and Thailand. The authors contend that the adoption of a free-floating exchange rate regime—and consequent temporary exchange rate fluctuations—by these two economies after the currency crisis may have been a further reason for the amplified ERPT in the post-crisis period.[13] (Chapter 3 of this volume offers a detailed study of ERPT in Korea and Thailand.)

McCarthy (2000) adopts a VAR approach to measure pass-through into aggregate import prices, CPI and PPI for Japan and other industrial countries during 1976:q1–1998:q4. The impulse response function shows that the response of import prices to exchange rate changes is greater than for PPI, while it is insignificant for CPI. The variance decomposition analysis shows that a variation in prices due to 1 percent exchange rate shock is about 6 percent for import prices and PPI but only 1.8 percent for CPI.

Sasaki (2002) examines the export pricing behavior of Japanese exporters to the US, Asia and the European Union (EU) by estimating PTM elasticities using monthly bilateral export price data for the period 1990–1995. PTM is found to be highest for Japan's exports to the US and lowest for exports to Asia. Specifically, Japanese exporters to the US market absorb about 50 percent of the yen–dollar exchange rate changes in their own currency denominated export prices, while for the EU and Asia the PTM elasticities are relatively lower at 0.24 and 0.32, respectively. In all likelihood, this result is due to the relatively large size and high level of competition in the US market, where exporters attempt to maintain their market share and are prepared to accept low mark-ups.[14] Another reason for the relatively low ERPT of Japanese exports (i.e. high PTM) to the US might be because of the large-scale dollar invoicing of Japanese exports to the US (about 84 percent of Japan's exports in the US are invoiced in dollars).[15]

Webber (1999) examines the nexus between bilateral exchange rates with USD and import prices in nine countries in the Asia-Pacific region, viz. Korea, Pakistan, the Philippines, Malaysia, Singapore, Japan, Australia and New Zealand. Using the Johansen cointegration methodology the author finds a long-run stable linear relationship between import prices and exchange rates for seven of the nine countries from 1978 to 1994, though the ERPT estimates vary between countries. ERPT is highest for the lowest income countries, Pakistan (109 percent) and the Philippines (89.6 percent), while ERPT is partial for the other six nations, ranging from 25 to 50 percent.[16] Notwithstanding macro level differences between countries, the author surmises that the different ranges of ERPT for the countries are due to the different varieties of goods imported by the countries. This emphasizes the need for studies using more disaggregated data (i.e. at industry or product levels). Section 2.3.2 studies disaggregated level analysis of ERPT in Asia.[17]

2.3.2 Selected disaggregate-level studies on ERPT in Asia

2.3.2.1 Japan

In one of the earlier works on ERPT at the disaggregate level (SITC 4-digit) involving any Asian nation, Marston (1990) examines the pricing behavior of Japanese exporters. The author estimates PTM elasticity for 17 products in the transportation and electrical machinery industry between 1980:m2 and 1987:m12. The impact of trade weighted real effective exchange rate on export-domestic price margin is found to be significant. PTM elasticities for selected products are: small passenger cars (0.52), tires and tubes (1.03), trucks (0.41), color TVs (0.51), tape recorders (0.95) and microwave ovens (0.28). This suggests that Japanese exporters partially pass-through exchange rate changes in foreign prices of their exports, apart from tires and tubes.

Takagi and Yoshida (2001) estimate the ERPT for Japanese exports and imports with selected East Asian trading partners, viz. Indonesia, Malaysia, the Philippines, Singapore, and Thailand, as well as for Germany and the US. The authors estimate ERPT using monthly export and import unit value series obtained from Japanese customs data spanning 1988:m1–1999:m6 for twenty (eleven exports and nine imports) at the 9-digit level of industrial commodities. Using a dynamic panel data and applying a fixed effects model for these categories aggregated together, as well as for the countries combined, the estimated ERPT for Japanese exports into the destination market currency is almost complete (0.97), while the ERPT into Japanese imports is almost nonexistent (only 0.01). On a bilateral country basis, for the individual commodity groupings, ERPT for Japanese exports in the majority of the cases is found to be complete or very high (i.e. low degree of PTM).[18] ERPT for Japanese imports is either absent or far from complete.[19] This suggests that foreign importers attempt to maintain price stability in yen terms while pricing their exports in Japanese markets, while Japanese exporters also maintain their unit prices stable in yen terms.

The authors go on to examine the impact of the Asian currency crisis on the pricing behavior by comparing ERPT estimates during the pre-crisis periods (1988:m1–1997:m6) with the entire sample period. They find little difference in ERPT before and after the crisis for most products and for most countries except for some imports to Malaysia. For these Asian countries, Japan is their dominant trade partner. In other words, exporters in these countries tend to preserve or increase their market share by actively PTM. This may explain the low Japanese import ERPT (also see Sato 1999, 2003).

Otani et al. (2003) estimate ERPT into Japanese import prices using monthly data for the period Jan 1978:m1–2002:m10. Using the IMF's nominal effective exchange rate (NEER) for Japan and employing a seemingly unrelated regression (SUR) estimation methodology, the authors find ERPT elasticities into aggregate prices for the entire time period to be complete. This appears to be at odds with the Takagi and Yoshida (2001) results noted above which examined ERPT for a shorter and more recent period (1988:m1–1999:m6). In fact, once Otani et al. (2003) decompose the time period into two subsamples—1978:m1–1989:m12 and 1990:m1–2001:m10—they find a decline in ERPT in the 1990s at the aggregate level as well as for most product categories.[20] The fact that the decline in ERPT occurred both in aggregate and disaggregate data implies that changing composition of Japan's imports is unlikely to be a key factor in explaining the declining ERPT in aggregate prices. An interesting hypothesis put forward by the authors for their finding is the rapid appreciation of the yen in the mid-1980s, which consequently led to a rise in Japanese FDI and overseas production by Japanese firms. The subsequent increase in intrafirm trade and reimports may have led to firms absorbing price changes internally and transferring the impact on margins between firms, thus reducing the extent of ERPT. The impact of FDI and multinational corporations (MNCs) on ERPT is clearly an issue in need of further research.[21]

2.3.2.2 Korea

We turn from Japan to the only other Asian OECD member, Korea. Athukorala (1991) is a pioneering study on ERPT for selected Korean manufacturing exports. His study focused on textiles, clothing and footwear, metal products and machinery and transport equipment over the period 1980:q1–1989:q1. Using a polynomial distributed lag model, the author finds ERPT into foreign prices for the NEER to be around 28 percent.

Adopting a similar methodology, Yang and Hwang (1994) estimate ERPT of the real sectoral exchange rate to Korean export prices in six manufacturing sectors for the period 1976:m12–1990:m12. ERPT estimates range between 18 percent and 60 percent—textiles (18 percent), chemical (19 percent), machinery (25 percent), metal products (41 percent), mineral products (46 percent) and wood (60 percent).

Lee (1997) estimates ERPT of the industry-specific real exchange rate into Korean import prices from OECD nations for the period

1980:q1–1990:q4. The author estimates ERPT elasticities for 24 industries. The ERPT estimates range between 0.43 for iron and steel and 0.92 for leather and fur; the average pass-through elasticity for all manufacturing imports is 0.38. The author also finds that the more concentrated the industries the smaller is the ERPT, possibly due to more competition.

Lee (1995) examines the response of export prices by Korean manufacturers to NEER changes into 16 industries, including auto, television sets, refrigerators, silk fabrics, car tires and integrated circuits for the period 1980:q1–1990:q4. The PTM estimates are automobiles (0.65), CTV (0.53) and tires (1.12), confirming that Korean firms seem to engage in active pricing strategies when exporting (other than tires).

2.3.2.3 Hong Kong

While most of the country-specific studies in Asia have been concentrated on Japan and Korea, there are a few other studies on specific economies in Asia. For instance, Parsley (2003) estimates ERPT into import prices for Hong Kong. The author estimates ERPT for 21 disaggregate 5-digit SITC imports from Hong Kong's top eight non-China exchange rate trading partners (viz. Germany, the Netherlands, France, United Kingdom, Taiwan, Japan, Singapore and Australia) spanning the period 1992–2000. The results indicate a high degree of ERPT of between 80 and 95 percent for the nominal exchange rate and 70 to 85 percent for the real exchange rate.[22] Parsley (2004) estimates ERPT for Hong Kong's exports (and reexports) to its top nine non-mainland China export partners (Canada, Germany, Netherlands, France, UK, Taiwan, Japan, Singapore and the US) for the same time period for 29 commodities at the disaggregated 5-digit level. He found a lack of evidence of PTM in Hong Kong's exports, suggesting high ERPT into foreign prices by exporters of Hong Kong.

2.3.2.4 Southeast Asia

Parsons and Sato (2005) estimates ERPT for four Southeast Asian countries, Indonesia, Thailand, Malaysia, and the Philippines, for 27 export commodities at the HS 6-digit level of disaggregation and to 13 destination (export) markets for 1999–2004.[23] Using a pooled regression model for each good, they do not find any ERPT for the majority of the goods for all the countries. With export prices denominated in the exporter's currency, their findings of insignificant exchange rate coefficient confirms the notion that small open economies are predominantly price takers in world markets, but could also reflect the fact that these economies invoice their exports in US dollars.

Sasaki (2005) examines the effects of changes in the US dollar and Japanese yen on import prices both at the aggregate level and for finer goods for selected Asian economies, viz. Hong Kong, Indonesia, Korea, Malaysia, the Philippines, Singapore, and Thailand for the period 1973:m2–2000:m12.[24] Empirically, at the aggregate level, changes in the US dollar appear to have been passed through to the import prices of the Asian countries, while there is little evidence of ERPT of Japanese yen changes into import prices for the Southeast Asian economies.[25] However, at the disaggregate commodity level there is significant ERPT for the Asian economies for imports from Japan for color photo papers and golf balls.[26] From a policy perspective, the paper recommends that Asian nations adopt a currency basket of the Japanese yen and the US dollar, as changes in both these currencies affect their import prices.[27]

2.3.2.5 India

Mallick and Marques (2006) examine the extent of PTM in the case of India's exports. They estimate ERPT into export prices of 34 SITC 2-digit commodities for the period 1980–2001 using the NEER of the Indian rupee comprising India's top 36 trading partners. Given that the Indian economy has been going through a significant liberalization program in 1991 (see Ahluwalia 2002 and Rajan and Sen 2002)—with a reduction in tariff rates, removal of capital controls and movement towards a managed floating exchange rate—the authors estimate ERPT coefficients for two subperiods (1980–1990 and 1991–2001) to detect any significant differences in pricing behavior by Indian exporters. The average ERPT into foreign prices of India's exports in the preliberalization period was 0.20, while for the postliberalization period it was 0.65. During the former subperiod the authors do not find any ERPT for most commodity categories with the exceptions of clothing (47 percent) and footwear (40 percent). This suggests that during the preliberalization period India acted predominantly like a small, price-taking country in world markets.

For the postliberalization period, the study found significant ERPT for most categories of products, ranging from 12 percent to 79 percent. ERPT estimates for individual products are: clothes (46 percent), cotton (79 percent), iron ore (12 percent), manufacturing metals (23 percent), spices 19 (percent), tobacco (15 percent), transportation equipment (28 percent) and yarn (49 percent). The authors argue that liberalization allowed India to gain some price-making power in some of these industries. In their opinion, this is because of the increasing share of manufacturing in India's exports (which rose from 68 percent of merchandise exports in 1986–1987 to 76 percent in 2001–2002).[28] However, this conclusion is at odds with much of the other literature examined above, which has argued that ERPT into import prices has declined over the years largely because of the changing composition of domestic trade towards manufactured goods.

2.4 ERPT and the role of production sharing

When thinking about trade in manufactured goods, especially in Asia, it is important to pay close attention to the role of cross-border "production sharing." This refers to the dispersion of separate production blocks of an integrated production process across different countries.[29] Thus, trade no longer just involves final goods and services, but also the international exchange of parts and components (PCAs).[30] The presence of production sharing suggests that it is insufficient to merely consider ERPT at a disaggregated commodity level (let alone at the aggregate level); it is especially important to consider ERPT at the level of the corresponding intermediate good.

As noted in Section 2.3.1, the simplest form of production sharing is bilateral in nature, whereby a representative firm in country B exports the final good (Y) to country A, while simultaneously procuring the parts and components (X) from country A.[31] In such a situation depreciation of B's currency (and ignoring PTM behavior for the moment) raises the country's exports of good Y but concurrently increases the imported input price of good X. Thus, changes in domestic costs following a currency change are higher with production sharing than without it, resulting in the firm in country B altering its foreign currency price of exports to a lesser extent. In other words, even without proactive PTM strategies or local currency pricing (LCP), one would expect *lower ERPT a priori* with production sharing.

The issue of production sharing and ERPT is a relatively underresearched area and there is consequently scant related literature in the area.

Gron and Swenson (1996) show that incomplete ERPT occurs when MNCs are able to acquire inputs from different sources internationally, hence allowing them to adjust their input prices in response to exchange rate changes.

Webber (1995) develops a partial equilibrium model of import ERPT in the presence of imported inputs. He also incorporates the role of currency invoicing. Not surprisingly, he shows that ERPT is incomplete or partial when imports are procured from another country and invoiced in a third nation's currency.

Athukorala and Menon (1994) examine ERPT for Japanese manufacturing exports that are characterized by the use of imported intermediate inputs for the period 1980:q1–1992:q1. As Japanese exports rely heavily on imported inputs, the authors estimate ERPT by separating out the direct PTM effects and the impact of exchange rate changes on input costs. Their results show that ERPT is lower when the impact of exchange rate changes on imported input costs is taken into account. Using an autoregressive distributed modeling technique, the results show that total pass-through estimates vary across industries. It is lowest for industries characterized by heavy concentration of imported parts and components (like textiles, electrical machinery and electronics) and highest for categories like chemicals where production sharing is not wisdespread.

2.5 Conclusion

This chapter has surveyed available empirical evidence on the extent of ERPT in selected Asian economies. It is apparent that results on the degree of ERPT depend on the time period horizon of analysis. This said, on a country-by-country basis, overall it appears that ERPT is highest for developing Asian economies like Thailand and Indonesia and somewhat lower for developed economies like Japan. Beyond levels of economic development, an interesting area for research would be the extent to which ERPT is impacted by a nation's macroeconomic fundamentals such as money supply growth, inflation rate and type of exchange rate regime.

Exchange rate regimes in Asia span a wide spectrum. A number of smaller Asian economies appear to prefer some form of single currency pegs. This is true of Hong Kong, SAR (currency board arrangement pegged to the US dollar), Brunei (currency board arrangement pegged to the Singapore dollar) and Bhutan and Nepal (pegged to the Indian Rupee). In contrast, Bangladesh, Sri Lanka, and the crisis-hit economies of Indonesia, Korea, Philippines, and Thailand officially operate flexible exchange rate regimes. The flexible exchange rates in the four East Asian countries are accompanied by inflation targeting frameworks. A number of other Asian countries like India, Pakistan, Singapore, Taiwan and Vietnam have adopted a variety of intermediate regimes (currency baskets, crawling bands, adjustable pegs, and such). Both China and Malaysia on July 21, 2005 officially shifted to what may be best referred to as a more mechanical version of a currency basket regime (i.e. keeping the trade-weighted exchange rate within a certain band as a goal in and of itself). Therefore, it is readily apparent that "one-size does not necessarily fit all" when it comes to the choice of exchange rate regimes in Asia (Cavoli and Rajan 2009, chapter 1). As such Asia provides an ideal setting to analyze the role of exchange rate regimes on ERPT.

In the final analysis, while the extent of ERPT has important macroeconomic implications, it is predominantly a microeconomic phenomenon. This consequently implies the need to pay more attention to ascertaining ERPT at the disaggregated level rather than at the broad macro level. At the disaggregated level, it is especially important to focus more research efforts on the role of production sharing and MNCs and their implications for ERPT. Given that the literature on ERPT and standard trade in Asia is relatively limited, it is not surprising that the empirical literature connecting fragmented trade with ERPT is virtually nonexistent. For future empirical research on ERPT in the context of cross-border production sharing involving Asia, the challenge lies in compilation of export (import) quantity and price data for both final goods and parts and components.

Notes

1. This chapter draws on an article originally published in *Asian Pacific Economic Literature*, 21 (2), 2007, 13–28 (Blackwell Publishing). Reprinted with permission.
2. Of course, there may be other real sector consequences of exchange rate changes via, for instance, balance sheet effects. See note 5 below
3. Low ERPT also has implications for the transmission of shocks (for instance, see Betts and Devereux 2001).
4. Of course, if $(\Delta \ln MKP_{Y}^{t}/\Delta \ln E_{B}^{A}) < -1$, then $\Delta \ln P_{Y}^{B} / \Delta \ln E_{B}^{A} < 0$, i.e. there is more than full ERPT.
5. If large exchange rate changes lead to sharp contractions (for instance, because of balance sheet effects following devaluation), there is less likely to be much if any ERPT (see Burnstein et al. 2002). Thus, Goldfajn and Werlang (2000) also emphasize the importance of business cycles in determining the extent of ERPT, i.e. firms are more willing to pass through increases in costs during a boom. Chapter 4 of this volume discusses the circumstances under which devaluations could be contractionary. Chapter 7 of this volume discusses macroeconomic policy management in the presence of balance sheet effects.
6. In addition to changing product composition, the authors also emphasize the role of competition from China as being a factor limiting the extent of ERPT into US import prices. In fact, Marazzi et al. (2005) do not find either the size of direction of exchange rate movements as having been significant determinants import prices pass-through in the US.
7. However, if the country is simultaneously importing and exporting to the same country, ERPT may be lower.

8. Using a data set on the cross-country (76 countries) prices of eight specific goods (Marlboro Cigarettes, Coca Cola, Cognac, Gilbey's gin, Time Magazine, Kodak Color Film, Cointreau Liqueur and Martini and Rossi Vermouth) for the period 1990–2001, Frankel et al. (2005) test some of the foregoing factors. They arrive at the conclusion that, while there is strong evidence that ERPT is slower and smaller in lower income countries, there is much weaker evidence in relation to the size effects. They also find transport and tariff barriers to have been important factors determining the extent of ERPT.
9. It is harder to say *a priori* whether Asia is potentially more susceptible to ERPT than Latin America in view of the relatively lower degree of monetary stability and higher consequent inflation rates in the latter. For instance, in a 71-country panel study of transmission of exchange rate changes into consumer prices between 1980 and 1988, Goldfajn and Werlang (2000) find ERPT to be highest in Latin America. Kamin and Klau (2003) find ERPT to be broadly similar across both regionals.
10. We have intentionally limited the scope of the survey of aggregate ERPT studies to those that are multi-country in nature. Single country studies (such as Ghosh and Rajan 2007, 2008 on India and Singapore, respectively) are not considered here due to space considerations.
11. The magnitude of response to these shocks for Indonesia appears to be larger than for the other economies.
12. Abeysinghe and Tan (1998) examine the relationship between export and import prices for Singapore and find a high degree of correlation and cointegration among export prices of final goods and import prices of intermediate goods for major commodity categories between 1980:q1 and 1993:q4.
13. On the other hand, it has been suggested that the greater the degree of exchange rate flexibility the lower will be ERPT, as firms may be less willing to pass on exchange rate changes to their customers when there is a chance that they will be subsequently reversed. The role of exchange rate regimes on ERPT is clearly an issue in need of further research (for instance, see Steel and King 2004).
14. The paper also examines the effect of unexpected exchange rate changes in export prices.
15. See Sato (1999) for a discussion of currency invoicing of Japanese trade and the dominance of the US dollars in East Asian intraregional trade. Also see Giovannini (1988) and Fukuda and Ji (1994) for formalizations of the impact of currency invoicing on the extent of ERPT.
16. The estimates of ERPT for the other countries are as follows: Korea (40.3 percent), Australia (26.3 percent), Japan (44.8 percent) and New Zealand (35.9 percent). The estimated ERPT for Singapore was 77.1 percent, far higher than most other estimates for the city-state.
17. In particular we consider four papers each on Japan and Korea and two papers each on Hong Kong, South East Asia and India. There are no papers to our knowledge that have examined ERPT in China using disaggregated data.
18. The exceptions are electricity boards to US and microscopes to Germany, where the ERPT rates are 30 percent and 42 percent, respectively.

19. The exceptions are wooden seats (75 percent) and wooden furniture (47 percent) from the US, appliance parts from Germany (53 percent) and wooden furniture from Singapore (93 percent).
20. These results are robust to variations in estimation techniques and data series. The ERPT coefficients for eight disaggregated commodities vary; it is highest for fuels (1.46), followed by material (1.11), metals (0.92), others (0.81), food (0.79), chemicals (0.78) and machinery (0.76).
21. Menon (1996) examines the role of MNCs in affecting ERPT for import prices of Australia's manufactured imports for the period 1981:q3–1992:q3. Noticeably the author finds MNCs' operations (as proxied by foreign control of imports) to have a negative effect on pass-through. This is clearly an area in need of much more analytical and empirical research. Sato (1999) briefly highlights the importance of Japanese multinationals and their role in pricing and trade invoicing with regard to Japan's trade with the rest of East Asia.
22. The country-specific ERPT estimates for the nominal exchange rate were: Germany (1.36), UK (0.24), Taiwan (0.97), Japan (0.86), Singapore (1.58) and Australia (0.05). ERPT estimates for the real exchange rate were: Germany (1.26), the Netherlands (1.09), France (1.13), UK (0.26), Taiwan (0.52), Japan (0.62), Singapore (1.28) and Australia (0.02).
23. The destination markets for these countries were Australia, Canada, China, France, Germany, Hong Kong, Indonesia, Japan, Korea, Malaysia, Singapore, Thailand, UK and the US.
24. The North Asian economies of Taiwan, Korea and Hong Kong are also included in the study.
25. From the US, ERPT into import prices of these nations were Hong Kong (0.52), Indonesia (0.28), Korea (0.29), Malaysia (0.19), the Philippines (0.90), Singapore (0.40), Thailand (0.91, Taiwan (1.67). ERPT coefficients of imports from Japan for the Asian nations were insignificant except for Hong Kong (0.04), Malaysia (–0.10) and Taiwan (0.06).
26. Interestingly, for US imports from Japan, yen changes appear to have little impact on US import prices. This suggests that Japanese exporters price their exports in US dollars and engage in PTM to maintain their market share in a competitive market like the US. However, this conclusion is at odds with some of the other studies of Japanese ERPT noted previously.
27. Also see Rajan (2002) and Williamson (2005) for discussions of the virtues of a currency basket regime for Asia and references cited within.
28. In another paper, Mallick and Marques (2005) estimates the ERPT of the dollar–rupee exchange rate into both India's import and export prices for nine SITC 1-digit commodities for the period 1980–2001. Using panel data estimations, they find that the average ERPT for imports is about 82 percent, and that for exports into dollar prices was 22 percent.
29. The literature on production sharing has used an array of terms to describe this phenomenon, including "recycling comparative advantage," "production fragmentation," "super-specialization," "vertical specialization," and "slicing the value chain," to name just a few.
30. Over the last decade production sharing based trade has expanded at a faster rate than growth in world trade and world GDP. See Athukorala (2005), Athukorala and Yamashita (2006) and Ng and Yeats (2001, 2003) for

excellent descriptions of trends and patterns of international production fragmentation across the globe and in Asia.

31. US–Mexico trade is a good case in point.

References

Abeysinghe, T. and L.Y. Tan (1998). "Exchange Rate Appreciation and Export Competitiveness: The Case of Singapore," *Applied Economics*, 30, 51–55.

Ahluwalia, M.S. (2002). "Economic Reforms in India Since 1991: Has Gradualism Worked?," *Journal of Economic Perspectives*, 16, 67–88.

Athukorala, P.C. (1991). "Exchange Rate Pass-through—The Case of Korean Exports of Manufactures," *Economics Letters*, 35, 79–84.

Athukorala, P.C. (2005). "Product Fragmentation and Trade Patterns in East Asia," *Asian Economic Papers*, 4, 1–27.

Athukorala, P.C. and J. Menon (1994). "Pricing To Market Behavior and Exchange Rate Pass-through in Japanese Exports," *The Economic Journal*, 104, 271–281.

Athukorala, P.C. and N. Yamashita (2006). "Production Fragmentation and Trade Integration: East Asia in a Global Context," *The North American Journal of Economics and Finance*, 17, 233–256.

Baldwin, R.E. (1988). "Hysteresis in Import Prices: The Beachhead Effect," *American Economic Review*, 78, 773–785.

Baldwin, R. and P. Krugman (1989). "Persistent Trade Effects of Large Exchange Rate Shocks," *Quarterly Journal of Economics*, 104, 635–654.

Betts, C. and M. Devereux (2001). "The International Effects of Monetary and Fiscal Policy," in G. Calvo and R. Dornbusch (eds), *Essays in Honor of Robert A. Mundell*, Cambridge, MA: MIT Press.

Bhagwati, J.N. (1991). "The Pass-through Puzzle: The Missing Prince from Hamlet," in D.A. Irwin (ed.), *Political Economy and International Economics*, Cambridge, MA: MIT Press.

Burnstein, A., B. Eichenbaum, and S. Rebelo (2007). "Modeling Exchange Rate Pass through After Large Devaluations," *Journal of Monetary Economics*, 54, 346–368.

Campa, J.M. and L.S. Goldberg (2005). "Exchange Rate Pass-through into Import Prices," *The Review of Economics and Statistics*, 87, 679–690.

Cavoli, T. and R.S. Rajan (2008). *Exchange Rate Regimes and Macroeconomic Management in Asia*, Hong Kong: Hong Kong University Press, 2009.

Dixit, A.K. (1989). "Hysteresis, Import Penetration and Exchange Rate Pass-through," *Quarterly Journal of Economics*, 104, 205–228.

Dornbusch, R. (1987). "Exchange Rates and Prices," *American Economic Review*, 77, 93–106.

Frankel, J., D. Parsley, and S.J. Wei (2005). "Slow Pass-through Around the World: A New Import for Developing Countries?," Working Paper No. 11199, NBER.

Froot, K. and P. Klemperer (1989). "Exchange Rate Pass-through When Market Share Matters," *American Economic Review*, 79, 637–654.

Fukuda, S. and C. Ji (1994). "On the Choice of Invoice Currency by Japanese Exporters: The PTM Approach," *Journal of the Japanese and International Economies*, 8, 511–529.

Ghosh, A. and R.S. Rajan (2007). "How High is Exchange Rate Pass Through in India?," *Journal of International Trade and Development*, 16, 373–382.
Ghosh, A. and R.S. Rajan (2008). "What is the Extent of Exchange Rate Pass-through in Singapore?," forthcoming in *Journal of the Asia Pacific Economy*.
Giovannini, A. (1988). "Exchange Rates and Traded Goods Prices," *Journal of International Economics*, 24, 45–68.
Goldberg, P. and M. Knetter (1997). "Goods Prices and Exchange Rates: What have we Learned?," *Journal of Economic Literature*, 35, 1243–1292.
Goldfajn, I. and S. Werlang (2000). "The Pass-through from Depreciation to Inflation: A Panel Study," Discussion Paper No. 423, Department of Economics, Pontifícia Universidad Católica do Rio de Janeiro (PUC-Rio).
Gron, A. and D. Swenson (1996). "Incomplete Exchange-rate Pass-through and Imperfect Competition: The Effect of Local Production," *American Economic Review*, 86, 71–76.
Ito, T., Y. Sasaki, and K. Sato (2005). "Pass-through of Exchange Rate changes and Macroeconomic Shocks to Domestic Inflation in East Asian Countries," Discussion Paper Series No. 05-E-020, Research Institute of Economy, Trade and Industry (RIETI), Japan.
Kamin, S. and M. Klau (2003). "A Multi-country Comparison between Inflation and Exchange Rate Competitiveness," *International Journal of Finance and Economics*, 8, 167–184.
Kang S. and Y. Wang (2003). "Fear of Floating: Exchange Rate Pass-through in East Asia," Working Paper No. 03-06, Korea Institute of Economic Policy.
Knetter, M. (1993). "International Comparisons of Pricing-to-Market Behavior," *The American Economic Review*, 83, 473–486.
Krugman, P. (1987). "Pricing to Market when the Exchange Rate Changes," in S.W. Arndt and D. Richardson (eds), *Real Financial Linkages Among Open Economies*, Cambridge, MA: MIT Press.
Lee, J. (1995). "Pricing-To-Market in Korean Manufacturing Exports," *International Economic Journal*, 9, 1–12.
Lee, J. (1997). "The Response of Exchange Rate Pass-through to Market Concentration in a Small Economy," *The Review of Economics and Statistics*, 79, 142–145.
Madhavi, S. (2002). "The Response of the US Export Prices to Changes in the Dollar's Effective Exchange Rate: Further Evidence from Industry Level Data," *Applied Economics*, 34, 2115–2125.
Mallick, S. and H. Marques (2006). "Sectoral Exchange Rate Pass-through: A Tale of Two Policy Regimes in India," *Scottish Journal of Political Economy*, 53, 280–303.
Mallick, S. and H. Marques (2005). "Exchange Rate Transmission at Two-digit Sectoral Level: A Tale of Two Policy Regimes in India," mimeo.
Marazzi, M., N. Sheets, R. Vigfusson, and J. Rogers (2005). "Exchange Rate Pass-through to U.S. Import Prices: Some New Evidence," International Finance Discussion, Papers No. 833, Board of Governors of the Federal Reserve System.
Marston, R. (1990). "Pricing to Market in Japanese Manufacturing," *Journal of International Economics*, 29, 217–236.
McCarthy, J. (2000). "Pass-Through of Exchange Rates and Import Prices to Domestic Inflation in Some Industrialized Economies," Staff Paper No. 111. Federal Reserve Bank of New York.

Menon, J. (1995). "Exchange Rate Pass-Through," *Journal of Economic Surveys*, 9, 197–231.

Menon, J. (1996). "The Degree and Determinants of Exchange Rate Pass-through: Market Structure, Non-tariff Barriers and Multinational Corporations," *Economic Journal*, 106, 434–444.

Meurers, M. (2003). "Incomplete Pass-through in Import Markets and Permanent versus Transitory Exchange Rate Shocks," mimeo.

Ng, F. and A.J. Yeats (2001). "Production sharing in East Asia: Who Does What For Whom, and Why?," in L.K. Cheng and H. Kierzkowksi (eds), *Global Production and Trade in East Asia*, Boston, MA: Kluwer Academic Publishers.

Ng, F. and A.J. Yeats (2003). "Major Trends in Asia—What are Implications for Regional Cooperation and Growth," Policy Research Paper No. 3084, The World Bank.

Otani, A., S. Shiratuka, and S. Shirato (2003). "The Decline in the Exchange Rate Pass-through: Evidence from Japanese Import Prices," *Monetary and Economic Studies*, 21, Institute for Monetary and Economic Studies, Bank of Japan, 53–81.

Parsley, D.C. (2003). "Exchange Rate Pass-through in a Small Open Economy: Panel Evidence from Hong Kong," *International Journal of Finance and Economics*, 8, 1–9.

Parsley, D.C. (2004). "Pricing in International Markets: a 'Small-Country' Benchmark," *Review of International Economics*, 12, 509–524.

Parsons, C. and K. Sato (2005). "Exchange Rate Pass-through of the ASEAN-4," Working Paper No. 2005-09, Centre for International Trade Studies (CITS), Yokohama National University.

Pollard, P.S. and C.C. Coughlin (2003). "Size Matters: Asymmetric Exchange Rate Pass-through at the Industry Level," Working Paper No. 2003-029b, Federal Reserve Bank of St. Louis.

Rajan, R.S. (2002). "Exchange Rate Policy Options for Post-Crisis Southeast Asia: Is There a Case for Currency Baskets?," *The World Economy*, 25, 137–163.

Rajan, R.S. and R. Sen (2002). "A Decade of Trade Reforms in India: How it Compares with East Asia," *World Economics*, 3, 1–14.

Sasaki, Y.N. (2002). "Pricing to Market Behavior: Japanese Exports to the US, Asia, and the EU," *Review of International Economics*, 10, 140–150.

Sasaki, Y.N. (2005). "Pass-through of Exchange Rates on Import Prices of East Asian Countries," *Keizai Kenyu, No. 132, The Society of Economics*, Meiji Gakuin University, 23–33.

Sato, K. (1999). "The International Use of the Japanese Yen: The Case of Japan's Trade with East Asia," *The World Economy*, 22, 547–584.

Sato, K. (2003). "Currency Invoicing in Japanese Exports to East Asia: Implications for Yen Internationalization," *Asian Economic Journal*, 17, 129–154.

Steel, D. and A. King (2004). "Exchange Rate Pass-through: The Role of Regime Changes," *International Review of Applied Economics*, 18, 301–322.

Takagi, S. and Y. Yoshida (2001). "Exchange Rate Movements and Tradable Goods Prices in East Asia: An Analysis Based on Japanese Customs Data, 1988–1999," *IMF Staff Papers*, 48, 266–289.

Webber, A. (1995). "Partial Small Country Import Pass-through, Currency Composition, and Imported Inputs," *International Economic Journal*, 9, 13–29.

Webber, A. (1999). "Dynamic and Long Run Responses of Import Prices to the Exchange Rate in the Asia-Pacific," *Asian Economic Journal*, 13, 303–220.

Williamson, J. (2005). "A Currency Basket for East Asia, Not Just China," *Brief No. 05-01*, Institute for International Economics, Policy, Washington D.C.

Yang, Y. and M. Hwang (1994). "Price Behavior in Korean Manufacturing," *The Review of Economics and Statistics*, 76, 461–470.

3
A Closer Examination of Exchange Rate Pass-through in Korea and Thailand[1]

(Co-authored with Amit Ghosh)

3.1 Introduction

There has been increasing discussion about the role of economic globalization in domestic inflation in various countries (for instance, see Borio and Filardo 2007 and Helbling et al. 2006). An important but age-old transmission channel of global factors into domestic prices is via exchange rate movements. As noted in Chapter 2 of this volume, the transmission of exchange rate changes into import (export) prices of goods into the destination-market currency as well as into aggregate domestic prices is referred to as exchange rate pass-through (ERPT). Small and open economies are generally viewed as being relatively more susceptible to ERPT effects in domestic prices. This in turn is a reason often cited for the "fear of floating" among such economies.

Following the financial crisis of 1997–1998, Korea and Thailand have officially moved towards flexible exchange rate regimes while adopting a monetary policy strategy based on inflation targeting (see Table 1 and Cavoli and Rajan 2009, chapter 2; See Table 3.1; also see Cavoli and Rajan, 2009, Chapter 1 of this volume). What has been the extent of ERPT in these two countries and has ERPT changed over time? These are among the set of questions examined in this chapter by estimating ERPT into Korea's and Thailand's consumer and import prices at the aggregate level for the period over the last two decades into the US dollar, the Japanese yen and the Nominal effective exchange rate (NEER).

The chapter is organized as follows. Section 3.2 estimates ERPT elasticities for Korea's and Thailand's import prices and consumer prices using bilateral exchange rates with the US dollar (USD) and the Japanese yen (JPY)

Table 3.1 Highlights of inflation targeting regimes in Korea and Thailand

Country	Date	Target price index	Target horizon	Escape clauses	Accountability	Target set by	Publication and accountability
Thailand	April 2000	Core CPI (excluding food and energy)	Indefinite	None	Public explanation of breach and steps taken to address it	Central Bank in consultation with Government	Inflation Report, inflation forecasts and publication of models used
Korea	January 1998	Core CPI (excluding non-cereal agricultural products and petroleum products)	Indefinite	Changes caused by major force	None	Central Bank in consultation with Government	Inflation report and submission to parliament, publication of monetary policy meetings

Source: Authors.

as well as the NEER for the period 1980:q1–2006:q4. Section 3.3 examines whether the ERPT has changed over time using simple recursive estimates. Section 3.4 investigates whether ERPT is endogenous to certain macro variables, including inflation and monetary and exchange rate volatility. We are particularly interested in whether the ERPT is endogenous to the extent of exchange rate variability. The final section concludes the chapter.

3.2 Empirics: point estimates

3.2.1 The model

We examine ERPT into the aggregate import prices of Korea and Thailand with regard to their bilateral nominal exchange rate with the US dollar and the Japanese yen, as well as their NEERs. To do so we follow Ghosh and Rajan (2007) by using the following estimating equation in our empirical specification for the bilateral exchange rates and NEER, respectively:

Bilateral exchange rate:

$$\ln (P^i)_t = \alpha_0 + \alpha_1 \ln (E^i_j)_t + \alpha_2 \ln (\mathrm{GDP}^i)_t + \alpha_3 \ln (\mathrm{PPI}^i)_t \quad (1)$$

$$\text{NEER: } \ln (P^i)_t = \beta_0 + \beta_1 \ln (\mathrm{NEER})_t + \beta_2 \ln (\mathrm{GDP}^i)_t + \beta_3 \ln (\mathrm{CPI}^w) \quad (2)$$

where: i = Korea or Thailand, j = US or Japan, P^i denotes either import prices (or CPI) of Korea or Thailand, E^i_j denotes the nominal exchange rate of Korea and Thailand per USD or JPY; NEER is the nominal effective exchange rate for each nation. A rise in either the bilateral or the NEER denotes a depreciation of the currency of either Korean won or Thai baht; PPI^i denotes the producer price index (PPI) of the US and Japan, respectively; CPI^w denotes world consumer price index (CPI).

The coefficients of particular interest are the ERPT elasticities, α_1 and β_1. If $\alpha_1 = 0$ there is no ERPT into import prices or CPI, while if $\alpha_1 = 1$ there is complete ERPT. If the coefficient lies anywhere in between 0 and 1 there is partial or incomplete ERPT. In estimating eqs. (1) and (2) we control for possible shifts in domestic demand and costs changes in the exporting nations. A rise in income implies an increase in demand for imported goods, thereby raising the import price. Thus α_2 and β_2 are generally expected to be positive.[2] While we have data on GDP for the entire time period of interest (1980–2006) for Korea, for Thailand we use an Industrial Production Index as a proxy for income.[3] The extent of ERPT may also be affected by the marginal costs of the exporters. We proxy foreign exporters' costs by using both the PPI and CPI of the US and Japan. For NEER pass-through, we use the world CPI as a proxy for the costs of all the combined exporters supplying to the two economies.

All data are sourced from the IFS. The data spans the period 1980:q1–2006:q4 with the exception of the NEER, which are only available from 1985:q1 onwards.

3.2.2 Stationarity tests

We conduct tests for stationarity in the variables in eqs. (1) and (2) using both the augmented Dickey-Fuller (ADF) test and the Phillip-Perron test (Table 3.2a). Both tests fail to reject the null hypothesis of unit root in the variables in their level form, suggesting that they are stationary in their first differenced form. Given that the variables are *I(1)*, we next perform cointegration among the variables in eq. (3) using the methodology developed by Johansen and Juselius (1990). Evidence of cointegration among variables rules out the possibility of the estimated relationship being spurious. The Johansen procedure involves identification of rank of a m by m matrix Π with the following specification:

$$\Delta X_t = \delta + \sum_{i=1}^{k-1} \Gamma_i \Delta X_{t-i} + \Pi X_{t-k} + \varepsilon_t \tag{3}$$

X_t is a column vector of the m variables. Γ and Π represent coefficient matrices. Δ is a difference operator. k denotes the lag length. δ is a constant. If Π has zero rank there is no linear combination of the variables, i.e. the variables are non-cointegrated. If the rank r of Π is greater than zero then the variables in eq. (3) are cointegrated.

The cointegration results for ERPT into import prices for bilateral exchange rates and NEER using the alternate measures of exporter's costs are shown in Table 3.2(b). The results indicate the presence of a cointegrating relationship.

3.2.3 Methodology

We obtain the long-run ERPT elasticities by using a recent methodology developed by Stock and Watson (1993). The dynamic OLS (DOLS) procedure involves regressing any variable with the regressors itself but also the leads and lags of the first differences of the regressors. Stock and Watson (1993) show that it is a robust methodology, particularly for small samples, as it allows for regressing variables which are integrated of different orders but are co-integrated. Moreover, by including the lagged and lead values of the changes in the regressors it corrects for potential simultaneity bias and small sample bias among the regressors.

Table 3.2(a) Unit root test results

	Korea				Thailand			
	Levels		1st difference		Levels		1st difference	
	ADF stat.	5% critical value	ADF stat.	5% critical value	ADF stat.	5% critical value	ADF stat.	5% critical value
Null hypothesis: variable has a unit root								
LIMPR$_i$	–3.472	–3.453	–8.613	–3.454	–2.526	–3.453	–8.589	–3.453
LEXRT$_i$/USD	–2.248	–3.452	–12.312	–3.453	–2.156	–3.452	–9.839	–3.453
LEXRT$_i$/JPY	–1.942	–3.452	–12.297	–3.453	–1.763	–3.452	–8.998	–3.453
LNEER$_i$	–1.652	–3.462	–7.347	–3.464	–2.868	–3.463	–5.284	–3.466
LGDP$_K$	–0.810	–3.456	–5.145	–3.456				
LIP$_T$					–2.168	–3.474	–2.555	–3.474
LPPI$_{USA}$	–2.659	–3.453	–6.500	–3.453	–2.659	–3.453	–6.500	–3.453
LCPI$_{USA}$	–1.847	–3.454	–4.464	–3.454	–1.847	–3.454	–4.464	–3.454
LPPI$_{JAP}$	–1.243	–3.453	–9.495	–3.453	–1.243	–3.453	–9.495	–3.453
LCPI$_{JAP}$	–0.811	–3.454	–3.510	–3.454	–0.811	–3.454	–3.510	–3.454
LCPI$_i$	–1.658	–3.454	–7.086	–3.453	–1.446	–3.453	–8.385	–3.453
LCPI$_W$	–0.426	–3.457	–.293	–3.457	–0.426	–3.457	–2.293	–3.457

	Levels		1st difference		Levels		1st difference	
	P-P stat.	5% critical value	P-P stat.	5% critical value	P-P stat.	critical value	P-P stat.	5% critical value
Null hypothesis: variable has a unit root								
LIMPR$_i$	–3.684	–3.453	–10.865	–3.453	–2.301	–3.453	–8.513	–3.453
LEXRT$_i$/USD	–2.075	–3.452	–12.318	–3.453	–2.250	–3.452	–9.919	–3.453
LEXRT$_i$/JPY	–1.935	–3.452	–12.355	–3.453	–1.790	–3.452	–9.945	–3.453
LNEER	–1.930	–3.462	–7.809	–3.463	–2.256	–3.462	–6.342	–3.463
LGDP$_K$	–9.736	–3.453	–52.782	–3.454				
LIP$_T$					–1.808	–3.468	-11.961	–3.468
LPPI$_{USA}$	–2.510	–3.452	–6.385	–3.453	–2.659	–3.453	–6.500	–3.453
LCPI$_{USA}$	–4.295	–3.452	–6.905	–3.453	–1.847	–3.454	–4.464	–3.454
LPPI$_{JAP}$	–3.108	–3.452	–9.157	–3.453	–3.108	–3.452	–9.157	–3.453
LCPI$_{JAP}$	–2.261	–3.452	–13.906	–3.453	–2.261	–3.452	–13.906	–3.453
LCPI$_i$	–3.672	–3.453	–7.035	–3.453	–2.714	–3.452	–8.437	–3.453
LCPI$_W$	0.924	–3.453	–3.954	–3.453	0.924	–3.453	–3.954	–3.453

Notes: LIMPR$_i$—import price of Korea or Thailand; LEXRT$_i$/USD—exchange rate of Korea or Thailand per unit of USD; LEXRT$_i$/JPY—exchange rate of Korea or Thailand per unit of JPY; LNEER$_i$—nominal effective exchange rate of Korea or Thailand; LGDP$_K$—GDP of Korea; LIP$_T$—industrial production index of Thailand; LPPI$_{USA}$—producer price index of USA; LCPI$_{USA}$—consumer price index of USA; LPPI$_{JAP}$—producer price index of Japan; LCPI$_{JAP}$—consumer price index of Japan; LCPI$_i$—consumer price index of either Korea or Thailand; LCPI$_W$—consumer price index of world.

Source: Authors.

Table 3.2(b) Cointegration test results

		Trace statistic				Maximum Eigenvalue statistic			
		r=0*	r=1	r=2	r=3	r=0	r=1	r=2	r=3
Korea									
Import price pass-through	Spec1—US PPI	83.866	18.534	4.589	0.522	65.332	13.945	4.066	0.522
	Spec2—US CPI	77.557	23.570	7.566	1.422	53.987	16.003	6.145	1.422
	Spec1—JAP PPI	77.145	31.194	13.894	3.091	45.951	17.300	10.803	3.091
	Spec2—JAP CPI	92.719	30.623	12.880	0.916	62.096	17.742	11.965	0.916
	NEER	57.496	29.310	13.465	0.797	28.185	15.845	12.668	0.797
CPI pass-through	Spec1—US PPI	88.379	27.576	6.453	0.849	60.803	21.123	5.605	0.849
	Spec2—US CPI	91.107	36.965	13.136	2.032	54.141	23.829	11.104	2.032
	Spec1—JAP PPI	79.730	38.834	20.444	6.665	40.896	18.390	13.779	6.665
	Spec2—JAP CPI	92.495	36.406	15.644	4.296	56.090	20.762	11.348	4.296
	NEER	70.211	39.227	12.510	0.344	30.984	26.717	12.166	0.344
Thailand									
Import price pass-through	Spec1—US PPI	61.731	19.349	7.199	1.004	42.382	12.150	6.194	1.004
	Spec2—US CPI	50.835	21.234	9.704	1.162	29.601	11.530	8.541	1.162
	Spec1—JAP PPI	62.743	26.010	11.645	2.696	36.734	14.364	8.949	2.696
	Spec2—JAP CPI	90.431	33.527	5.413	0.886	56.904	28.113	4.527	0.886
	NEER	89.834	23.442	10.656	0.140	66.391	12.786	10.516	0.140
CPI pass-through	Spec1—US PPI	105.522	28.584	13.191	3.156	76.938	15.392	10.035	3.156
	Spec2—US CPI	73.592	40.729	20.441	8.008	32.863	20.288	12.433	8.008
	Spec1—JAP PPI	100.844	28.641	12.605	3.741	72.203	16.037	8.864	3.741
	Spec2—JAP CPI	85.963	30.080	9.165	1.052	55.883	20.915	8.113	1.052
	NEER	84.010	26.735	10.108	0.792	57.275	16.627	9.316	0.792

Note: * r denotes number of cointegrating vectors.
Source: Authors.

The empirical estimating version of eq. (3) is given by:

$$\ln\left(P^i\right)_t = B'X_t + \sum_{k=-1}^{k=+1} \eta_k \Delta \ln\left(E_j^i\right)_{t-k} + \sum_{k=-1}^{k=+1} \lambda_k \Delta \ln\left(\mathrm{GDP}^i\right)_{t-k} + \sum_{k=-1}^{k=+1} \gamma_k \Delta \ln\left(\mathrm{PPI}^j\right)_{t-k} + \zeta_t \quad (4)$$

where: $B = [\alpha_0, \alpha_1, \alpha_2, \alpha_3]'$, $X = [(1), \ln(E_j^i), \ln(\mathrm{GDP}^i), \ln(\mathrm{PPI}^j)]$.

The results presented are with one period leads and lags of the regressors.[4] Tables 3.3(a)–(b) show the results for import price pass-through of Korea and Thailand while Tables 3.4(a)–(b) show the results for CPI

Table 3.3(a) Dynamic OLS (DOLS)—import price ERPT for Korea

	Won–USD		Won–JPY		NEER
C	**–3.634*** **	**–3.379*** **	**11.677*** **	**10.690*** **	**5.196*** **
	0.704	0.924	3.899	2.352	0.884
LEXRTK	**0.508*** **	**0.438*** **	0.062	**0.240* **	
	0.049	0.065	0.163	0.139	
LNEER					**0.534*** **
					0.138
$LGDP_K$	0.007	**–0.289* **	0.169	**0.501*** **	**0.610*** **
	0.044	0.155	0.135	0.132	0.168
$LPPI_j$	**0.992*** **		**–1.754** **		
	0.160		0.773		
$LCPI_j$		**1.331*** **		**–1.961*** **	
		0.379		0.589	
$LCPI_W$					**–0.211* **
					0.085
ΔLEXRT(1)	0.033	0.031	–0.168	–0.028	
	0.059	0.076	0.108	0.093	
ΔLEXRT(–1)	0.160	0.155	0.152	0.183	
	0.110	0.094	0.161	0.162	
ΔLNEER(1)					**–0.234* **
					0.131
ΔLNEER(–1)					0.151
					0.121
$\Delta LGDP_K(1)$	0.022	–0.134	0.116	**0.309*** **	**0.261** **
	0.045	0.083	0.070	0.085	0.099
$\Delta LGDP_K(-1)$	–0.012	–0.005	–0.031	–0.034	0.011
	0.034	0.030	0.054	0.092	0.065
$\Delta LPPI_j(1)$	**1.110** **		0.969		
	0.486		1.872		
$\Delta LPPI_j(-1)$	**1.478*** **		1.158		
	0.535		1.642		

Continued

Table 3.3(a) Continued

	Won–USD		Won–JPY		NEER
$\Delta LCPI_j(1)$		**4.028*** **		0.753	
		1.044		1.775	
$\Delta LCPI_j(-1)$		**5.349*** **		**–3.227***	
		1.222		1.915	
$\Delta LCPI_W(1)$					–0.824
					0.911
$\Delta LCPI_W(-1)$					–0.912
					0.880
Adj. R^2	0.956	0.939	0.834	0.858	0.908

Notes: Terms below coefficient denote standard errors. *, **, *** indicates significance at the 10%, 5%, 1% levels. Δ denotes first differenced operator; L denotes log of variables; (–) denotes one period lag of the variables; (1) denotes one period lead of the variables; j denotes either the US or Japan.

Source: Authors.

Table 3.3(b) Dynamic OLS (DOLS)—import price ERPT for Thailand

	Baht–USD		Baht–JPY		NEER
C	**–6.767*** **	**–7.526*** **	**13.424** **	**11.114*** **	**8.256*** **
	0.585	1.827	5.276	3.606	0.723
LEXRT	**0.909*** **	**0.625*** **	**0.533*** **	**0.796*** **	
	0.065	0.113	0.182	0.147	
LNEER					**1.255*** **
					0.134
LIPT	**0.104*** **	–0.209	**0.393*** **	**0.572*** **	**0.370*** **
	0.060	0.193	0.082	0.124	0.133
$LPPI_j$	**1.643*** **		**–2.188***		
	0.156		1.158		
$LCPI_j$		**2.336*** **		**1.807***	
		0.646		0.887	
$LCPI_W$					0.100
					0.085

Continued

Table 3.3(b) Continued

	Baht–USD		Baht–JPY		NEER
ΔLEXRT(1)	**0.228****	0.071	−0.200	0.022	
	0.103	0.106	0.188	0.175	
ΔLEXRT(−1)	**0.247****	**0.331*****	−0.259	−0.258	
	0.106	0.094	0.286	0.279	
ΔLNEER(1)					0.184
					0.126
ΔLNEER(−1)					0.171
					0.111
$\Delta LIP_T(1)$	−0.013	−0.177	−0.240	−0.115	0.081
	0.073	0.154	0.239	0.399	0.112
$\Delta LIP_T(-1)$	−0.061	−0.020	**−0.349***	−0.416	−0.040
	0.054	0.080	0.208	0.357	0.089
$\Delta LPPI_j(1)$	−0.561		1.642		
	0.380		2.684		
$\Delta LPPI_j(-1)$	**−1.192*****		5.194		
	0.434		3.298		
$\Delta LCPI_j(1)$		**3.998***		0.082	
		2.228		3.063	
ΔLCPIj(−1)		**6.056****		−1.238	
		2.542		3.049	
$\Delta LCPI_W(1)$					−0.786
					0.726
$\Delta LCPI_W(-1)$					**−1.244***
					0.694
Adj. R^2	0.985	0.974	0.896	0.892	0.975

Notes: Terms below coefficient denote standard errors. *, **, *** indicates significance at the 10%, 5%, 1% levels. Δ denotes first differenced operator; L denotes log of variables; (–) denotes one period lag of the variables; (1) denotes one period lead of the variables; j—denotes either the US or Japan.

Source: Authors.

pass-through.[5] In order to capture the impact of the currency crisis the estimations were also run using a dummy with a value of 1 for 1997:q1–1998:q2 and 0 otherwise. The ERPT elasticities were unchanged, while the dummy itself was found to be positive but insignificant.

3.2.4 Result: ERPT into import prices

With respect to the USD bilateral rate for Korea we find ERPT elasticities of 51 percent when we use the US PPI, and 44 percent when we use the US CPI. The corresponding elasticities for Thailand are 91 and 63 percent, respectively, as shown in Table 3.3(b). With respect to the JPY, the ERPT elasticity for import prices of Korea is statistically insignificant when we use Japanese PPI, while it is 24 percent when we use the Japanese CPI. For Thailand the corresponding ERPT elasticities are 53 and 80 percent, respectively. Using NEER we find the ERPT for Korea is 53 percent while for Thailand ERPT seems to be complete. These results are broadly consistent with the findings of Sasaki (2005) and Ito et al. (2005) (also see Chapter 2 of this volume).

With regard to the other independent variables, for ERPT with respect to the USD we find the coefficient on Korea's GDP to be negative and significant, while this coefficient with respect to the JPY and NEER is positive. The coefficients on both the US PPI and CPI are positive and significant, while the PPI and CPI of Japan are both negative. For Thailand we find the industrial production index to be positive in all cases. Here again we find the coefficients of the US PPI and CPI to be positive, while those on the Japanese PPI and CPI are negative. The world CPI is negative for Korea's NEER pass-through, while it is insignificant for Thailand's NEER pass-through.

3.2.5 Results: ERPT into CPI

With respect to the USD bilateral rate for Korea we find ERPT elasticities to be 21 percent when we use the US PPI, and 14 percent when we use the US CPI (Table 3.4a). For Thailand we estimate the ERPT elasticity to be 31 percent using either US or Japan's PPI, but statistically insignificant in the case of either US or Japan's CPI (Table 3.4b). With respect to the JPY, we do not find any significant ERPT into CPI for Korea, while for Thailand ERPT is in the range of 30 percent in both specifications. NEER pass-through into CPI for Korea is 14 percent, while it is 29 percent for Thailand.[6]

With regard to the other independent variable, the Korean GDP is found to be positive. Here again, as in the case of import price pass-through, the coefficients for both the US PPI and US CPI are positive

Table 3.4(a) Dynamic OLS (DOLS)—CPI ERPT for Korea

	Won–USD		Won–JPY		NEER
C	**–2.649*** **	**–3.543*** **	0.255	1.270	**2.569*** **
	0.814	0.522	2.691	1.512	0.316
LEXRT	**0.210*** **	**0.135*** **	0.066	0.038	
	0.044	0.041	0.083	0.093	
LNEER					**0.144** **
					0.058
$LGDP_K$	**0.436*** **	–0.085	**0.676*** **	**0.666*** **	**0.429*** **
	0.061	0.092	0.096	0.071	0.069
$LPPI_j$	**0.819*** **		0.232		
	0.232		0.515		
$LCPI_j$		**1.644*** **		0.036	
		0.192		0.352	
$LCPI_W$					**0.159*** **
					0.041
ΔLEXRT(1)	0.043	**0.099*** **	–0.040	–0.040	
	0.047	0.036	0.071	0.077	
ΔLEXRT(–1)	**0.076* **	0.041	0.056	0.054	
	0.044	0.031	0.076	0.078	
ΔLNEER(1)					–0.035
					0.050
ΔLNEER(–1)					0.070
					0.053
$\Delta LGDP_K(1)$	**0.250*** **	–0.027	**0.361*** **	**0.373*** **	**0.233*** **
	0.039	0.048	0.049	0.051	0.041
$\Delta LGDP_K(-1)$	**–0.029* **	–0.014	–0.028	–0.020	–0.012
	0.018	0.014	0.029	0.054	0.020
$\Delta LPPI_j(1)$	0.303		1.429		
	0.285		1.209		
$\Delta LPPI_j(-1)$	**–0.809* **		–1.105		
	0.457		0.882		

Continued

Table 3.4(a) Continued

	Won–USD		Won–JPY		NEER
$\Delta LCPI_j(1)$		1.305		1.075	
		0.858		1.341	
$\Delta LCPI_j(-1)$		1.563		–1.883	
		1.005		1.422	
$\Delta LCPI_W(1)$					–0.115
					0.282
$\Delta LCPI_W(-1)$					–0.100
					0.263
Adj. R^2	0.987	0.992	0.971	0.971	0.992

Notes: Terms below coefficient denote standard errors. *, **, *** indicates significance at the 10%, 5%, 1% levels. Δ denotes first differenced operator; L denotes log of variables; (–) denotes one period lag of the variables; (1) denotes one period lead of the variables; j denotes either the US or Japan.

Source: Authors.

Table 3.4(b) Dynamic OLS (DOLS)—CPI ERPT for Thailand

	Baht-USD		Baht-JPY		NEER
C	**2.338*** **	**–3.485*** **	**3.826** **	0.725	**4.411*** **
	0.581	0.826	1.827	1.392	0.227
LEXRT	**0.305*** **	0.017	**0.300*** **	**0.312*** **	
	0.050	0.054	0.076	0.054	
LNEER					**0.286*** **
					0.040
LIPT	**0.446*** **	**–0.250** **	**0.338*** **	**0.287*** **	0.070
	0.047	0.107	0.034	0.048	0.051
$LPPI_j$	–0.202		–0.105		
	0.175		0.409		
$LCPI_j$		**1.996*** **		**0.625* **	
		0.318		0.342	
$LCPI_W$					**0.259*** **
					0.034

Continued

Table 3.4(b) Dynamic OLS (DOLS)—CPI ERPT for Thailand

	Baht-USD		Baht-JPY		NEER
ΔLEXRT(1)	**0.169*** **	0.053	**0.129***	0.072	
	0.044	0.043	0.073	0.058	
ΔLEXRT(−1)	−0.028	0.066	−0.120	−0.169	
	0.062	0.059	0.084	0.066	
ΔLNEER(1)					−0.032
					0.036
ΔLNEER(−1)					−0.041
					0.056
$\Delta LIP_T(1)$	**0.174*** **	**−0.152** **	0.058	0.055	0.049
	0.051	0.071	0.082	0.101	0.032
$\Delta LIP_T(-1)$	**−0.108***	**−0.065***	**−0.165***	**−0.169** **	-0.003
	0.055	0.038	0.088	0.105	0.026
$\Delta LPPI_j(1)$	**−0.839** **		−0.405		
	0.346		0.844		
$\Delta LPPI_j(-1)$	−0.538		−0.887		
	0.388		1.247		
ΔLCPIj(1)		−0.472		0.578	
		0.777		1.178	
$\Delta LCPI_j(-1)$		**−2.572** **		−0.840	
		1.107		0.895	
$\Delta LCPI_W(1)$					−0.169
					0.238
$\Delta LCPI_W(-1)$					**−0.371***
					0.208
Adj. R^2	0.972	0.985	0.957	0.962	0.991

Notes: Terms below coefficient denote standard errors. *, **, *** indicates significance at the 10%, 5%, 1% levels. Δ denotes first differenced operator; L denotes log of variables; (–) denotes one period lag of the variables; (1) denotes one period lead of the variables; j enotes either the US or Japan.

Source: Authors.

and significant. For Thailand's CPI pass-through its industrial production index coefficient is positive for specification 1 with respect to the US, while it is negative for the second specification. It is positive for both specifications with respect to Japan. The coefficients on the US and Japanese CPI are both positive. The coefficient for the world CPI is also positive for both Korea and Thailand's NEER pass-through.

3.3 Has ERPT declined over time?

Recent literature on ERPT has found that it has declined since 1980s for the industrialized countries (see Chapter 2 of this volume and references cited within). Can the same be said of ERPT in these two Asian economies? To test this we used the recursive estimation methodology to plot the dynamic ERPT elasticities over time. While the DOLS methodology used in the earlier section provides a point estimate of ERPT elasticities over the entire sample period, the recursive methodology involves adding one data point to the sample in the DOLS model and rerunning the regression. A downward trend in the estimated pass-through coefficient is suggestive of declining ERPT. As such the last data points in the recursive ERPT elasticity plots exactly match the value of the point elasticities reported in Tables 3.3(a) and 3.3(b) and Tables 3.4(a) and 3.4(b), as both are based on the entire sample size. But, given that the initial recursive estimates for the initial period are based on too few observations, we present the recursive plots for Korea's ERPT from 1992:q1. For Thailand, with the sample size starting from 1987, we begin all the recursive plots from 1996:q1.[7]

Figures 3.1(a)–(b) show the recursive estimates of ERPT for Korea's Won–USD into import prices and CPI, respectively. With regard to import prices, we see evidence of stable ERPT prior to 1996, followed by a spike upwards until the end of the financial crisis and relative stability thereafter at a higher level. In the case of Korean CPI, the upward trend in ERPT began much earlier in 1992 and continued till about the start of the crisis in 1996. There was a further upward spike during the crisis. Since then the ERPT has been fairly stable till the last sample period.

Figures 3.1(c)–(d) show the recursive plots for Won–JPY rate into Korea's import prices and CPI. Trends in this case are somewhat less clear, though there appears to be evidence of rising ERPT just after the crisis period followed by a gradual decline since 2000.

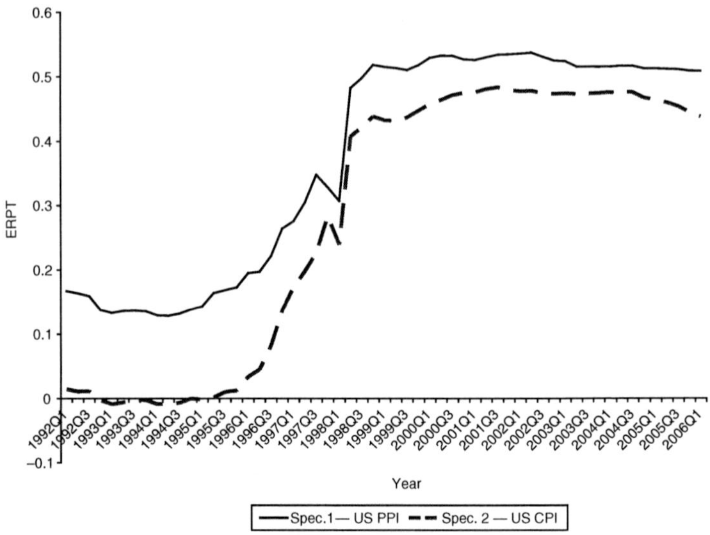

Figure 3.1(a) Recursive estimates of ERPT elasticities of Won–USD into Korea's import prices

Source: Authors.

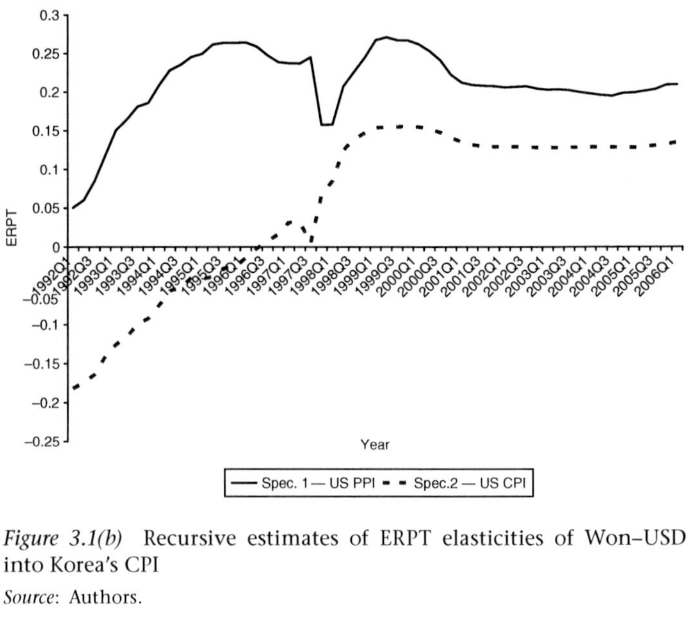

Figure 3.1(b) Recursive estimates of ERPT elasticities of Won–USD into Korea's CPI

Source: Authors.

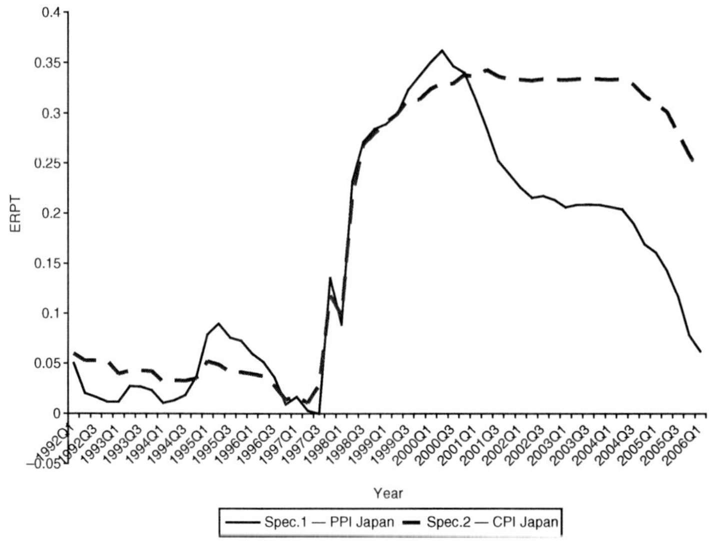

Figure 3.1(c) Recursive estimates of ERPT elasticities of Won–Yen into Korea's import prices

Source: Authors.

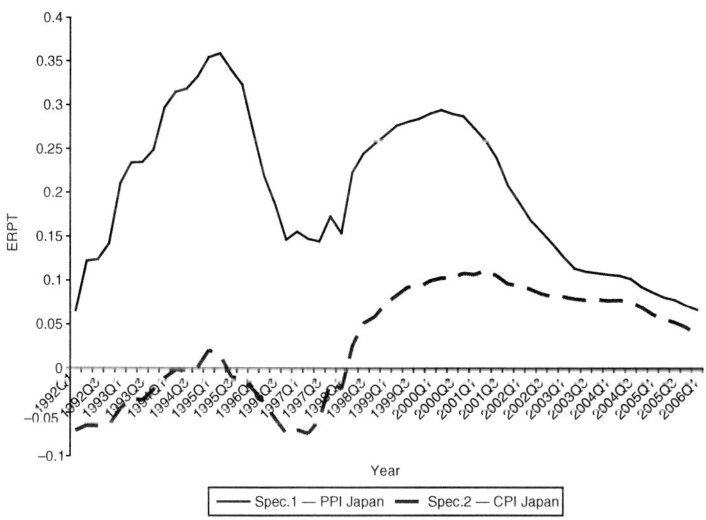

Figure 3.1(d) Recursive estimates of ERPT elasticities of Won–Yen into Korea's CPI

Source: Authors.

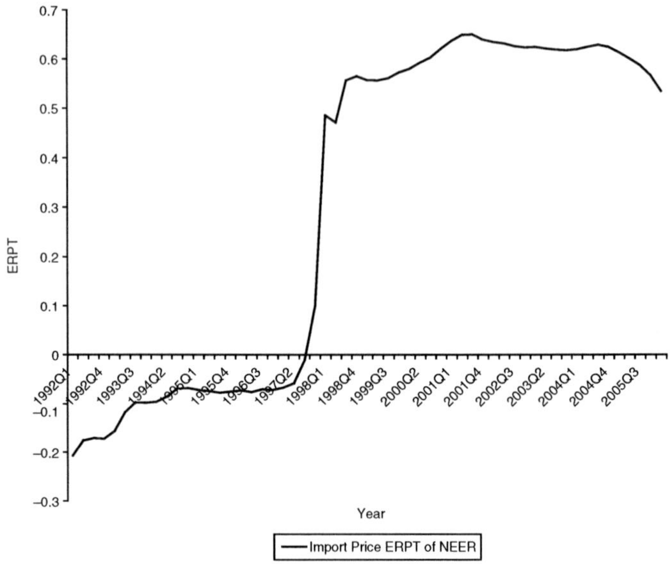

Figure 3.1(e) Recursive estimates of ERPT elasticities of NEER into Korea's import prices

Source: Authors.

Figure 3.1(f) Recursive estimates of ERPT elasticities of NEER into Korea's CPI

Source: Authors.

Figures 3.1(e)–(f) clearly reveal that the ERPT of NEER was stable in Korea prior to the crisis, followed by a spike upwards during the crisis period. This in turn was followed by a degree of stability in the case of import price ERPT at a higher level till the end of the sample period. In the case of Korea's CPI, the spike following the crisis was followed by a period of rising ERPT till the end of the sample period, where the elasticity is 0.14.

Next we plot the dynamic elasticities for Thailand. Figures 3.2(a)–(b) show the ERPT of the Baht–USD rate. In all cases there appears a clear spike in ERPT during the crisis and relative stability thereafter. This pattern is even more distinct in Figures 3.2(c)–(d) for the Baht–JPY rate. A drop in ERPT just prior to the crisis is followed by a distinct rise in ERPT and stability at the higher level thereafter. A broadly similar pattern is apparent in the case of ERPT using Thai NEER (Figures 3.2(e)–(f)), into both import prices and CPI with the last data points being 1.25, 0.29, respectively, the same as the corresponding point elasticities shown in Tables 3.3(b) and 3.4(b).

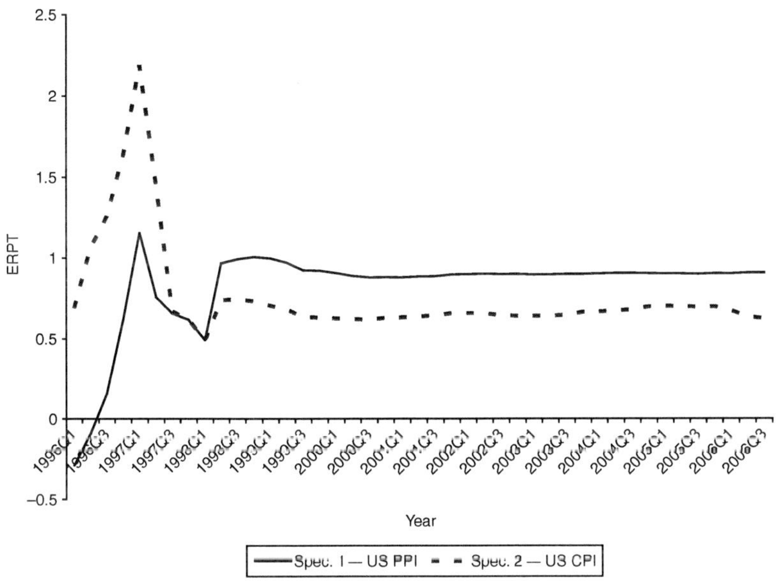

Figure 3.2(a) Recursive estimates of ERPT elasticities of Baht–USD into Thailand's import prices

Source: Authors.

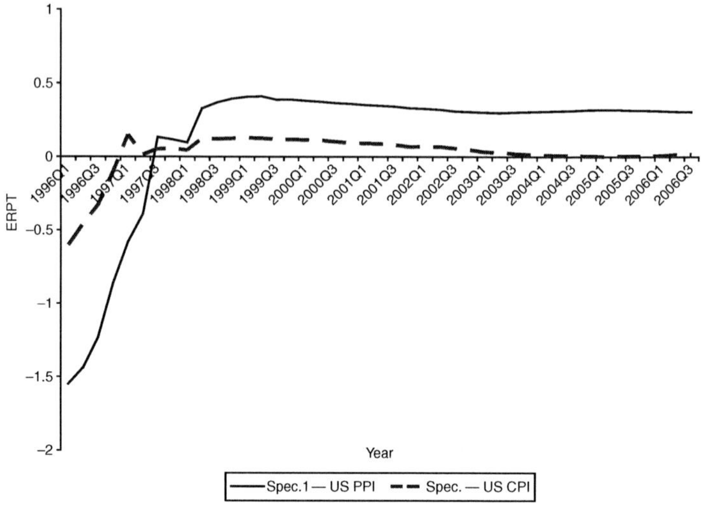

Figure 3.2(b) Recursive estimates of ERPT elasticities of Baht–USD into Thailand's CPI

Source: Authors.

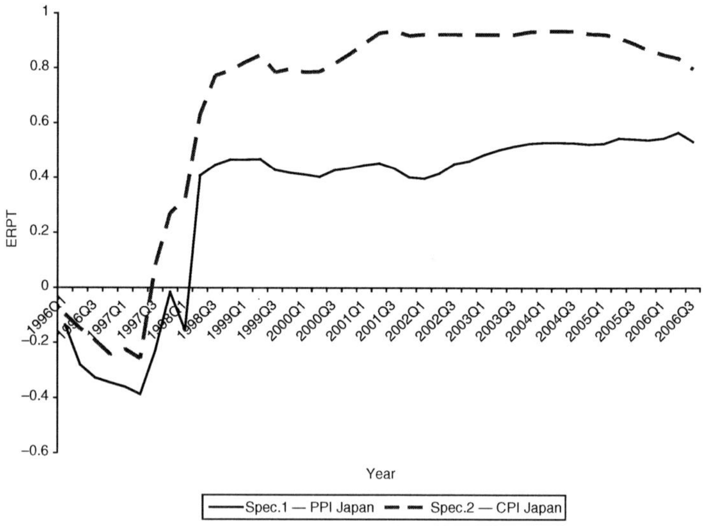

Figure 3.2(c) Recursive estimates of ERPT elasticities of Baht–Yen into Thailand's import prices

Source: Authors.

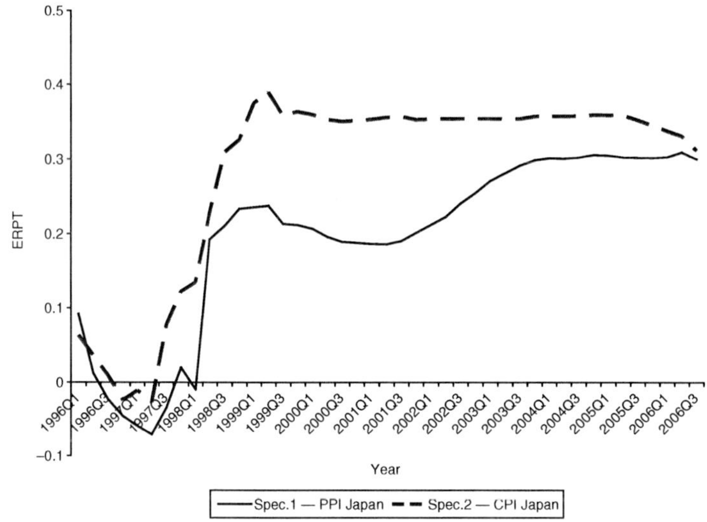

Figure 3.2(d) Recursive estimates of ERPT elasticities of Baht–Yen into Thailand's CPI

Source: Authors.

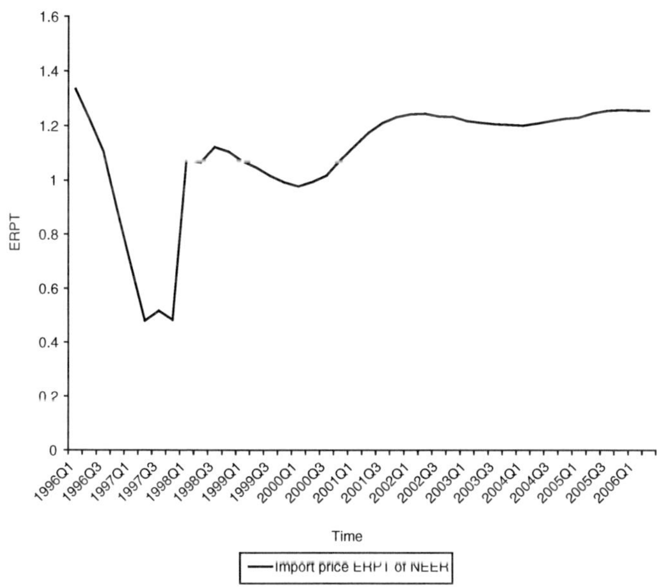

Figure 3.2(e) Recursive estimates of ERPT elasticities of NEER into Thailand's import prices

Source: Authors.

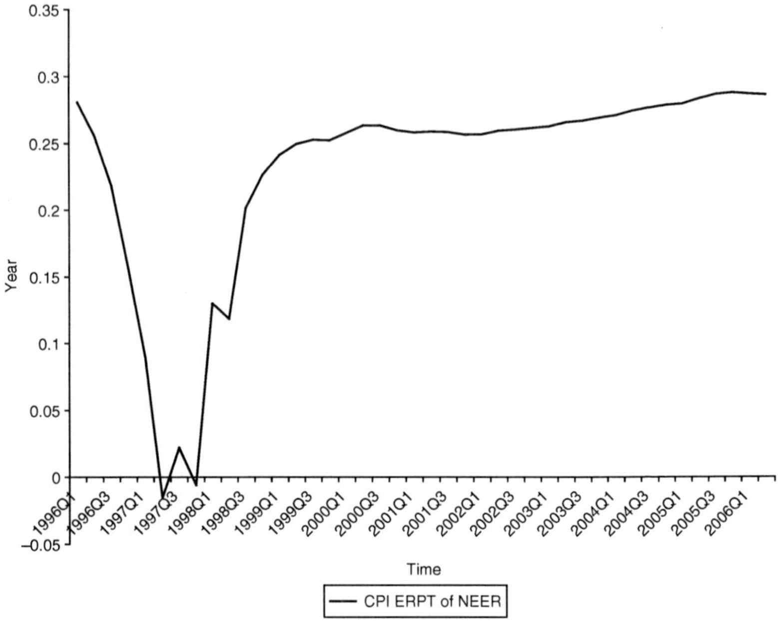

Figure 3.2(f) Recursive estimates of ERPT elasticities of NEER into Thailand's CPI
Source: Authors.

3.4 Endogeneity of pass-through rates with macroeconomic variables

Overall the foregoing results suggest that ERPT increased after the currency crisis period and appears to have remained somewhat more stable post-crisis. But was the rise in the ERPT during the crisis a result of the crisis *per se*, or because of changes in underlying fundamentals? To answer this question we next turn our attention to the macroeconomic factors that impact ERPT. In particular we are interested in the question as to whether ERPT is endogenous to a country's underlying macroeconomic fundamentals.

Taylor (2000) argues that ERPT is endogenous to a nation's exchange rate and monetary policy. ERPT rates are endogenous to a nation's monetary policy and monetary stability, i.e. the more stable is a country's monetary policy and the lower its inflation the lower will be the extent of ERPT. Some empirical evidence of this has been reported by Gagnon and Ihrig (2004), Choudri and Hakura (2001) and Frankel et al. (2005) using macro level data for industrial countries.

Another important macro variable that may affect the ERPT elasticities is exchange rate volatility. Devereux and Engel (2001) argue that if exporters set their prices in the currency of the country that has stable monetary policy (i.e. local currency pricing as opposed to producer currency pricing) then ERPT into import prices in local currency terms will be low for countries with low monetary and exchange rate variability.[8] In contrast, Froot and Klemperer (1989) contend that ERPT is low when nominal exchange rate volatility is high as exporters try to preserve market share. They view exchange rate volatility as temporary fluctuations in exchange rates in any one direction, leading exporters to absorb these shocks in their mark-ups and profit margins. We also examine whether the extent of trade openness impacts ERPT. On the one hand, greater openness ought to imply that domestic prices are more directly and significantly impacted by exchange rate changes. Thus, one would expect ERPT to be higher. On the other hand, greater openness may also imply higher degree of competition for market share, thus implying lower ERPT.

We test for the role of these macroeconomic variables by regressing the time varying ERPT elasticities obtained from the recursive estimations on lagged inflation rate, lagged exchange rate volatility and trade openness.[9] Moreover, we use a dummy that has a value of 1 for 1997:q2–1998:q2 and 0 otherwise to capture any impact of the specific period of the currency crisis.

$$\hat{\alpha}_1^i - \delta' x_t \tag{5}$$

where $\delta = [\delta_0, \delta_1, \delta_2, \delta_3,]$, x_t = [lagged inflation rate, lagged exchange rate volatility, trade openness, crisis dummy]. For inflation rate we use percentage change of CPI for both Korea and Thailand. For ERPT elasticities into both import prices and CPI of the bilateral rate with the USD and the JPY as well as the NEER we use the corresponding exchange rate series to obtain the measure of volatility. We capture exchange rate volatility by using a moving average standard deviation of the exchange rate series:

$$V = \left[\left(\frac{1}{m} \right) \sum_{i=1}^{m} \left(\log E_{t+i-1} - \log E_{t+i-2} \right)^2 \right]^{1/2} \tag{6}$$

where $m = 4$ is the number of lags and E = exchange rate (either bilateral or effective). We measure openness by the ratio of the volume of exports and imports to GDP.

The results for the impact of macro variables on import price and CPI ERPT elasticities are shown in Tables 3.5(a)–(b).[10] Focusing on the case of import prices, we find that exchange rate volatility has a positive impact on ERPT elasticities. This holds for Korea and Thailand's bilateral rate with the USD and JPY as well as for their NEERs. The effect of volatility is much stronger for Thailand. This finding seems to argue in favour of the endogeneity thesis of Devereux and Engel (2001) that ERPT is positively related to exchange rate volatility. Higher openness leads to higher ERPT in both nations, and consistently so in the case of import price pass-through. Higher lagged inflation rates tend to lower ERPT elasticities, though this variable is only statistically significant in the case of Thailand for import price pass-through. This is a rather odd finding as one would have expected lower inflation rates in both economies to reduce rather than increase the extent of ERPT. A possible reason behind this is that higher inflation may lead an inflation targeting regime to undertake contractionary monetary policy measures to curb inflation, which in turn leads to lower ERPT.[11] The Asian currency crisis dummy is negative for Korea, suggesting that the general rise in ERPT during the crisis as discussed previously may have been more due to changes in other macroeconomic factors such as higher exchange rate

Table 3.5(a) Effect of macro variables on ERPT elasticities into import prices

	Korea			Thailand		
	Won–USD	Won–Yen	NEER	Baht–USD	Baht–Yen	NEER
Constant	**–0.351****	**–0.303*****	**–0.396****	0.049	**–1.194*****	–0.009
	0.151	0.107	0.156	0.497	0.287	0.542
Inflation rate$_{(t-1)}$	–0.024	–0.013	–0.023	**–0.144***	**–0.116*****	–0.142*
	0.016	0.015	0.014	0.077	0.038	0.079
Exrt volatility$_{(t-1)}$	**0.617*****	**0.572*****	**0.862*****	**1.882***	**2.534*****	2.616
	0.157	0.129	0.208	1.047	0.851	1.61
Trade openness	**1.255*****	**0.755*****	**1.327*****	**0.658***	**1.246*****	0.709*
	0.239	0.202	0.255	0.383	0.22	0.422
Crisis_dummy	**–0.159***	**–0.148*****	**–0.129***	0.021	**–0.231*****	0.052
	0.081	0.04	0.069	0.145	0.079	0.161
Adj. R^2	0.614	0.445	0.6	0.342	0.775	0.31

Note: *, **, *** indicates significance at the 10%, 5%, 1% levels

Source: Authors.

Table 3.5(b) Effect of macro variables on ERPT elasticities into CPI

	Korea			Thailand		
	Won–USD	Won–Yen	NEER	Baht–USD	Baht–Yen	NEER
Constant	**0.226*** **	**0.374*** **	**0.22*** **	**–2.031*** **	**–0.327*** **	**–2.209*** **
	0.067	0.117	0.069	0.494	0.11	0.556
Inflation rate$_{(t-1)}$	–0.011	–0.002	–0.011	**–0.321*** **	**–0.029***	**–0.320*** **
	0.008	0.011	0.008	0.087	0.015	0.091
Exrt volatility$_{(t-1)}$	0.069	**0.346** **	0.12	**4.668*** **	**0.608***	**6.973*** **
	0.055	0.145	0.092	1.075	0.355	1.558
Trade openness	–0.014	–0.331	–0.007	**1.803*** **	0.438	**1.949*** **
	0.101	0.206	0.108	0.389	0.085	0.44
Crisis_dummy	–0.004	–0.031	–0.001	0.284	**–0.116***	**0.349***
	0.02	0.032	0.02	0.195	0.027	0.198
Adj. R^2	–0.028	0.138	–0.025	0.735	0.76	0.708

Note: *, **, *** indicates significance at the 10%, 5%, 1% levels

Source: Authors.

volatility. The crisis itself appears to have imparted a contractionary-cum-deflationary effect on the Korean economy (see Burstein et al. 2002). The same is true when we consider Thai ERPT using the Baht–JPY exchange rate. However, the crisis does not appear to have had a separate direct impact on ERPT in Thailand when using the Thai Baht–USD rate or the Thai NEER.

While the foregoing results broadly hold for the case of CPI in Thailand, most of the variables are insignificant in the case of Korea. *A priori* this is not surprising as Thailand is a much smaller and open economy with a relatively smaller nontradables sector and greater dependence on imports. Thus, factors impacting import prices may also feed directly into CPI.

3.5 Conclusion

This chapter has estimated ERPT elasticities for two Asian economies, Korea and Thailand, both of which have moved towards greater exchange rate flexibility since the currency crisis of 1997–1998. We considered ERPT for three exchange rates, viz. bilateral nominal exchange rate per unit of the USD and the Japanese yen as well as for their NEER.

We also examined the dynamics of ERPT over time and the possible impact of macro fundamentals on these time varying ERPT elasticities. Certain results warrant summarizing.

First, the ERPT into Thailand is higher than in Korea in all cases under consideration. Given that Thailand is a relatively small and open economy compared with Korea, this is consistent with one's priors in that it is generally acknowledged that ERPT tends to be greater in lower income economies and relatively smaller and more open economies where there is a high share of traded goods, high import content, limited domestic substitutes (thus limiting the extent of "flight from quality" *a la* Burstein et al. 2002), and high degree of integration with the global trading system.

Second, it is apparent that ERPT is much larger into import prices than CPI for both countries. This is also consistent with priors in that typically CPI ERPT is less sensitive to changes in exchange rate changes, as CPI includes nontradables and is also impacted by other factors such as distribution channel and market structure of retail chains. Therefore, the impact of exchange rate changes on CPI is much more indirect than it is on import prices (i.e. "prices at the border") only.

Third, we find that for both Korea and Thailand pass-through of the bilateral rate vis-à-vis the USD is higher than their bilateral exchange rate with respect to the yen. This may be partly explained by the fact that much of Japan's trade with Asia tends to be invoiced in US dollars, which automatically implies lower ERPT (for details, see Sato 1999, 2003 and Fukuda and Ono 2005).

Fourth, unlike studies on the US and some other industrialized nations, we find no evidence that pass-through has been declining over time for Korea and Thailand. In fact we find ERPT to have risen during the crisis period. The question that follows is whether the rise was because of the crisis *per se*, or due to changes in the underlying macroeconomic factors. On analyzing the macro determinants of ERPT into import prices, we find evidence that higher trade openness and greater exchange rate volatility raise ERPT for import prices into both Korea and Thailand. Independent of the macroeconomic variables, the currency crisis dummy itself appears in general to have imparted a deflationary impact on import prices into the Korean economy, though the evidence for Thailand's ERPT is mixed.

Given our results, the next stage of research on ERPT, especially in the context of Asian economies, needs to pay more attention to the impact of different exchange rate regimes on the extent of ERPT.

Notes

1. This chapter draws on an article originally forthcoming in *Japan and the World Economy*, 21 (1), 55–79 (Elsevier B.V.). Reprinted with permission.
2. However, a rise in output could also imply less demand for imported goods and a decline in the import prices. So it is plausible that α_2 and β_2 might be negative as well.
3. For Thailand GDP data are available only from 1993, while data on Industrial Production are available from 1987. As such we used the latter as it provided a longer time series.
4. We also used higher order lags and leads but they were statistically insignificant. As such we restrict our analysis to the most parsimonious model specification.
5. With one period lag and lead of the regressors the final estimation sample ranged from 1983:q1–2006:q1 for bilateral ERPT and from 1985:q3–2006:q1 for NEER pass-through.
6. Instead of Thailand's Industrial Production index, when we used its GDP starting from 1993 the ERPT elasticities into import prices from the USD were 88 and 41 percent, respectively, for the two specifications. For the Baht–JPY rates they were 99 and 100 percent. For NEER it was 93 percent. For CPI pass-through of Baht–USD the elasticities were 34 and 11 percent, respectively, for the two specifications. For Baht–JPY they were 37 and 35 percent. NEER pass-through into CPI of Thailand using its GDP was insignificant.
7. For Korea as such we have 60 observations while for Thailand we have 44 observations in the recursive plots.
8. We also tried the variability in monetary growth but this is consistently statistically and economically insignificant so we dropped it.
9. For both Korea's and Thailand's ERPT of their bilateral rates with the USD and JPY we use the specification 1 with either US or Japanese PPI.
10. To be consistent with our graphical illustration of the time-varying elasticities, for Korea we run the impact of macro variables on ERPT elasticities starting from 1992, while for Thailand we start from 1996.
11. Of course, the implicit assumption here is that the policies do not directly impact any of the control variables in eq. 3 such as output or costs.

References

Borio, C. and A. Filardo (2007). "Globalization and Inflation: New Cross-country Evidence on the Global Determinants of Domestic Inflation," Working Paper No. 227, Bank for International Settlements.

Burstein, A., B. Eichenbaum, and S. Rebelo (2002). "Why is Inflation so Low After Large Contractionary Devaluations," Working Paper No. 8748, NBER.

Cavoli, T. and R.S. Rajan (2009). *Exchange Rate Regimes and Macroeconomic Management in Asia*, Hong Kong: Hong Kong University Press.

Choudri, E. and D. Hakura (2001). "Exchange Rate Pass-through to Domestic Prices: Does the Inflationary Environment Matter," Working Paper No. 01/194, IMF.

Devereux, M. and C. Engel (2001). "Endogenous Currency of Price Setting in a Dynamic Open Economy Model," Working Paper No. 8559, NBER.

Frankel, J., D. Parsley, and S.J. Wei (2005). "Slow Pass-through Around the World: A New Import for Developing Countries?," Working Paper No. 11199, NBER.

Froot, K. and P. Klemperer (1989). "Exchange Rate Pass-through When Market Share Matters," *American Economic Review*, 79, 637–654.

Fukuda, S. and M. Ono (2005). "The Choice of Invoice Currency under Exchange Rate Uncertainty: Theory and Evidence from Korea," *The Journal of the Korean Economy*, 6, 161–193.

Gagnon, J. and J. Ihrig (2004). "Monetary Policy and Exchange Rate Pass-through," International Finance Discussion Paper No. 704, Federal Reserve Board.

Ghosh, A. and R.S. Rajan (2007). "How High is Exchange Rate Pass Through in India?," *Journal of International Trade and Development*, 16, 373–382.

Helbling, T., F. Jaumotte, and M. Sommer (2006). "How has Globalization Affected Inflation?" *IMF World Economic Outlook*, Washington, DC: IMF, April, Chapter 3.

Ito, T., Y. Sasaki, and K. Sato (2005). "Pass-through of Exchange Rate Changes and Macroeconomic Shocks to Domestic Inflation in East Asian Countries," Discussion Paper Series No. 05-E-020, Research Institute of Economy, Trade and Industry (RIETI), Japan.

Johansen, S. and K. Juselius (1990). Maximum Likelihood Estimation and Estimation and Inference on Cointegration with Applications to Money Demand, *Oxford Bulletin of Economics and Statistics*, 52, 169–210.

Sasaki, Y.N. (2005). "Pass-through of Exchange Rates on Import Prices of East Asian Countries," Keizai Kenyu (The Papers and Proceedings of Economics), The Society of Economics, Meiji Gakuin University No. 132, 23–33.

Sato, K. (1999). "The International Use of the Japanese Yen: The Case of Japan's Trade with East Asia," *The World Economy*, 22, 547–584.

Sato, K. (2003). "Currency Invoicing in Japanese Exports to East Asia: Implications for Yen Internationalization," *Asian Economic Journal*, 17, 129–154.

Stock, J.H. and M. Watson (1993). "A Simple Estimator of Cointegrating Vectors in Higher Ordered Systems," *Econometrica*, 61, 783–820.

Taylor, J.B. (2000). "Low Inflation, Pass-through, and the Pricing Power of Firms," *European Economic Review*, 44, 1389–1408.

Part II

Impact of Currency Crisis and Monetary Policy

4

Are Crisis-Induced Devaluations Contractionary? If so, Why?[1]

(Co-authored with Shen Chung-Hua)

4.1 Introduction

The Mexican crisis of 1994–1995 followed by the East Asian crisis of 1997–1998 and the other crises in Brazil, Russia and Turkey in 1999–2000 have generated a great deal of academic and policy interest in the causes of currency crises in emerging and developing economies. The main focus of this literature has been on whether the crisis was "inevitable" (first generation models) or "self-fulfilling" (second generation models). A common element in both these two genres of crisis models is that, if a speculative attack is successful in breaking down the currency peg, the resulting devaluation ought to mark the end of the crisis. Real devaluation, according to the conventional view, would have expansionary effects because it increased the demand for tradables (Dornbusch 1988). In practice, the postdevaluation experiences have varied markedly among countries. Some countries, like Brazil, seemed to recover smartly following the initial devaluation of the real. Others underwent a considerable output contraction immediately following flotation of the respective currencies. Kamin and Rogers (2000) and Santaella and Vela (1996) confirm this (contraction) to have been the case for Mexico following the 1994–1995 crisis and Moreno (1999) shows it to have held for East Asia in general.[2]

In view of the above, Dooley and Walsh (2000) have commented, "(w)e are unsure why some crises are followed by long periods of economic recession while others are not" (p. 3). This chapter is an attempt at answering this query. In particular, we investigate two closely related issues. We first explore whether there is a difference in the output effects of a devaluation during "normal" periods versus crisis ones; after all, during non-crisis periods, real exchange devaluation is seen as an important policy option for promoting exports and output growth.[3]

Yet, the literature has not made a distinction between crisis and non-crisis periods. To preview the main conclusion, we find that the contractionary effects tend to exist only during the crisis period. Building on this, we go on to explore the factors that cause a crisis-induced devaluation to be contractionary.

The remainder of this chapter is organized as follows. Drawing upon recent analytical literature on currency crises and capital flows, the next section synthesizes the reasons for and channels via which a devaluation is contractionary. This section outlines the specific hypotheses to be tested. Sections 4.3 and 4.4 respectively describe the econometric model and the data to be used in the analysis. The main results are summarized in Section 4.5. The final section offers a summary and a few concluding remarks.

4.2 Devaluation in emerging and developing economies: contractionary channels

4.2.1 New structuralist school: current account channels

There exists a rich early literature that has detailed the various channels through which a devaluation might be contractionary in emerging and developing economies due to their unique economic structures, a point stressed by the so-called "New Structuralist" school (Taylor 1981). There are various well-established routes via which devaluation may, in principle, have a contractionary effect that spans both aggregate demand and aggregate supply (see the well-cited papers by Edwards 1989; Lizondo and Montiel 1989 and van Wijnbergen 1986 for comprehensive reviews; Cooper 1971 provides one of the earliest systematic surveys).

On the demand side, and with both a high average propensity to import and a low price elasticity of demand for imports, devaluation will tend to divert domestic monetary demand away from home produced goods. The income redistributive effects of devaluation will favour profits in the traded goods sector—the mechanism through which devaluation affects the current account—and disfavour real wages, as the price level rises. However, spending and savings propensities may differ as between those receiving profits and wages. If the marginal propensity to save is higher from profits than from wages the economy's average propensity to save will rise and this will tend to be demand contractionary (Diaz-Alejandro 1963 and Knight 1976). On the supply side, there are again a number of channels through which devaluation may exert a recessionary impact. To name one, the domestic currency costs of imported inputs will rise, leading to stagflationary effects.

Regardless of the exact channels, this New Structuralist School opines that devaluation is more likely the lower the income level of the country. Thus, *Hypothesis 1* is as follows: *The lower the per capita income level of a country the more likely that devaluation is contractionary.* We refer to this as the "Income effect."[4]

4.2.2 Regional contagion effects

An important characteristic of emerging and developing economies is that a currency crisis tends to be accompanied by contagion or negative spillover effects that are largely *regional* in scope (consequently, they are also referred to as "neighbourhood effects"). For instance, while the East Asian crisis did threaten to turn global, it did not. Similarly, while the currencies of Thailand, Hong Kong and the Philippines underwent brief periods of speculative attacks during the Tequila crisis, the crisis predominantly affected Mexico's neighbouring economies (such as Argentina). In a recent study using a sample of twenty countries covering the periods of the 1982 Mexican debt crisis, the 1994–1995 Tequila crisis and the 1997–1998 Asian crisis, De Gregario and Valdes (2001) found contagion to be directly dependent on *geographical horizon.* Using a panel of annual data for nineteen developing economies for the period 1977–1993, Krueger et al. (2000) concluded that a currency crisis in a *regional economy* raises the probability of a speculative attack on the domestic currency by about 8.5 percentage points.[5] Thus, even if the New Structuralist arguments are rejected, it is possible that devaluation may fail to boost exports if regional contagion effects accompany it. In other words, currency devaluation in one economy may provoke a devaluation in one or more trade competitors (i.e. other economies with similar export structures/comparative advantage) that suddenly find themselves at a competitive disadvantage.

Gerlach and Smets (1995) is a pioneering attempt at modeling the phenomenon of competitive devaluation. Their trade spillover model consists of two channels via which a trade partner is impacted. In the primary channel, devaluation in an export competitor leads to a deterioration in the trade balance in the partner country, causing a speculative attack on the latter. In the secondary channel, devaluation lowers the aggregate price level and demand. This leads to the domestic currency being substituted for foreign currency, depleting international reserves and making the economy vulnerable to a classic speculative attack. Two other recent models of competitive devaluation are by Huh and Kasa (1997) and Corsetti, Pesenti and Roubini (2000), which is built on microfoundations. The Corsetti–Pesenti–Roubini model shows how a game of competitive devaluation could generate currency overshooting if market participants, anticipating that a series of competitive devaluations will occur once there is a successful speculative attack in one country, flee altogether from the trade competitors.[6]

This leads to *Hypothesis 2: Devaluation may be contractionary in the presence of regional "contagion."* We dub this the "Regional effect."

4.2.3 "Twin" crisis

An important channel ignored by the older literature is the so-called "balance-sheet effect" due to sizable unhedged exposures to short term foreign currency denominated debt (Aghion et al. 2000 and Krugman 1999a,b).[7] The rise in corporate bankruptcies due to an escalation in domestic currency liabilities inevitably leads to large-scale domestic "credit rationing," as decapitalized banks, burdened by large non-performing loans (NPLs), curtail their lending.[8] It is therefore not surprising that currency crises in emerging and developing economies often tend to be accompanied by banking crises. The coexistence of banking and currency crises has been found to be the norm during the late 1980s and early 1990s (Kaminsky and Reinhart 1999), and these twin crises seem to be far more pervasive in developing economies than developed ones (Glick and Hutchison 1999).[9]

This leads to *Hypothesis 3: Other things equal, devaluation accompanied by a banking crisis is more likely to be contractionary.* We refer to this as the "Banking Crisis effect."

4.2.4 Short term indebtedness

Krugman (1999b) has noted that the positive pro-competitive effects of a devaluation would dominate for "small" variations in the exchange rate, resulting in a devaluation being expansionary; while the negative balance sheets effects may dominate for "large" devaluations, resulting in an income contraction. The conundrum is that even a small devaluation in emerging and developing economies may act as a trigger leading to sharp capital outflows and an outright economic collapse after the initial devaluation. Thus, Krugman (1998) has noted,

> nobody who looks at the terrible experiences of Mexico in 1995 or Thailand in 1997 can remain a cheerful advocate of exchange rate flexibility. It seems that there is a double standard on these things: when a Western country lets its currency drop, the market in effect says "Good, that's over" and money flows in. But when a Mexico or Thailand does the same, the market in effect says "Oh my God, they

> have no credibility" and launches a massive speculative attack. So the question for...(emerging and developing economies)...is, do you think that the market will treat you like Britain, or do you think it will treat you like Mexico? And this is not an experiment that any responsible policymaker wants to try.[10]

In other words, if devaluation damages confidence it may result in additional capital outflows. This in turn could cause a further decline in the currency's value than was anticipated, leading to a vicious spiral of crisis-induced devaluation, illiquidity and insolvency of financial institutions and corporates, and eventual outright economic collapse.

Received wisdom linking the composition of international capital flows to economic instability and financial crises is quite straightforward. Short term inflows (or "hot money"), it is argued, can be easily reversed. Thus, Fernández-Arias and Hausmann (2000, 2001) refer to short term debt as "bad cholesterol" as it is motivated by "speculative considerations" such as interest rate differentials and exchange rate expectations.[11] This type of financing is the first to exit in times of trouble, the resulting boom-bust cycle of capital flows in the 1990s having inflicted great damage to small and open economies. The extent of short term indebtedness has been found to be a robust predictor of financial crises (Dadush et al. 2000; Rodrik and Velasco 1999 and World Bank 2000). The extreme reversibility of short term debt in the event of negative shock exposes borrowers to liquidity runs and systemic crises.

This implies a further hypothesis to be tested. *Hypothesis 4: The larger the level of short term indebtedness,* ceteris paribus, *the greater the likelihood that devaluation will be contractionary.* We refer to this as the "Excessive Debt effect."

4.2.5 Composition of capital flows and corruption

The preceding emphasis on short term debt leaves the analysis open to two criticisms.

One, short term debt is by no means the only form of liquid liability. An alternative—more complete—measure of illiquidity is given by "mobile capital" or international capital markets, which refers to short term bank loans plus portfolio investment in the form of equity and bond issues in offshore markets. Unfortunately, significant data problems exist in the case of components of international capital flows. These take the form of data unavailability as well as concerns regarding possible substitutability between various types of capital flows (see Fernández-Arias and Hausmann 2000, 2001 and Rajan and Siregar 2002).

Two, there is an active parallel area of research that has identified insolvency caused by poor public governance or "crony capitalism" as an important reason for crises in emerging and developing economies, especially in East Asia in 1997–1998. Wei (2001) and Wei and Wu (2001) provide a way of resolving the illiquidity versus crony capitalism debate. Countries that are corrupt, and are therefore vulnerable to insolvency, tend also to have capital inflows that are biased away from more "secure" forms of financing (like FDI) towards the highly mobile variety, hence making them susceptible to illiquidity crises.

This leads us to *Hypothesis 5: The higher the level of corruption, ceteris paribus, the greater the likelihood that devaluation will be contractionary.* We refer to this as the "Corruption effect."

4.2.6 State-contingent devaluation

An important but oft-ignored analytical point is that the New Structuralist hypothesis (*Hypothesis 1*) opines that devaluations in emerging and developing economies will be contractionary regardless of whether they occur during a period of "crisis" or a relatively tranquil (i.e. non-crisis) period. In contrast, the other hypotheses noted here are more specifically relevant to the currency crisis periods. Therefore, before going on to test the five hypotheses set out above, we first investigate whether the output effects of devaluations in economies vary between crisis and non-crisis periods, that is "state contingent devaluation."

4.3 Model design and sample countries

4.3.1 Econometric model

On the basis of the discussion in the previous section, we take a two-step approach in our econometric model. We first explore whether output does contract after a currency crisis. We then investigate the reasons for contraction based on the five hypotheses outlined in the previous section. The two-step method is as follows:

$$y_{it} - \tilde{y}_{it} = \left(\alpha_0^{(1)} + \alpha_1^{(1)} \left(e_{it} - \tilde{e}_{it}\right)\right) I_{it} + \left(\alpha_0^{(2)} + \alpha_1^{(2)} \left(e_{it} - \tilde{e}_{it}\right)\right)(1 - I_t) + \beta\left(X_{it} - \tilde{X}_{it}\right) + \varepsilon_t \quad i = 1, \ldots, N, \quad t = 1, \ldots, T \tag{1}$$

$$\alpha_1^{(k)} = \theta_0^{(k)} + \theta_1^{(k)} z_{t,} \quad k = 1, 2 \tag{2}$$

where I_{it} is the indicator function and

$$I_{it} = 1 \quad \textit{if there is no crisis}$$
$$= 0 \quad \textit{if there is a crisis}$$

y_t is the real output, e is the real exchange rate, X is the vector of controlled variables, including government expenditure (g), domestic interest rate (r) and monetary policy (m). This is based on Agenor (1991) and Moreno (1999).[12] The tilde (~) denotes the expected trend, i refers to the country and t is the time period. All variables are adjusted using deviation from the expected trend. z denotes our hypothesized variables, i.e. proxies for GNP per capita (income), regional effect (region), banking crisis (*bc*), excessive short term debt hypothesis (debt), and poor public governance (proxied by corrupt), which *represent* the five hypotheses mentioned in the previous section. The coefficients $\alpha_0^{(k)}$, $\alpha_1^{(k)}$, $\theta_0^{(k)}$ and $\theta_1^{(k)}$ are unknown parameters, where $k = (1, 2)$ denotes the crisis regimes.

The intuition guiding our econometric model is straightforward. The first step measures the responses of output to exchange rate movements in the "normal time" (non-crisis period) and the responses during the crisis period, respectively, separated by indicator I. That is, the output effects of exchange rate variations are different across the two regimes (i.e. crisis versus non-crisis).

$$\frac{\partial y_t}{\partial e_t} = \alpha_1^{(1)} = 0 \quad \text{if there is no crisis, or no "successful attack"}$$
$$\alpha_1^{(2)} < 0 \quad \text{if there is a crisis, or a "successful attack."}^{13}$$

In this step, the exchange rate response of output is constant *within each* regime but differs *across* regimes. We expect significant negative responses of output to exchange rate variations during the currency crisis, and no response or even a positive one in the absence of a crisis (we define what we mean by "currency crisis" in the next section). This specification differentiates this chapter from past studies which do not distinguish the output responses during normal times and chaotic times. Failure to make this distinction could lead to misleading results and conclusions.

The second step concerns the reasons causing the output collapse. We relate the response coefficient $\alpha_i^{(k)}$ to a constant $\theta_0^{(k)}$ and z_t. That is, the response coefficients are:

$$\alpha_1^{(1)} = \theta_0^{(1)} + \theta_1^{(1)} z_t \quad \text{if there is no crisis, or no successful attack}$$
$$\alpha_1^{(2)} = \theta_0^{(2)} + \theta_1^{(2)} z_t \quad \text{if there is a crisis, or a successful attack}$$

where z_t is the proxy of the above mentioned five hypotheses alternatively, viz.,

$$z_t = \{\text{income, region, banking crisis, debt, corrupt}\}$$

The Income effect hypothesis is proxied by GNP per capita. Based on the New Structuralist arguments, we expect the coefficient to be positive, that is, the lower the income level the more likely it is that devaluation is contractionary.

The Regional effect is proxied by regional dummies for Latin America, Asia, Nordics, Southern Europe and others (sample used is described in the next section).

The third hypothesis pertains to the "twin crisis," that is, coincidence of currency and banking crises. This banking crisis hypothesis is proxied by a variable containing dates of banking crisis of each country. This dummy variable is denoted as *bc*, which is equal to one if there is a banking crisis simultaneously with a currency crisis, otherwise it takes on a zero value.

The Excessive debt hypothesis is proxied by short term debt as a proportion of total external debt. Unfortunately, such data are only available for developing countries in the World Bank's databank. As such, the Nordic countries are excluded when this hypothesis is tested. The coefficient is expected to be negative for reasons already outlined.

The Corruption hypothesis is proxied by a dummy variable ranging from 0 to 10. This dummy is taken from LaPorta, Lopez-de-Silanes, Shleifer and Vishny (hereafter LLSV) (1998). The index is based on the International Country Risk's assessment of government corruption levels across countries. A lower score indicates that "high government officials are likely to demand special payments" and "illegal payments are generally expected throughout lower levels of government." Thus, a higher score indicates less corruption and vice versa.

4.4 Data and descriptive statistics

4.4.1 Sample countries

We consider 25 countries in this study. There are nine Latin American countries, including Argentina, Bolivia, Brazil, Chile, Columbus, Mexico, Peru, Uruguay, Venezuela; five Asian countries, including Indonesia, Malaysia, Philippines, South Korea and Thailand; four Nordic countries, including Denmark, Finland, Norway and Sweden; three South European countries, including Czech Republic, Greece and Spain; and others including Egypt, Israel, South Africa and Turkey. These 25 countries are selected based on the monograph by Goldstein, Kaminsky and Reinhart (2000), which provides dates of currency and banking crises of the above 25 sample countries.

Goldstein et al. (2000) define the date of currency crisis as a situation in which an attack on the currency leads to a "substantial reserve loss" or to a "sharp depreciation of the currency." Insofar as our five hypotheses ought, strictly speaking, to pertain only to a successful speculative, i.e. actual devaluation, we consider the case of a currency crisis as defined above as well as the case of only a "successful attack," that is, actual devaluation. We date an attack as "successful" if the percentage change of the exchange rate exceeds 1.65 times one standard deviation of the percentage change of the exchange rate. While many researchers also use 1.65 times one standard deviation of the percentage change of exchange rate as the criteria for defining a crisis, such a technical rule is not without its flaws. Nonetheless, different mechanical criteria, such as using 1.96, do not alter the results significantly.

The date of a banking crisis is characterized by two types of events: bank runs that lead to the closure, merger, or takeover by the public sector of one or more financial institutions; and, if there are no bank runs, the closure, merging, takeover, or large-scale government assistance of an important financial institution. Admittedly, there may be a selection bias since floating exchange countries and developed countries are excluded. As such, countries like the United Kingdom, which suffered from a currency crisis during September 1992, are not listed in Goldstein et al. (2000).

The sample initially spans the period 1981 to 1999; annual data is used. All data are taken from *International Financial Statistics* published by the International Monetary Fund and the *World Development Indicator* published by the World Bank. Following Moreno (1999) we consider two expected trends to remove non-stationary of variables. We first use the polynomial trended method. The expected trend method is obtained by regressing the variables on constant, linear, quadratic, cube and quadruplet trends to obtain filtered variables. We then consider the Hodrick-Prescott trend method. The two filters yield broadly similar results.

4.4.2 Descriptive statistics

Table 4.1 reports the average growth rate of GDP and the five hypothetical proxies over the sample period for the countries under consideration. Since the numbers in Table 4.1 are averages over 25 years, their information may be limited due to the wide variations over these years. The first column is the average growth rate across countries. Note that the Asian countries experienced a higher rate of growth than other countries in our sample despite the severe output contractions in 1997–1998 by virtue of the phenomenal pre-crisis expansions. The next two columns are the currency and banking crises. The GNP per capita values are shown

Table 4.1 Country information: average GDP growth and proxies for the five hypotheses

Countries	GDP growth (%)	Currency crisis (Dates)	Banking-cum-currency crises (Dates)	Short term debt/total (%)	Corruption index
Argentina	1.543	1981, 1982, 1986, 1989, 1990	1981, 1986	20.15	6.02
Bolivia	1.912	1982, 1983, 1985		10.91	6.00
Brazil	3.252	1983, 1986, 1989 1990, 1998	1986	15.33	6.32
Chile	5.080	1976, 1982, 1984	1982	16.98	5.30
Colombia	3.458	1982, 1985	1983, 1985	21.51	5.00
Denmark	1.943	1979, 1993		NA	10.00
Egypt	1.593	1979, 1989, 1990		16.19	5.00
Finland	2.524	1982, 1991, 1992	1991, 1992	NA	10.00
Greece	2.282	1976, 1980, 1984		NA	7.27
Indonesia	5.170	1978, 1983, 1986 1997		15.43	2.27
Israel	3.874	1977, 1983, 1984	1983	NA	8.33
Malaysia	6.576	1975, 1997	1997	17.03	7.38
Mexico	3.271	1976, 1982, 1994	1982, 1994	16.95	4.77
Norway	3.215	1978, 1986, 1992	1986	NA	10.00
Peru	1.731	1987		21.09	4.70
Philippines	2.928	1983, 1984, 1997	1983, 1997	25.00	2.92
South Africa	5.039	1981, 1984, 1996		43.68	8.92
Korea	6.956	1984, 1997		30.73	5.30
Spain	2.430	1977, 1982, 1986 1992, 1993	1977	NA	7.38
Sweden	1.593	1981, 1982, 1992	1992	NA	10.00
Thailand	6.344	1978, 1981, 1984 1997	1978, 1992	29.86	5.18
Turkey	3.698	1980, 1994	1994	21.57	5.18
Uruguay	2.419	1982	1982	20.75	4.00
Venezuela	1.840	1984, 1986, 1989 1994, 1995	1994	23.35	4.70

Source: Table based on data from various sources. Dates of currency and banking crises are taken from Goldstein et al. (2000); Corruption Index is taken from LLSV (1998).

in the next column. The highest short term debt ratio is South Africa (43.68), followed by South Korea (30.73). The final column shows the corruption index.

4.5 Estimation results

4.5.1 Contractionary devaluation hypothesis

We estimate eq. 1 for each country (excluding Czech Republic) and collect the estimated response coefficient of α_1. Thus, we have 24 response coefficients. 18 out of 24 coefficients are negative and 10 out of the 18 negative coefficients are significant at the 10 percent level. Hence, while negative coefficients are typically observed, seeming to support the contractionary hypothesis, the trend is blurred by the large variations.

Table 4.2 reports the estimation results of pooling 24 countries. Three distinct models are estimated—a single regime or linear model (i.e. encompassing the entire sample period), and a pair of two-regime models. The first two-regime model is based on the currency crisis index (i.e. both successful and unsuccessful speculative attacks) and the second two-regime model is based on only the cases of a successful attack. Regime 1 in both models is the normal period and regime 2 is the crisis period.

With respect to the single regime model, while the response of output to exchange rate changes is negative, it is statistically insignificant.

Table 4.2 Contractionary depreciation during currency crisis

	Linear/Single regime model	Two-regime model 1 (currency crisis)	Two-regime model 2 (successful attack)
Constant × I	−0.0033 (0.945)	−0.0070 (0.935)	0.0070 (0.959)
$(e-\tilde{e}) \times I$	−0.0493 (1.013)	0.0008 (0.325)	0.0011 (0.458)
Constant × $(1 - I)$		−0.0243 (1.403)	−0.0034** (2.196)
$(e-\tilde{e}) \times (1 - I)$		−0.0474* (4.799)	−0.0521* (4.986)
$g-\tilde{g}$	−0.2234 (0.889)	0.0131 (1.614)	0.0093 (1.132)
$m-\tilde{m}$	0.1204*** (1.832)	0.0248* (2.534)	0.0254* (2.592)
$r-\tilde{r}$	0.0308 (1.602)	−0.0121 (1.466)	−0.0117 (1.416)
R^2	0.054	0.069	0.073

Notes: *, **, *** denote the significance at 1, 5 and 10 percent levels. Variables are deviated from expected trend, which uses polynomial trend method here. $I = 1$ denotes that there is no currency crisis or there is no successful attack; $I = 0$ denotes that there is a currency crisis or there is a successful attack.

Source: Authors.

Hence, using the single regime model leads us to reject the contractionary devaluation hypothesis. This is consistent with the negative trend and wide variations of sample in the previous figures.

With respect to the first two-regime model, using the currency crisis periods to separate samples into the two regimes, the response coefficient turns out to be positive but is still insignificant in the normal regime. This is more consistent with the conventional wisdom that devaluation typically facilitates an output rebound. However, strongly negative responses are discernible in the crisis regime. While the coefficient (–0.0474) is close to that of a single regime model, it *is* significant at the 1 percent level. Hence, the contractionary devaluation does not exist during the normal time. It only does so during the crisis period. This validates our emphasis on state-contingent devaluation, a point that appears to have been largely ignored by the New Structuralist School.

There is not much alteration in the results in the second two-regime model, where the crisis index is limited to the cases of a successful attack. The coefficient becomes slightly higher at –0.0521 and is also significant at the 1 percent level. Finally, the coefficient also increases slightly from 0.054 in the single regime model to 0.069 in the first two-regime, and to 0.073 in the second two-regime model.

4.5.2 Testing the five hypotheses

Table 4.3 reports the estimation results assuming that response coefficients are functions of the five hypotheses alternatively. After plugging eq. (2) into eq. (1), the right hand side of the equation contains four interactive terms:

$$\theta_0^{(1)}(e_{it}-\tilde{e}_{it})I_{it}+\theta_1^{(1)}z_i(e_{it}-\tilde{e}_{it})I_{it}+\theta_0^{(2)}(e_{it}-\tilde{e}_{it})(1-I_{it})+\theta_1^{(2)}z_i(e_{it}-\tilde{e}_{it})(1-I_{it})$$

The coefficients of $\theta_0^{(1)}$ and $\theta_0^{(2)}$ represent the response of output to exchange rate variations with the presence of z during the normal and the crisis periods, respectively. Since output does not drop during the normal period, our primary interest is the coefficient on the latter variable. In other words, for all the five hypotheses, the primary coefficient of interest is $\theta_0^{(2)}$. I_{it} is first proxied by the currency crisis index which encompasses the cases when a crisis is unsuccessful in the sense that it does not lead to a devaluation.

When z is the GNP per capita, the coefficient is 0.0121 and is insignificantly different from zero. The positive coefficient means that the lower the GNP per capita, the lower the output for a given devaluation.

Table 4.3 Testing the five hypotheses of output contraction during currency crisis

	GNP Per capita	Regional effect	Twin crises	Short term debt/ total	Corruption
const. $\times I$	−0.0037 (0.543)	−0.0052 (0.7814)	−0.0032 (0.460)	0.0095 (1.302)	−0.0036 (0.541)
$(e\text{-}\tilde{e}) \times I$	−0.0404 (0.324)	−0.3955* (7.8652)	−0.0240 (1.263)	−0.0095 (0.119)	0.0117 (0.118)
$(e\text{-}\tilde{e}) \times z \times I$	0.0024 (0.142)		−0.0003 (0.006)	−0.0075 (0.221)	−0.0063 (0.384)
$(e\text{-}\tilde{e}) \times I \times D_{Latin}$		0.2916 (2.0955)			
$(e\text{-}\tilde{e}) \times I \times D_{Asia}$		4114 (2.6976)			
$(e\text{-}\tilde{e}) \times I \times D_{Nordic}$		2950 (1.1711)			
$(e\text{-}\tilde{e}) \times I \times D_{MiddleE}$		2855** (1.9877)			
const. $\times (1-I)$	0.0005 (0.208)	−0.002 (0.0763)	0.0003 (0.154)	−0.0029 (1.108)	0.0004 (0.169)
$(e\text{-}\tilde{e}) \times (1-I)$	−0.1435*** (1.841)	−0.3166* (2.2893)	−0.0479* (4.785)	0.0152 (0.328)	−0.1487* (5.733)
$(e\text{-}\tilde{e}) \times z \times (1-I)$	**0.0121 (1.240)**		**−0.1205 (0.095)**	**−0.0271** (1.695)**	**0.0202* (4.182)**
$(e\text{-}\tilde{e}) \times (1-I) \times D_{Latin}$		**−0.44394* (8.6783)**			
$(e\text{-}\tilde{e}) \times (1-I) \times D_{Asia}$		**−0.6140* (10.2428)**			
$(e\text{-}\tilde{e}) \times (1-I)\ (1-I) \times D_{Nordic}$		**−0.5849* (6.4071)**			
$(e\text{-}\tilde{e}) \times (1-I) \times D_{MiddleE}$		**−0.4256** (7.8448)**			
$g-\tilde{g}$	0.0120 (1.444)	0.0134*** (1.8326)	0.0123 (1.495)	0.0074 (1.036)	0.0160* (2.008)
$m-\tilde{m}$	0.0245* (2.460)	0.0233* (2.5381)	0.0252* (2.506)	0.0364* (4.010)	0.0240* (2.460)
$r-\tilde{r}$	−0.0122 (1.400)	−0.0124*** (1.6573)	−0.0120 (1.399)	−0.0029 (0.380)	−0.0121 (1.488)
R^2	0.072	0.265	0.093	0.179	0.120

Notes: Absolute value in parenthesis; *,**, *** denote the significance at 1, 5 and 10 percent levels. All variables are deviated from expected trend, which uses polynomial trend method here. $I = 1$ if there is no currency crisis; $I = 0$ if there is a currency crisis.

Source: Authors.

While the sign is consistent with the New Structuralist hypothesis, it is statistically insignificant and is rejected.

We have four regional dummies, D_{Latin}, D_{Asia}, D_{Nordic} and $D_{MiddleE}$. The dummies equal unity if the countries are in that region, otherwise they are zero. As seen in Table 4.3, in the absence of a currency crisis, the coefficients are significantly positive for Latin American, Asian and Middle Eastern countries, but insignificantly different from zero for Nordic countries. This suggests that, during the non-crisis period, while the overall effect is negative for currency devaluation, this negative effect is lessened in the first three regions, but remains unchanged for the Nordic countries. Results are sharply reversed during the currency crisis periods. Coefficients on the four regional dummies are overwhelmingly negative and highly significant at the 1 percent level, suggesting that the negative effect is exacerbated for the four regions if a currency crisis occurs. The regional effect does exist for the devaluation effect when there is the currency crisis.

When z is the GNP per capita, the coefficient is –0.1205. Though this coefficient is negative, suggesting that the banking crisis aggravates the declines of output, it is not significantly different from zero. Also, the response coefficient of $(e - \tilde{e}) \times I(cc = 1)$ changes little compared with that presented in Table 4.2. Thus, the coincidence of a banking and a currency crisis appears to be of little help in accounting for a devaluation-induced output collapse.

When the ratio of short debt to total external debt ratio is used, the coefficient of interest is –0.0271, and significant at only the 10 percent level. Hence, when there is a currency crisis, the higher the short term debt, the greater the drop in output.[14]

Lastly, the corruption hypothesis is also confirmed. The primary coefficient of interest is significantly positive at the 1 percent level. Because the *corrupt* indicator ranges from 1 to 10, where a higher number indicates less corruption (better public governance), the positive response implies that the better the quality of public governance, the less likely that a currency crisis will be contractionary.

When I_{it} is replaced by successful attack, there are a few variations in the findings which warrant highlighting. In Table 4.4, GNP per capita becomes significant at the 10 percent level, which confirms the New Structuralist Hypothesis. The four regional dummies are again highly significant regardless of the sample period. In other words, the coefficients on the various regional dummies are negative even during the non-crisis period. The regional effect is significant at all times (i.e. during both crisis and non-crisis periods). The twin crisis variable is the incorrect sign but remains statistically insignificant. Results of the remaining two hypotheses are unaltered.

Table 4.4 Testing the five hypotheses of output contraction during successful attack

	GNP Per capita	Regional effect	Twin crises	Short term debt/ total	Corruption
const. $\times I$	0.0064 (0.838)	−0.0017 (0.2307)	0.0077 (1.061)	0.0075 (1.031)	0.0075 (1.054)
$(e\text{-}\tilde{e}) \times I$	−0.0717 (0.589)	−0.0014* (0.6012)	−0.0303** (2.166)	0.0415 (0.792)	−0.2302* (3.788)
$(e\text{-}\tilde{e}) \times z \times I$	0.0058 (0.348)		−0.1418 (1.361)	−0.0311 (1.623)	0.0367* (3.404)
$(e\text{-}\tilde{e}) \times I \times D_{\text{Latin}}$		−0.2623* (4.6068)			
$(e\text{-}\tilde{e}) \times I \times D_{\text{Asia}}$		−0.4297* (6.5268)			
$(e\text{-}\tilde{e}) \times I \times D_{\text{Nordic}}$		−0.3954* (4.1446)			
$(e\text{-}\tilde{e}) \times I \times D_{\text{MiddleE}}$		−0.2446* (4.0783)			
const. $\times (1 - I)$	−0.0011 (0.433)	0.5930* (6.0480)	−0.001 (0.415)	−0.0028 (1.070)	−0.0014 (0.581)
$(e\text{-}\tilde{e}) \times (1 - I)$	−0.2038* (2.239)	−0.6272* (6.3570)	−0.0553* (5.166)	0.0221 (0.440)	−0.1604* (4.845)
$(e\text{-}\tilde{e}) \times z \times (1 - I)$	**0.0188*** (1.685)**		**0.0648 (1.318)**	**−0.0306*** (1.720)**	**0.0194* (3.454)**
$(e\text{-}\tilde{e}) \times (1 - I) \times D_{\text{Latin}}$		**−0.6273* (6.3570)**			
$(e\text{-}\tilde{e}) \times (1 - I) \times D_{\text{Asia}}$		**−0.5859* (5.2179)**			
$(e\text{-}\tilde{e}) \times (1 - I)\ (1 - I) \times D_{\text{Nordic}}$		**−0.7178* (2.8799)**			
$(e\text{-}\tilde{e}) \times (1 - I) \times D_{\text{MiddleE}}$		**−0.6209* (6.0190)**			
$g - \tilde{g}$	0.0085 (1.029)	0.0134*** (1.7319)	0.0091 (1.105)	0.0074 (1.018)	0.0085 (1.063)
$m - \tilde{m}$	0.0248* (2.504)	0.0212* (2.2528)	0.0282* (2 .805)	0.036* (3.909)	0.0225* (2.347)
$r - \tilde{r}$	−0.0125 (1.463)	−0.0144*** (1.8848)	−0.0136 (1.613)	−0.0034 (0.446)	−0.0118 (1.466)
R^2	0.078	0.231	0.093	0.178	0.120

Notes: Absolute *t* value in parenthesis; *, **, *** denote the significance at 1, 5 and 10 percent levels. All variables are deviated from expected trend, which uses polynomial trend method here. $I = 1$ if there is no successful attack; $I = 0$ if there is a successful crisis.

Source: Authors.

4.6 Conclusion

This chapter has examined whether output declines when a fixed exchange rate regime is devalued. We find the output increases insignificantly during a "normal period" but drops during a "crisis period." In other words, the impact of devaluation is state-contingent. This in itself seems to be an important finding and has implications for an exit strategy between a pegged regime and a more flexible one. In particular, our analysis suggests that such a transition is best made during a period of relative calm (Eichengreen et al. 1999).[15]

Having linked a currency crisis and exchange rate devaluation with economic collapse, we proceeded to establish the circumstances under which a crisis-induced devaluation may exert a recessionary influence. Drawing on the recent literature on currency crisis, we outlined five hypotheses to explain the reasons for a crisis-induced output contraction. The five hypotheses are: the "Income effect," based on the New Structuralist hypothesis; "Regional effect" to capture regional contagion effects; "twin crisis," to denote the coincidence of a banking crisis and a currency crisis; "Excessive Debt effect" and "Corruption effect," both of which capture aspects of composition of capital flows (i.e. short term capital flows are more easily reversible and potentially damaging to the real economy). The Corruption effect serves a dual purpose, also acting as a proxy for particular attributes of insolvency.

While all estimated coefficients have the anticipated signs, we reject outright the twin crisis hypothesis on the basis of the data and proxies available. This may be partly due to difficulties in accurately dating banking crises, let along twin crises. Our results are broadly supportive of the other three hypotheses which emphasize the importance of contagion and composition of capital flows. There is also weak evidence in support of the New Structuralist thesis. Taken as a whole, these findings may provide reason to pause before recommending devaluation to every country in the midst of a crisis, and to think carefully about what policies should accompany such an expenditure switching policy if implemented.

Notes

1. The chapter draws on an article originally published in *Journal of Economic Integration*, 21 (3), 2006, 526–550 (Center for International Economics, Sejong Institution, Sejong University). Reprinted with permission.
2. Bird and Rajan (2004) discuss the case of Thailand.

3. For instance, Rodrik (2000) has noted:

   there is every reason to think that...(the)...real depreciations were an important boost to economic activity, particularly in tradables, and not simply something that went alongside higher growth. They unleashed energies and focused them on world markets, boosted exports, and set the stage for economic transformation. (8–9)

4. Regression analysis of twelve developing economies for the period 1965–1980 by Edwards (1986) suggested that real devaluations have a small contractionary effect in the short run but are neutral in the long run. However, in a broad survey of the empirical evidence, Kamin (1988) concluded that there was no empirical evidence to support the claim that devaluation *per se* was contractionary. He found that, more often that not, recessions preceded devaluation. Also see Kamin and Klau (1998).
5. Other recent empirical studies confirming this regional dimension of currency crises include Calvo and Reinhart (1996), Frankel and Schmukler (1996), Glick and Rose (1999) and Kaminsky and Reinhart (2000).
6. The Corsetti–Pesenti–Roubini model also consists of a "bilateral trade" or "cheap imports" effect which is welfare enhancing, as it allows the importing country to enjoy a higher level of consumption, *ceteris paribus*, is also formally captured. As they show, if this effect dominates the welfare reducing effect due to loss of product competitiveness, devaluation in one country may not necessarily lead to a net welfare loss to its trading partner. In other words, devaluation may not necessarily be "beggar-thy-neighbour."
7. Over 50 percent of long term external debt in developing economies (for which data are available) is held in US dollar, with the remainder being held primarily in euros and Japanese yen. This inability by developing economies to borrow externally in their local currency has come to be referred to as the "original sin" hypothesis, a term attributed to Hausmann (1999). For a discussion of the implications of this original sin hypothesis on exchange rate policy in Southeast Asia, see Rajan (2002) and references cited within.
8. We do not enter here into the controversial debate of defining what is meant by a "credit crunch" and how it is most appropriately measured, only recognizing that credit growth reflects both the demand for and the supply of credit (see Lane and Associates 1999; Lindgren et al. 1999 and Furman and Stiglitz 1998).
9. These "twin crises" have inspired a number of recent theoretical contributions to the literature on financial crises in emerging and developing economies. The pioneering work in this area is Velasco (1987), who introduced a banking sector within a conventional Krugman (1979) framework. Also see Shen (1999).
10. Calvo (1996) makes a similar point. It is actually interesting to recall the debate prior to the Mexican crisis documented in the *Brookings Economic Papers* in 1994. While Rudiger Dornbusch and Andrew Werner had proposed a devaluation of the peso of about 20 percent prior to the Mexican crisis, Guillermo Calvo (1994) was on record as opposing the peso devaluation, arguing that "(t)his is not the time to implement a Dornbusch-Werner devaluation. The forces that have held together the 'good' equilibrium... may dissipate overnight" (p. 303).

11. Prominent examples of illiquidity models include Chang and Velasco (1999) and Goldfajn and Valdes (1997), which are essentially open economy extensions of the Diamond and Dybvig (1983) bank panic model.
12. In a study of IMF-supported stabilization programs, Hutchison (2001) considers a somewhat different specification. The variables he includes in his specification are inflation, credit growth and real GDP growth, external growth rate and the real exchange rate overvaluation at *t-1*.
13. We define these states of nature more precisely in the next section.
14. We can only conjecture that this mildly significant result may be a result of two possibilities. First, our data has not distinguished between short debt denominated in local currency versus foreign currency. The high short term debt may not necessarily lead to significant output losses if it is denominated in local currency since the devaluation does not automatically worsen the net worth of the economy (i.e. so-called "balance sheet effect"). Second, high short term debt and the currency crisis dummy may be highly correlated since the response coefficient of $\Theta_0^{(2)}$ becomes insignificant.
15. A related issue is: if a currency peg is abandoned, what alternative form of nominal anchor will need to replace it (Bird and Rajan 2002 and Eichengreen et al. 1999)?

References

Agenor, P. (1991). "Output, Devaluation, and the Real Exchange Rate in Developing Countries," *Weltwirtschaftliches Archiv*, 127, 18–41.

Aghion, P., P. Bacchetta and A. Banerjee (2000). "A Simple Model of Monetary Policy and Currency Crises," *European Economic Review*, 44, 728–738.

Bird, G. and R. Rajan (2002). "Optimal Currency Baskets and the Third Currency Phenomenon: Exchange Rate Policy in Southeast Asia," *Journal of International Development*, 14, 1053–1073.

Bird, G. and R.S. Rajan (2004). "Does Devaluation Lead to Economic Recovery or Economic Contraction? Examining the Analytical Issues with Reference to Thailand." *Journal of International Development*, 16, 141–156.

Calvo, G. (1994). "Comments on Dornbusch-Werner," *Brookings Papers on Economic Activity*, 2, 299–303.

Calvo, G. (1996). "Capital Flows and Macroeconomic Management: Tequila Lessons," *International Journal of Finance and Economics*, 1, 207–223.

Calvo, S. and C. Reinhart (1996). "Is there Evidence of Contagion Effect," in G. Calvo, M. Goldstein, and E. Hochreiter (eds), *Private Capital Flows to Emerging Economies After the Mexican Crisis*, Washington, DC: Institute for International Economics.

Chang, R. and A. Velasco (1999). "Liquidity Crises in Emerging Markets: Theory and Policy," in B. Bernanke and J. Rotemberg (eds), *NBER Macroeconomics Annual 1999*, Cambridge, MA: MIT Press.

Cooper, R. (1971). "Currency Devaluation in Developing Countries," *Princeton Essays in International Finance No. 86*, International Economic Section, Princeton University.

Corsetti, G., P. Pesenti and N. Roubini (2000). "Competitive Devaluations: Toward a Welfare-Based Approach," *Journal of International Economics*, 51, 217–241.

Dadush, U., D. Dasgaupta, and D. Ratha (2000). "The Role of Short-term Debt in Recent Crises," *Finance and Development*, 37, 54–57.

De Gregario, J. and R. Valdes (2001). "Crisis Transmission: Evidence from the Debt, Tequila, and Asian Flu Crises," in S. Claessens and K. Forbes (eds), *International Financial Contagion*, Boston: Kluwer Academic Publishers.

Diamond, P. and P. Dybvig (1983). "Bank Runs, Deposit Insurance, and Liquidity," *Journal of Political Economy*, 91, 401–419.

Diaz-Alejandro, C. (1963). "A Note on the Impact of Devaluation and the Redistributive Effects," *Journal of Political Economy*, 71, 577–580.

Dooley, M. and C. Walsh (2000). "Capital Controls and Crises: Theory and Experience," mimeo. Paper presented at AEA Meetings (June).

Dornbusch, R. (1988). *Open Economy Macroeconomics*, 2nd edition, New York: Basic Books.

Edwards, S. (1986). "Are Devaluations Contractionary?," *Review of Economics and Statistics*, 68, 501–508.

Edwards, S. (1989). *Real Exchange Rates, Devaluation, and Adjustment: Exchange Rate Policy in Developing Countries*, Cambridge, MA: MIT.

Eichengreen, B., P. Masson, M. Savastano, and S. Sharma (1999). "Transition Strategies and Nominal Anchors on the Road to Greater Exchange-Rate Flexibility," *Essays in International Finance*, International Economics Section, Princeton University.

Fernández-Arias, E. and R. Hausmann (2000). "Foreign Direct Investment: Good Cholesterol?," Working Paper No. 417, Inter-American Development Bank.

Fernández-Arias, E. and R. Hausmann (2001). "Is FDI a Safer Form of Financing?" *Emerging Markets Review*, 2, 34–49.

Frankel, J. and S. Schmukler (1996). "Crisis, Contagion, and Country Funds: Effects on East Asia and Latin America," Working Paper No. 96–04, Center for Pacific Basin Monetary and Economics Studies, Federal Reserve of San Francisco.

Furman, J. and J. Stiglitz (1998). "Economic Crises: Evidence and Insights from East Asia," *Brookings Papers on Economic Activity*, 2, 1–114.

Gerlach, S. and F. Smets (1995). "Contagious Speculative Attacks," *European Journal of Political Economy*, 11, 5–63.

Glick, R. and M. Hutchison (1999). "Banking and Currency Crises: How Common Are Twins?," Working Paper No. PB99–07, Center for Pacific Basin Monetary and Economic Studies, Federal Reserve Bank of San Francisco.

Glick, R. and A. Rose (1999). "Contagion and Trade: Why are Currency Crises Regional?," *Journal of International Money and Finance*, 18, 603–617.

Goldfajn, I. and R. Valdes (1997). "Capital Flows and the Twin Crises: The Role of Liquidity," Working Paper No. 97/87, IMF.

Goldstein, M., G. Kaminsky, and C. Reinhart (2000). *Assessing Financial Vulnerability: An Early Warning System for Emerging Markets,* Washington, DC: Institute of International Economics.

Hausmann, R. (1999). "Currencies: Should there be Five or One Hundred and Five," *Foreign Policy*, 116, 65–79.

Hutchison, M. (2001). "A Curse Worse Than the Disease?: Currency Crises and the Output Costs of IMF-supported Stabilization Programs," Working Paper No. 8305, NBER.

Huh, C. and K. Kasa (1997). "A Dynamic Model of Export Competition, Policy Coordination, and Simultaneous Currency Collapse," Working Paper No. 97–08, Center for Pacific Basin Monetary and Economics Studies, Federal Reserve of San Francisco.

Kamin, S. (1988). "Devaluation, External Balance, and Macroeconomic Performance: A Look at the Numbers," Princeton Studies in International Finance No. 62, International Economics Section, Princeton University.

Kamin, S. and M. Klau (1998). "Some Multi-Country Evidence on the Effects of Real Exchange Rates on Output," International Finance Discussion Papers No. 611, Board of the Governors of the Federal Reserve.

Kamin, S. and J. Rogers (2000). "Output and the Real Exchange Rate in Developing Countries: An Application to Mexico," *Journal of Development Economics*, 61, 85–109.

Kaminsky, G. and C. Reinhart (1999). "The Twin Crises: The Causes of Banking and Balance-of-Payments Problems," *American Economic Review*, 89, 473–500.

Kaminsky, G. and C. Reinhart (2000). "Bank Lending and Contagion: Evidence from the Asian Crisis," in T. Ito and A. Krueger (eds), *Regional and Global Capital Flows: Macroeconomic Causes and Consequences*, Chicago: University of Chicago Press.

Knight, J. (1976). "Devaluation and Income Distribution in Less Developed Economies," *Oxford Economic Papers*, 28, 208–227.

Krueger, M., P. Osakwe, and J. Page (2000). "Fundamentals, Contagion and Currency Crises: An Empirical Analysis," *Development Policy Review*, 18, 257–274.

Krugman, P. (1979). "A Model of Balance of Payments Crises," *Journal of Money Credit and Banking*, 11, 311–328.

Krugman, P. (1998). "Latin America's Swan Song," mimeo (undated).

Krugman, P. (1999a). "What Happened to Asia?," in R. Sato, R. Ramachandran, and K. Mino (eds), *Global Competition and Integration*, Boston: Kluwer Academic Publishers, 315–328.

Krugman, P. (1999b). "Balance Sheets, The Transfer Problem, and Financial Crisis," in P. Isard, A Razin, and A. Rose (eds), *International Finance and Financial Crises*, Boston: Kluwer Academic.

La Porta, R., F. Lopez-de-Silanes, A. Shleifer, and R.W. Vishny (1998). "Law and Finance," *Journal of Political Economy*, 106, 1113–1155.

Lane, T., A. Ghosh, J. Hamann, S. Phillips, M. Schultze-Ghattas and T. Tsikata (1999). "IMF-Supported Programs in Indonesia, Korea, and Thailand: A Preliminary Assessment," Occasional Paper 178, IMF.

Lindgren, C.T. Balino, C. Enoch, A. Gulde, M. Quintyn, and L. Teo (1999). *Financial Sector Crisis and Restructuring: Lessons from Asia*, Washington, DC: IMF.

Lizondo, S. and P. Montiel (1989). "Contractionary Devaluation in Developing Countries," *IMF Staff Papers*, 36, 182–227.

Moreno, R. (1999). "Depreciation and Recessions in East Asia," *Economic Review*, 3, Federal Reserve Bank of San Francisco, 27–41.

Rajan, R.S. (2002). "Exchange Rate Policy Options for Southeast Asia Revisited: Is There a Case for Currency Baskets?," *The World Economy*, 25, 137–163.

Rajan, R.S. and R. Siregar (2002). "Private Capital Flows in East Asia: Boom, Bust and Beyond," in G. de Brouwer (ed.), *Financial Markets and Policies in East Asia*, London: Routledge.

Rodrik, D. (2000). "Exchange Rate Regimes and Institutional Arrangements in the Shadow of Capital Flows," mimeo (September).

Rodrik, D. and A. Velasco (1999). "Short-Term Capital Flows," Working Paper No. 7364, NBER.

Santaella, J. and A. Vela (1996). "The 1987 Mexico Disinflation Program: An Exchange-rate Based Stabilization," Working Paper No. 96/49, IMF.

Shen, C.H. (1999). "Are They Really Twin: Evidence from Panel Cointegration," paper presented at 9th Security and Capital Market, Kaushiong, Taiwan (December).

Taylor, L. (1981). "IS/LM in the Tropics: Diagrammatics of the New Structuralist Macro Critique," in W. Cline and S. Weintraub (eds), *Economic Stabilization in Developing Countries*, Washington, DC: The Brookings Institution.

van Wijnbergen, S. (1986). "Exchange Rate Management and Stabilization Policies in Developing Countries," *Journal of Development Economics*, 23, 227–247.

Velasco, A. (1987). "Financial Crises and Balance of Payments Crises: A Simple Model of the Southern Cone Experience," *Journal of Development Economics*, 27, 263–283.

Wei, S.J. (2001). "Corruption and Globalization," Policy Brief No. 79, The Brookings Institution.

Wei, S.J. and Y. Wu (2001). "Negative Alchemy? Corruption, Composition of Capital Flows, and Currency Crises," Working Paper No. 8187, NBER.

World Bank (2000). *Global Development Finance 2000*, New York: Oxford University Press.

5

Financial Crisis, Capital Outflows and Monetary Policy Responses: Simple Analytics with Reference to East Asia[1]

Ramkishen S. Rajan

5.1 Introduction

Financial crises seem to have become the norm rather than the exception since 1992.[2] Specifically, in 1992–1993, Europe was faced with the very real possibility of a complete collapse of the European Exchange Rate Mechanism (ERM). The Italian lira and British pound withdrew from the ERM, three other currencies (the Spanish peseta, Irish pound and Danish krona) were devalued, and there was a substantial widening of the bands within which the currencies could fluctuate. In 1994–1995, the Mexican currency crisis, which saw a steep devaluation of the peso, brought Mexico to the brink of default. There were also spillover effects on Argentina and Brazil. Between July 1997 and mid-1998, the world experienced the effects of the East Asian crisis, which started somewhat innocuously with a run on the Thai baht, but spread swiftly to a number of other regional currencies, most notably the Indonesian rupiah, Malaysian ringgit and Korean won. Other large emerging economies such as Russia and Brazil also experienced periods of significant market weakness and required the assistance of the IMF. The Russian ruble was devalued in August 1998—during a period of exceptional financial market turbulence (Bank for International Settlements 1999)—and the Brazilian real's peg was eventually broken in January 1999. A number of other smaller emerging economies such as Turkey and Ecuador also experienced currency crises in the 1990s; Argentina and Venezuela were the most recent victims.

Most undergraduate textbooks in Money and Banking include a section on financial crisis in emerging economies (for instance, see chapter 24 in

Mishkin 2003 and chapter 20 in Hubbard 2005). Although these texts offer useful and up-to-date discussions of concepts such as financial crises and sterilization of international capital flows, the discussions generally seem to be "stand alones." No attempt is made to link the discussion of these important contemporary issues to the age-old analytics of the money market and money multiplier (chapters 15, 16 and 21 in Mishkin and chapters 17, 18 and 23 in Hubbard).

In this chapter I examine the impact of a crisis of confidence and resultant capital outflows from a small and open economy and the possible policy options in response to such outflows using simple tools and definitions that should be familiar to any student who has successfully completed a money and banking course or even one in intermediate macroeconomics. To facilitate the discussion, examples are drawn from the East Asian crisis of 1997–1998 (Indonesia, Korea, Malaysia and Thailand), although the analysis remains pertinent to emerging economies in general.[3]

5.2 Analytical framework

5.2.1 Preliminaries

Consider a semi-open economy (foreign country) in the sense that the risk adjusted interest parity holds (eq. 1):

$$i_t = i_t^* + \Delta e_{t+1}^e + rp_t \tag{1}$$

where e = foreign currency per US$; $\boldsymbol{i}$ = Thai/emerging economy interest rates; $\boldsymbol{i^*}$ = London interbank offer rate (LIBOR); $\boldsymbol{rp}$ = currency or country risk premium of the emerging economy.

Consider the domestic money market equilibrium:

$$\frac{M_t^s}{P_t} = M_t^d = f(y_t, i_t, V_t) \tag{2}$$

where: $\boldsymbol{M_t^s}$ = nominal money stock, $\boldsymbol{M_t^d}$ = real money demand, $\boldsymbol{P_t}$ = price level, y_t = real income and $\boldsymbol{V_t}$ = vector of other factors affecting money demand (financial innovations, inflation, etc.). Assume, for simplicity, that $\boldsymbol{P_t}$ is normalized to 1 at the start.

5.2.2 Crisis of confidence: causes and consequences

Assume the economy is originally in equilibrium at point 0 (Figure 5.1). Assume the country's equilibrium is disturbed because of a crisis of confidence, such that $(\Delta e_{t+1}^e + rp_t)$ rises sharply. This leads to a rise in

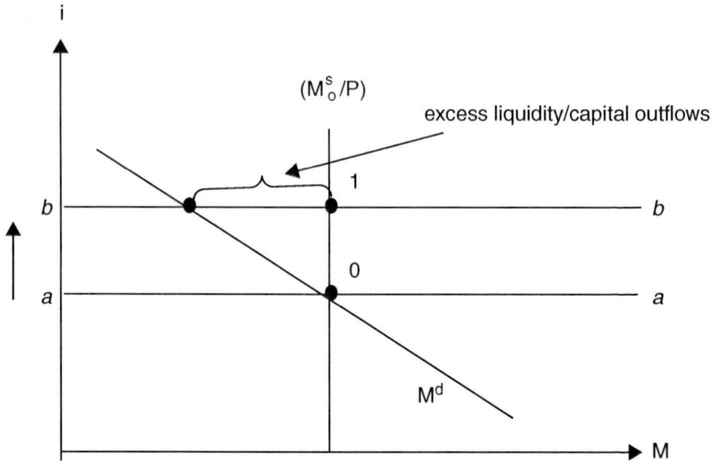

Figure 5.1 Impact of crisis of confidence
Source: Author.

the horizontal parity line from *aa* to *bb*. The rise in local interest rates implies a reduction in money demand. Thus, at 1, $M^s > M^d$. This excess liquidity in the economy is translated into a capital outflow. This is usually the beginning of a crisis.

But what might trigger a crisis of confidence and consequent capital reversals? Crisis triggers can be broadly divided into "country-specific" and "spread" factors. Country-specific factors might include: (a) concerns about export and overall growth prospects (possibly because of a sudden deterioration in the country's terms of trade or a marked appreciation of the real exchange rate as happened in Southeast Asia in 1996–1997);[4] (b) a bust in domestic asset markets (such as real estate) and the negative repercussions of that on the rest of the economy; (c) sociopolitical uncertainty or concerns about the commitment of the government to the reform program; or (d) revelation of new information—"bad news"—such as the extent of bad loans of the domestic financial system; the extent of implicit liabilities of the financial system or government; or the level of forward reserve commitments of the central bank (which effectively reduces the available reserves that can be used for balance of payments financing).

Spread factors triggering a crisis of confidence, leading to sharp capital reversals (i.e., booms turn to bust), could also be manifold. Indeed, as noted, an important characteristic of the East Asian crisis has been the rapid pace at which it spread from Thailand to many other East Asian economies—so-called contagion. This term broadly refers to the simultaneous occurrence of currency crises in two or more economies. While there are many channels that cause the contagious spread of crises involving both financial and trade linkages (Rajan 2003),[5] the pertinent question here is: what are the available policy options available to a monetary authority faced with such a crisis scenario?

5.2.3 The "do nothing" option

If the monetary authority does nothing and wants to defend the pegged exchange rate, the drain in liquidity in the economy implies a reduction in real money stock. Eventually, M^s declines from M_0^s to M_1^s such that the domestic money market is back in equilibrium at point 2 in the near term (Figure 5.2).[6] This is fully consistent with the so-called "Impossible Trinity," which maintains that a country cannot simultaneously maintain an open capital account, fixed exchange rate and monetary policy autonomy (sometimes referred to as the unholy trinity). Thus, in the above case, because the authority chose to defend the peg, it eventually had to forsake monetary policy autonomy. In practice, however, many countries attempt to maintain control of their domestic money supply while simultaneously fixing the exchange rate. (The consequences of forsaking the peg will be discussed later.) Is this possible? What are the

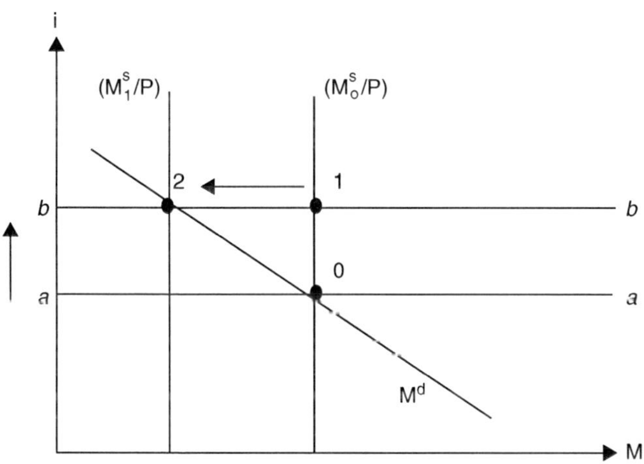

Figure 5.2 The "do nothing" option
Source: Author.

consequences of doing so? To answer these questions, let us examine in more depth the impact of capital outflows on money supply.

5.2.4 Impact of capital outflows on domestic money supply

Consider the following set of equations:

$$M^s = mm^* \text{ MB} \tag{3}$$

$$\text{MB} = \text{NDA} + \text{NFA} \tag{4}$$

$$\text{NFA} = e \times R \tag{5}$$

where: ***mm*** = money multiplier, ***MB*** = monetary base, ***NDA*** = net domestic assets, ***NFA*** = net foreign assets, ***R*** = foreign exchange reserves and ***e*** = nominal exchange rate. Equation (3) states that the aggregate money supply equals the money base multiplied by the money multiplier. Equation (4) states that the monetary base consists of two components, net domestic assets and net foreign assets. Equation (5) states that the stock of net foreign assets equals the stock of foreign exchange reserves multiplied by the nominal exchange rate (foreign currency per US dollar).

Recall that our maintained assumption is of a fixed exchange rate regime. With appropriate substitutions and taking the first derivative of M^s with respect to K (which denotes capital inflows) derives:

$$\begin{aligned}\frac{\partial M^s}{\partial K} &= \text{MB}\left(\frac{\partial mm}{\partial K}\right) + mm\left(\frac{\partial MB}{\partial K}\right) \\ &= \text{MB}\left(\frac{\partial mm}{\partial K}\right) + mm\left[\left(\frac{\partial \text{NDA}}{\partial K}\right) + e\left(\frac{\partial R}{\partial K}\right)\right]\end{aligned} \tag{6}$$

$\partial \text{NDA}/\partial K$: During a financial crisis this term is usually negative as capital outflows ($dK < 0$) are sterilized by the monetary authority ($dNDA > 0$) from the domestic financial system, especially deposit taking ones. What might motivate this bailout (i.e. lender of last resort)? Capital flows tend to be largely intermediated via the banking system, and bank lending is the dominant form of funding in most developing countries. Consequently, a sustained drop in bank lending following sharp capital outflows and declines in net worth will be severely detrimental to real economic activity. Figure 5.3 offers some indication of the increase in claims by the domestic monetary authority in Thailand on the domestic financial institutions during the period of massive capital outflows in 1997 and early 1998.[7]

$\partial mm/\partial K$: During a financial crisis this term is usually positive (see Mishkin, chapter 16, 428–429). The reason for this is clear if one

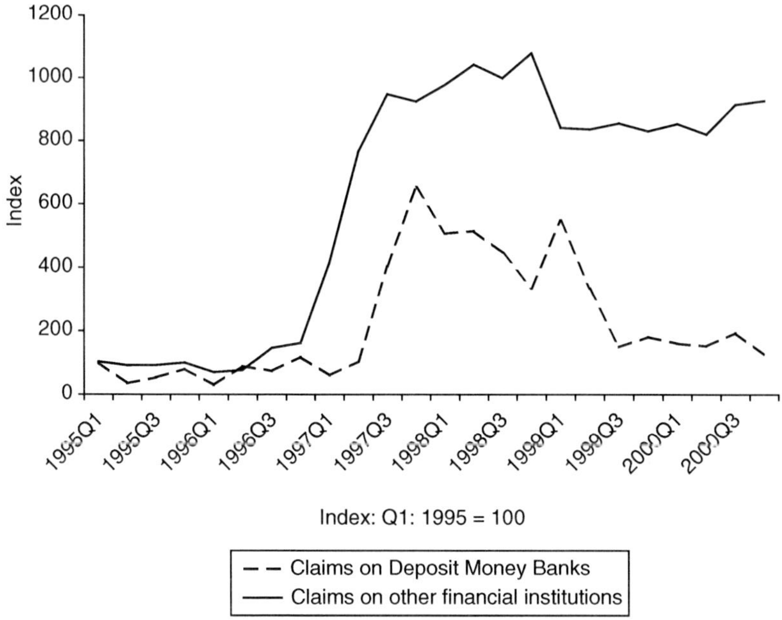

Figure 5.3 Liquidity infusion into Thai financial system
Note: Valuation in Thai Baht.
Source: Based on data from *International Financial Statistics*, IMF.

considers the definition of the *M2* multiplier. To be sure, let the narrow money (*M1*) = currency in circulation (C) plus demand/checking deposits (D). Let *M2* = *M1* + savings deposits and small denomination time deposits (referred to as *S*). Let *BR* denote reserve holdings by banks, which are made up of required reserves and excess reserves. Thus, the *M2* multiplier = $mm = [c + d + s]/[c + br]$, where all italicized variables in small letters are denoted as a proportion of demand/checking deposits. During a financial crisis, individuals will prefer to ensure their financial savings are as liquid as possible, leading to a shift of funds from *s* to *d*. In addition, if there are concerns about the viability of the banking system, there may be a sharp increase in *c* at the expense of all types of deposits. In addition, during the period of capital outflows, banks on their part may prefer to maintain a degree of liquidity, resulting in an increase in *br*.

$\partial R/\partial K$: This term refers to the impact of capital flows on foreign exchange reserves. Even in the case of a fixed exchange rate regime, this effect is generally ambiguous. Why? Consider eq. (7), which is the usual balance of payments accounting identity.

$$dR = \text{CAB} + dK \tag{7}$$

If there is no change in the current account balance (*CAB*), $\partial R/\partial K > 0$. This is straightforward—capital outflows ($dK < 0$) lead to a drain on foreign exchange reserves ($dR < 0$) and capital inflows ($dK > 0$) lead to foreign exchange reserve accumulation ($dR > 0$).[8] However, with capital outflows, governments may restrict imports such that the *CAB* rises. If the rise in *CAB* outweighs the capital outflows, foreign exchange reserves could actually grow.[9] A likely scenario is that initially the direct impact of the capital outflows exceeds the indirect effects via the current account such that foreign exchange reserves decline (i.e. $\partial R/\partial K > 0$). Over time, however, as capital flows stabilize, the decline in the current account balance continues to improve (because of curbs on imports and a resurgence in exports following a real exchange rate devaluation—see following section). This is apparent from Figures 5.4 and 5.5, which

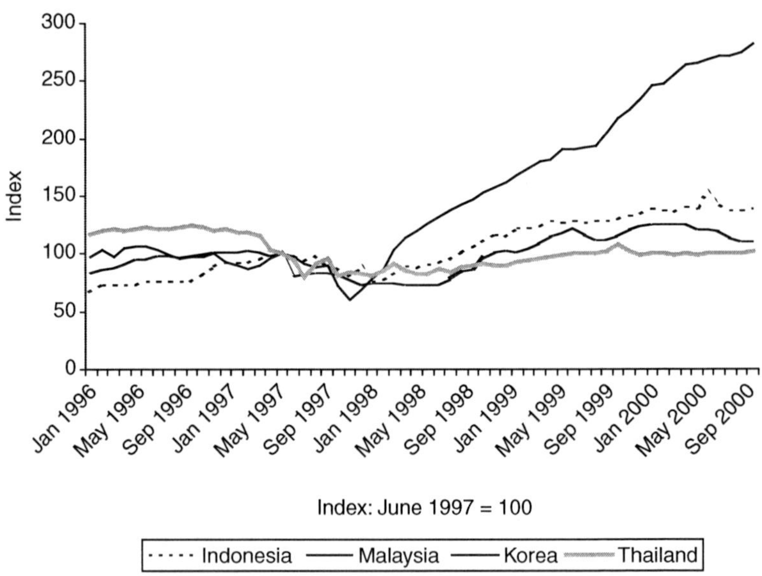

Figure 5.4 Foreign exchange reserve holdings in East Asia

Note: Valuation in US dollars.

Source: Based on data from the Asian Development Bank-Asia Recovery Information Centre (http://aric.adb.org/).

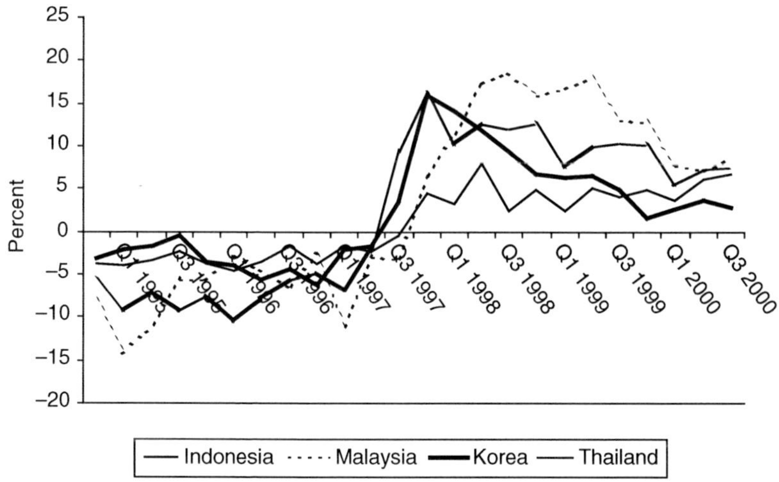

Figure 5.5 Current account balances as a proportion of GDP in East Asia (percentage)

Source: Based on data from the Asian Development Bank-Asia Recovery Information Centre (http://aric.adb.org/).

reveal an initial decline or stagnation in gross foreign exchange reserves in East Asia between mid-1997 and mid-1998 before they began to be replenished as the region's current account balances improved.[10]

Putting this all together, the net impact of capital flows on money supply is an empirical issue. The monetary base (*MB*) is more or less constant as the increase in domestic credit (*NDA*) to accommodate a run on the financial institutions offsets the fall in reserves (*NFA*), but the money multiplier (*mm*) declines sharply such that overall money supply (M^S) falls. There are always exceptions to this stylization. For instance, during the East Asian crisis of 1997–1998, Korea's and Thailand's monetary bases remained more or less constant between 1996 and 1998, that of Indonesia saw a sustained rapid expansion, and Malaysia's monetary base experienced sharp jumps between 1996Q2 and 1997Q4 before falling sharply (Figure 5.6).

5.2.5 Devaluing the currency

Consider the case where the monetary authority continues to sterilize capital outflows in order to resist the fall in the MB, as in Thailand, for instance. The persistent monetary disequilibrium in turn implies capital outflows continue unabated. MacIntyre (1999, 14) succinctly

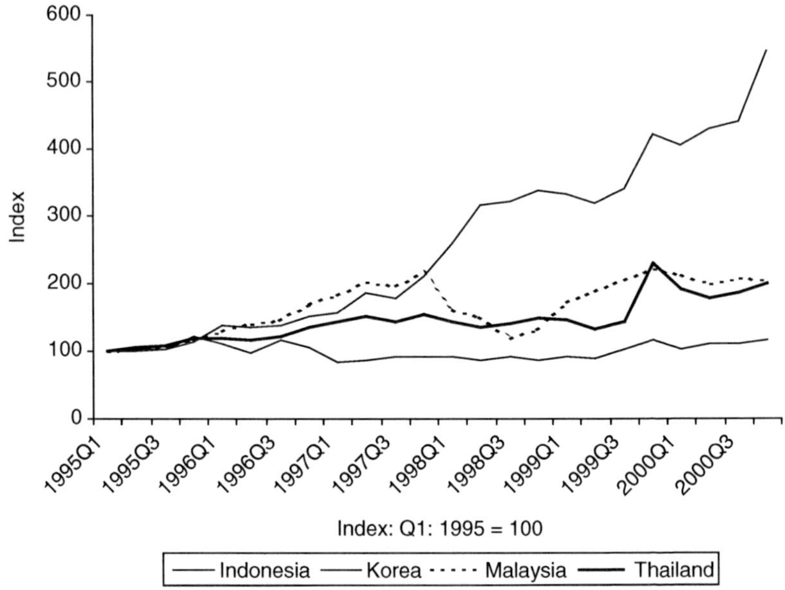

Figure 5.6 Trends in monetary base in East Asia

Note: Valuation in local currencies.

Source: Based on data from International Financial Statistics, IMF.

summarized the course of events in Thailand during the period of capital outflows in 1997:

> A side effect of injecting large scale emergency funding into the…failing finance companies was blowing out the money supply…This served to sharpen the fundamental contradiction in the government's overall macroeconomic position. At the same time as it was pumping money into insolvent finance companies to keep them afloat, the central bank was also spending down…(foreign exchange)…reserves to prop up the exchange rate…(T)his was not a sustainable strategy.

Indeed, at some stage, the country's stock of foreign exchange reserves declines to some minimum level (zero for simplicity), necessitating a break in the currency peg (i.e. currency devaluation).[11] That a fixed exchange rate cannot be sustained while attempting to control domestic monetary supply is fully consistent with the Impossible Trinity previously noted. But what might happen following this devaluation or expenditure switching policy? Two possibilities need to be considered.

One, in the conventional case, (a) devaluation is expansionary such that output rises, so money demand increases from M_0^d to M_1^d and (b) because the expected devaluation has materialized, $\Delta e_{t+1}^e \rightarrow 0$, such that there is a consequent shift down of the parity line from *bb* to *cc* (Figure 5.7). Eventually a new equilibrium (point 3) is attained corresponding to stability of the capital account, improvement in the current account balance and an increase in output. In other words, *devaluation is the end of the crisis*.[12] Indeed, it is trivial to note that, depending on the magnitude of the movements of the interest parity line and the money demand curve, the economy could be faced with capital inflows and resulting increase in domestic money supply/expected exchange rate appreciation. This is consistent with the boom–bust–boom scenario that seems to plague emerging economies.

Two, it is possible that the exchange rate devaluation leads to a hike in the risk premium such that the right hand side of eq. (1) remains unchanged or even rises postdevaluation, thus intensifying capital outflows (from *bb* to *dd* in Figure 5.8). This in turn may occur for a number

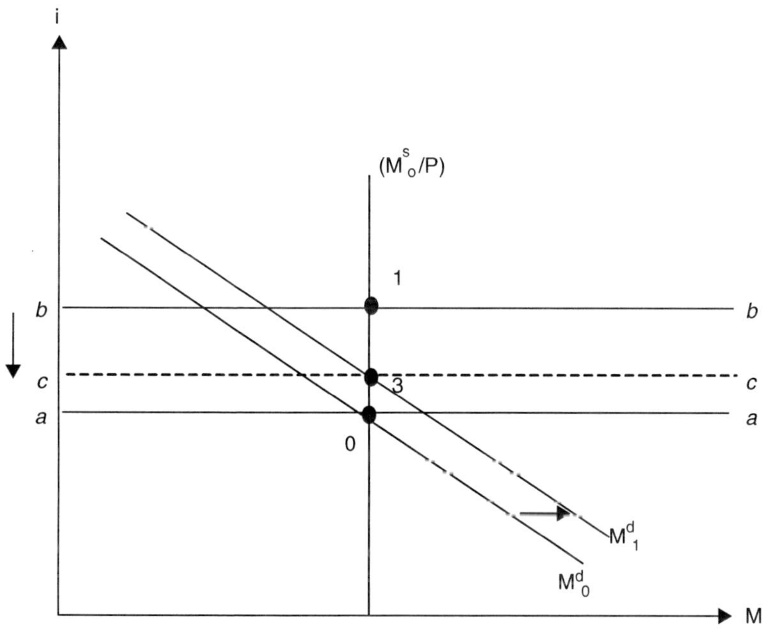

Figure 5.7 Exchange rate depreciation: conventional expansionary effects
Source: Author.

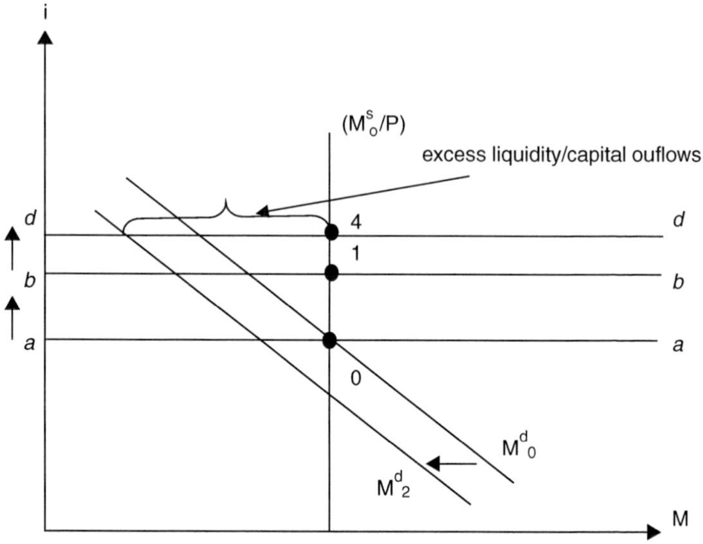

Figure 5.8 Exchange rate depreciation: perverse contractionary effects
Source: Author.

of reasons, including loss of credibility of the monetary authority; concerns about the impact of the currency devaluation of the financial and real sectors (elaborated upon below); loss of exchange rate anchor or shock of revelation of the dramatic decline in foreign exchange reserves and general weak state of the economy (as in the case of Thailand in June–July 1997), etc.

In other words, where devaluation is part of a credible macroeconomic strategy, combined with appropriate counterinflationary fiscal and monetary policy, and leads to a new exchange rate that is perceived by private capital markets to be close to the equilibrium real rate or below it, it will have a positive effect on creditworthiness and capital flows. Where, on the other hand, it is perceived as a panic measure, combined with excessively expansionary fiscal and monetary policy, and leads to a new rate that is still seen as involving currency overvaluation, it will be associated with further capital outflows.[13]

It is possible that a preemptive devaluation in the early stages of the crisis may reduce this shock impact, thus precluding as large a rise in the risk premium term. Maximum effort needs to be exerted so that devaluation does not appear to be a panic measure. Governments, in liaison with the IMF, need to address the risk that devaluation may spook private capital markets. Devaluation must be presented as part of a credible economic strategy. The monetary authority must carefully manage financial market expectations to ensure that expected future devaluations and risk premia come down and interest rates can be reduced. In addition to committing unequivocally to necessary structural adjustment programs (which is important in its own right but also because it signals availability of sufficient liquidity from the IMF), country experiences (e.g. Brazil in 1999 and Korea in 1998) suggest that market confidence can best be regained if the monetary authority swiftly moves to a transparent and credible monetary framework postdevaluation, such as open economy inflation targeting. Fraga, Goldfajn and Minella (2003) stress that the weak credibility of monetary policy institutions in emerging economies necessitates greater transparency and formality in the inflation-targeting regime compared with advanced economies.[14]

Apart from the shock impact noted above, devaluation may also be contractionary in and of itself such that output (y_t) declines (Figure 5.9). The recessions ranged from 7 percent in Korea to 17 percent in Indonesia in 1998. The Bank of Thailand (1998) report on the Thai crisis outlined

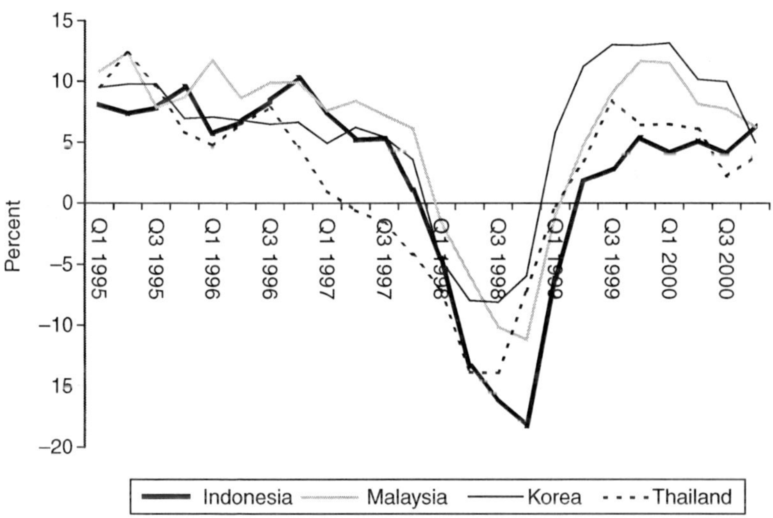

Figure 5.9 GDP growth rate (percentage)

Note: Year-on-year changes in US dollar terms.

Source: Based on data from International Financial Statistics, IMF.

the official reasons behind why a devaluation of the baht was perceived as doing more harm than good: high import content of Thai exports implying limited competitiveness benefit from a weakened currency; inflationary effects of devaluation leading to wage–price spiral; and unhedged foreign currency debts of corporates leading to bankruptcies, unemployment, and deterioration in asset quality of financial institutions because of a weakened corporate sector. The balance sheet effects resulting from large unhedged exposure to short-term foreign currency denominated debt were particularly important in the East Asian crisis.[15]

If devaluation does prove to be contractionary, money demand contracts further from M_0^d to M_2^d, such that domestic disequilibrium is further exacerbated (Figure 5.8). In this case, therefore, devaluation worsens the crisis, leading possibly to outright economic collapse.[16] This seems to have been the experience of a number of emerging economies in recent times, including those in East Asia.

5.2.6 Interest rate policy

Another common policy response to currency bearishness is to raise interest rates sharply, which effectively involves a leftward shift of the money supply (M^S) curve. Note that if the monetary authority is keen on building foreign exchange reserves via capital inflows, there is a need for a sufficiently contractionary monetary policy such that domestic money market equilibrium exceeds interest rates given by the interest parity condition (point 5 in Figure 5.10).

Once again, however, the impact of this policy response is not unambiguous. This contractionary or expenditure reducing policy may in fact have severe contractionary effects, thus reducing M^d. Apart from the conventional transmission channels via which tight interest rate policy may affect output (see chapter 25 in Mishkin and chapter 27 in Hubbard), in highly leveraged economies, high interest rates may make it impossible for a country to service its debt, further swelling the share of nonperforming loans (NPLs) held by financial institutions.[17] Decapitalized banks can in turn curtail their lending, intensifying the recession (supply side effect). In addition, the collapse in asset prices that tends to accompany—in fact precede—devaluation could deepen the credit crunch caused initially by loss of access to international capital markets (see Table 5.1) (Bank of Thailand 1998).

Thus, where tight monetary policy leads to increased concerns regarding the perceived riskiness and depreciation of collateral due to the balance sheet effects of the crisis (Boorman et al. 2000), it will prove to be

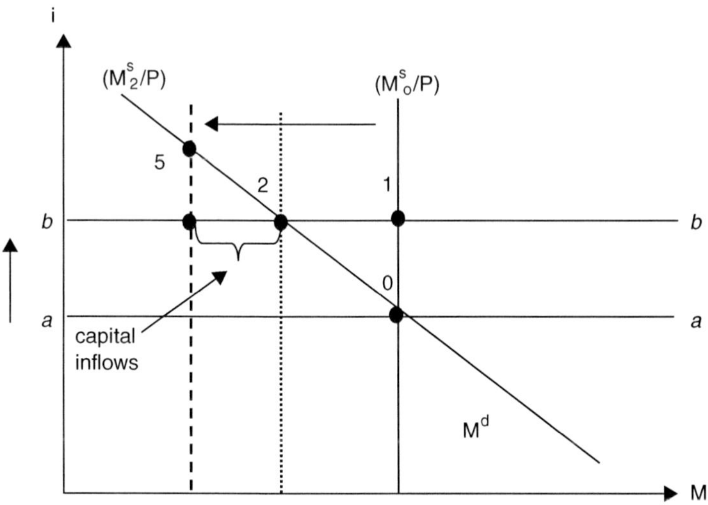

Figure 5.10 Impact of interest rate hike

Source: Author.

Table 5.1 Thailand: composition of net private capital inflows (US$ billions), 1997–1999

	1997	1998	1998		1999
			q1	q4	q1
Banks	**–6,640**	**–13,944**	1,244	–4,368	**–5,497**
Commercial banks	–1,727	–4,310	881	–2,445	–3,375
of which recapitalization	0	1,986	952	0	21
BIBFs	–1,913	–9,634	–2,125	–1,924	–2,123
Non-banks	**–1,912**	**–2,024**	–2,777	1,248	**–469**
Direct investment	3,201	4,688	1,066	1,218	902
Foreign direct investmenta	3,641	4,810	1,067	1,248	996
Thai direct investment abroad	–440	–123	–1	–30	–94
Other loans	–3,783	–4,279	–1,981	–734	–1,239
Portfolio investment	1,494	539	437	–15	221
Equity securities	3,869	354	434	–75	230
Debt securities	625	185	3	60	–9
Nonresident baht account	–5,839	–2,714	–2,269	779	–315
Trade credits	–242	–494	–186	–160	0
Others	256	237	156	160	–38
Total	**8,552**	**–15,967**	–4,021	–3,120	–5,966

Note: [a] Excluding US$ 2.1 billion in bank recapitalization.

Source: Based on data from Bank of Thailand.

counterproductive. Rather than domestic monetary policy neutralizing the recessionary effects of devaluation, it may lead to additional capital outflows that enhance them. On the other hand, if the monetary authority relaxes domestic monetary policy in order to at least partially offset the effects of capital outflows on domestic liquidity, it will neutralize the recessionary effects and may avoid a potential collapse in output. However, the current account effect will then be moderated and it will take longer to replenish depleted foreign exchange reserves. Moreover, since the rise in the interest rate will be less pronounced, this could delay the return of foreign capital.

In circumstances where governments are anxious to avoid a severe recession in the aftermath of devaluation immediately following a crisis, it is easy to see how they may be persuaded to combine currency devaluation with some degree of domestic monetary relaxation (for instance, see Aghion, Bacchetta and Banerjee 2000). The problem then is that monetary relaxation may be interpreted by markets as representing exactly the kind of macroeconomic laxity that they fear. Yet there

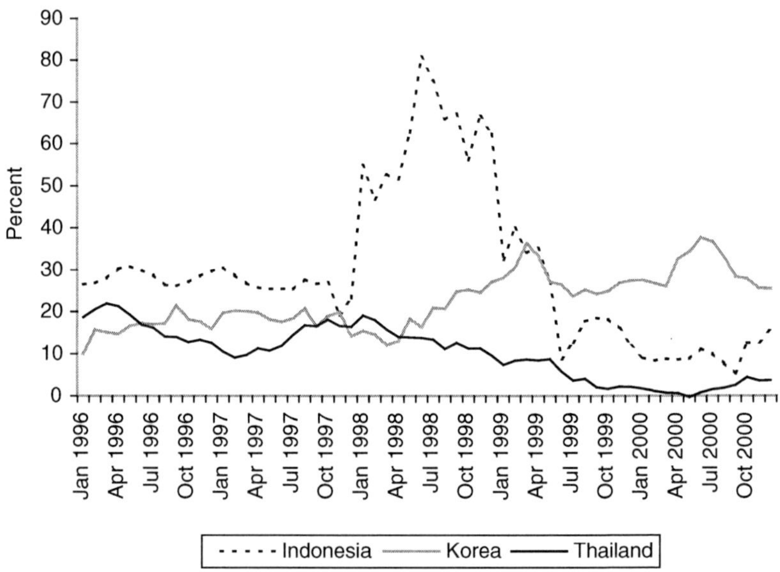

Figure 5.11 Growth in broad money supply (M2) (percentage)

Note: Year-on-year change in US dollars.

Source: Based on data from the Asian Development Bank-Asia Recovery Information Centre (http://aric.adb.org/).

remain Lucas-type dangers with this strategy, because capital markets may respond negatively if they perceive monetary policy as being insufficiently tight (see Chapters 6 and 7 of this volume for elaboration).

This conundrum helps explain the initial policy vacillations by the countries that first raised but then quickly lowered interest rates, only to raise them again substantially following intensified bearish pressures between 1997 and 1998. Specifically, while Korea and Thailand did eventually raise interest rates in 1998 to curb the selling pressures, Indonesia continued with its policy of monetary laxity primarily to infuse liquidity to the financial system (Figure 5.11). This inevitably led to inflationary pressures and heightened expectations of an exchange rate devaluation over time.[18] From eq. (1), it is apparent that interest rates in Indonesia ought to spike upwards (Figure 5.12).

Thus, Boorman, Lane and Schultze-Ghattas (2000, 32) correctly note:

> It would be highly misleading to interpret Indonesia's high nominal interest rates in late 1997 and the early months of 1998 as an indication of tight policy; rather, they signalled a loss of confidence in the currency as well as in the country's credit-worthiness.

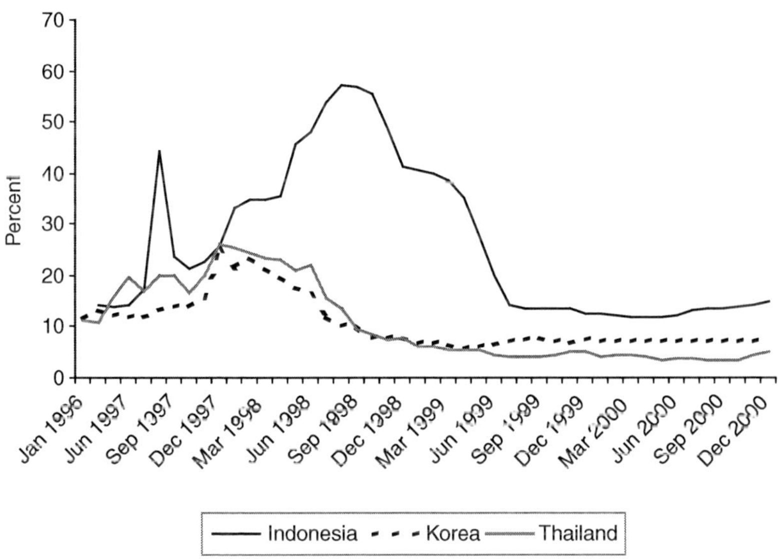

Figure 5.12 Three-month interbank lending rate in East Asia (percentage)

Source: Based on data from the Asian Development Bank-Asia Recovery Information Centre (http://aric.adb.org/).

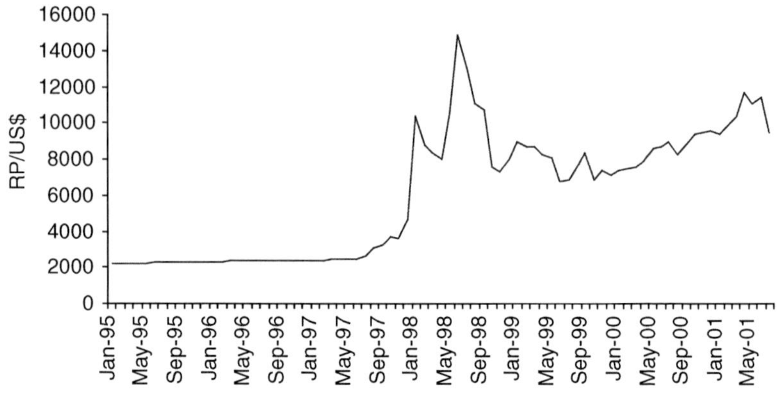

Figure 5.13 Bilateral nominal exchange rate: Rupiah per US Dollar

Source: Based on data from International Financial Statistics, IMF.

The large and growing disequilibrium in the domestic money market in turn predictably implied large-scale capital outflows and further exchange rate devaluations that were self-validating (Figure 5.13).[19] It is no surprise, therefore, that Indonesia was the country most severely impacted by the crisis.[20]

5.2.7 Capital controls

In the face of persistent capital outflows and concerns about the impact of currency devaluations, the monetary authority could also attempt to curb capital outflows by breaking the link between domestic and international financial markets (eq. 1) via capital controls. Recalling the constraints imposed by the Impossible Trinity, if the country wants to maintain a fixed exchange rate and monetary policy autonomy, it must forsake capital account openness. This was the case of Malaysia, which imposed wide-ranging capital controls to penalize offshore currency trading and short-term portfolio flows in September 1998 (Bird and Rajan 2000).[21]

A number of concerns were initially raised about the Malaysian controls. For instance, it had been argued in some quarters that, insofar as there has been a global trend towards economic liberalization (with many alternative investment opportunities), adopting exchange controls may lead Malaysia to be overlooked by the international community as a viable investment destination. There was also a feeling that the unilateral introduction of such controls may have been unwise in the midst of prevailing bearishness as it might be interpreted as a sign of weak economic fundamentals or the unsustainability of prevailing economic policies, hence exacerbating the situation.[22] Reluctance to specify early on whether the controls were temporary or permanent created an additional degree of uncertainty.

There is surely an element of truth in these concerns. For instance, immediately following the imposition of the restraints, Malaysia was removed from a number of key investment benchmarks. Malaysia's risk premium in international markets appreciated; Malaysia's sovereign ratings were downgraded; and FDI levels to Malaysia fell despite being exempted from the controls (Ariyoshi et al. 2000).

However, early empirical work on the administrative controls imposed between September 1998 and year end 1999 suggests that they in fact did accomplish the goal of providing greater policy autonomy. This allowed Malaysia to pursue independent (i.e., loose) monetary policy and a fixed exchange rate regime (Edison and Reinhart 2001). This in turn might possibly have contributed to the early recovery of the Malaysian economy from the crisis (Ariyoshi et al. 2000 and Kaplan and Rodrik 2001).

Many observers have drawn inspiration from Malaysia's experience to suggest that an appropriate policy response to sharp capital outflows is some combination of restoration of confidence quickly via large-scale liquidity financing, imposing standstills on external creditors and imposing capital controls to try to prevent capital flight. But how replicable is the Malaysian experience?

Experiences with illiberal regimes (trade or finance) in emerging economies have suggested that there is inevitably much inertia in removing controls. In other words, an illiberal regime, once initiated, tends to become a permanent feature, rather than a temporary tool that "buys time" to undertake the necessary institutional and policy reforms; many emerging economies may be characterized as being "soft" states (Rodrik 1992), being easily captured by interest groups. However, Malaysia, being a relatively "hard" or autonomous state, was able to ensure that there was a fairly quick and smooth transition to a relatively more transparent and less onerous set of restraints (price-based). There are the well-known problems relating to the potential for rent-seeking activities (bribery, corruption and so forth) that persistent controls generate, not to mention the high enforcement costs, the inevitable creation of a black market and the general porousness of quantitative restrictions, particularly in the medium and longer terms (Bird and Rajan 2000).

This, along with the fact that much more detailed empirical work remains to be done on the Malaysian experience of restraining capital movements, suggests the need for significant caution in advocating it as a panacea to other crisis-hit economies. Indeed, Malaysian economic recovery *per se* cannot necessarily be interpreted as a sign of success of the policy; Thailand and South Korea, both of which pursued the IMF programs and maintained open capital accounts, were able to gradually relax nominal interest rates and enjoyed rapid economic recoveries, as did Malaysia (Asian Development Bank 2000). In addition, Malaysia entered the crisis in a stronger macroeconomic position than the other two economies (also see Eichengreen and Leblang, 2003).

5.3 Conclusion

Using simple tools that are taught in any typical undergraduate money and banking course, this chapter has attempted to rationalize the impact of financial crisis and capital outflows in emerging economies, and the possible policy options and dilemmas thereof. Examples have been drawn freely from East Asia, which was faced with such a crisis and series of policy conundrums in 1997–1998.

From a policy perspective, an important conclusion from the preceding analysis is that, although managing a conventional current account crisis involves a judicious combination of adjustment and financing, resolving a crisis involving sharp capital outflows (capital account crisis) predominantly involves restoring confidence by managing/anticipating expectations. It is therefore a much more imprecise and messy task. Accordingly, the emphasis is best placed on crisis *prevention* to stem the build-up of weaknesses in the first instance.

Whereas capital controls might be one crisis preventive measure, as discussed previously, another measure commonly proposed is that countries move towards relatively greater exchange rate flexibility. Thus, in the context of a crisis of confidence, if the country maintained a flexible exchange rate, the exchange rate could be allowed to weaken without loss of reserves. The concern, however, is that devaluation/depreciation could be contractionary. Indeed, many developing countries have historically been unable or unwilling to borrow overseas in their domestic currencies, leading them to accumulate foreign currency debt liabilities that are primarily dollar denominated and unhedged (i.e. liability dollarization).[23] In such countries, large depreciations magnify the domestic currency value of their external debt and hence sharply reduce the net worth of individuals, corporations and the overall domestic financial system. This balance sheet effect could lead to massive bankruptcies, as it did in Mexico in 1994–1995 and East Asia in 1997–1998 (see Chapters 4, 6 and 7 of this volume). This, along with concerns about the inflationary consequences of currency depreciations (because of the high import content of domestic production), may explain the fear of floating exhibited by many developing countries (Calvo and Reinhart 2002 and Rajan 2002).

Although there may be some validity in both the above points, they do not automatically suggest that a fixed exchange rate is the best option. Indeed, the maintenance of a fixed US dollar peg may be self-fulfilling in that it blunts the incentives for agents to undertake appropriate risk management to hedge against exchange rate movements. Conversely, the introduction of some transactions costs and exchange rate risks by permitting a degree of currency variability may also help moderate the extent of capital inflows, consequently dampening the intensity of boom and bust cycles that have plagued so many developing countries in Asia and elsewhere.

The age-old issue of design of an appropriate exchange rate regime for small and open economies is set to remain a highly debated topic in academic and policy arenas.

Notes

1. This chapter draws on an article originally published in *Journal of Economic Education*, 38 (1), 2007, 92–108 (Heldref Publications). Reprinted with permission.
2. The term financial crisis is used here generically to imply a dual crisis of the financial system (banking crisis) and the balance of payments (currency crisis). The coexistence of banking and currency crises has been found to be the norm during the late 1980s and early 1990s. Most frequently banking crises appear to have taken the lead (Kaminsky and Reinhart 1999), and these twin crises seem to be far more pervasive in developing economies than in developed ones (Glick and Hutchison 2000). Banking crises themselves seem to be more likely following financial liberalization, with sharp increases in domestic (bank) lending acting as significant predictors of currency crises.
3. No attempt is made here to offer a detailed discussion of the East Asian crisis. Interested readers are referred to Berg (1999), Corsetti, Pesenti and Roubini (1999) and Rajan (1999).
4. If a country like Thailand had given greater weight to the yen in its currency management pre-crisis, there would not have been as large a real exchange rate overvaluation of the baht following the sharp nominal appreciation of the US dollar relative to the yen between June 1995 and April 1997 (from 85 to 125 yen/US$). Pegging against the US dollar was, in hindsight, clearly suboptimal, whereas pegging against a more diversified composite

basket of currencies would have enabled the regional countries to better deal with the so-called "third currency phenomenon" (i.e. yen–US$ and euro–US$ fluctuations) which contributed in part to the crisis (Bird and Rajan 2002).

5. A distinction should be made between transmission channels that are related to investor sentiment or psychology (termed "pure contagion") and linkages between countries that are measurable/observable *ex ante* (referred to as spillovers or interrelatedness). Masson (1998) shows how it is conceptually possible for pure contagion to make an economy relatively more susceptible to a currency crisis.
6. Over time, the domestic deflationary pressures ought to lead to an anticipated currency appreciation (assuming that purchasing power parity (PPP) holds), leading to a downward shift of the interest parity line. This will be followed by capital inflows and an increase in money supply until a new equilibrium is attained (the equilibrium will be below point 2 but may or may not coincide with point 0).
7. For details on the Thai crisis and policy response thereto, see Bank of Thailand (1998) and Rajan (2001).
8. This is akin to the classic first generation currency crisis model of Krugman (1979). See review of currency crisis models by Rajan (2001).
9. Though this inevitably is accompanied by sharp recessions, as in the case of East Asia in 1997–1998.
10. See Rajan and Siregar (2003) for a discussion of international reserve management in East Asia post-crisis. The data on reserves excludes swap liabilities. Also see Chapters 9 and 10 of this volume.
11. Devaluation occurred in Thailand in July 1997, and in Indonesia in August 1997 and other regional currencies soon after.
12. Insofar as the devaluation also has some inflationary effects, it is expected that the new equilibrium (3) will be higher than the initial one (0).
13. For instance, in the case of Thailand, in the period leading up to the devaluation (i.e. first quarter of 1997) only the nonbank sector experienced capital outflows. More precisely it was the nonresident baht accounts (NRBAs) in particular, but also the "other loans" component that recorded net outflows. Net foreign direct investment (FDI) inflows remained positive throughout 1997 and portfolio flows only changed direction in November and December 1997. Private bank capital flows turned around sharply by over US$10 billion between the first and second halves of 1997. This reversal intensified in 1998, with outflows reaching almost US$14 billion. Of significance here is the fact that funds were still flowing into the country during the first half of 1997 right up to the devaluation. It was only *after* the devaluation that there was a massive exodus of these banking sector flows (Rajan 2001).
14. Apart from provision of timely and detailed information to the public, Fraga et al. (2003) emphasize the need for a formal process for monetary policy decisions with regular monetary policy committee meetings.
15. There is also a large body of literature that developed in the 1960s and 1970s that explains why devaluation in emerging economies may be contractionary. It is, however, unlikely that the conventional contractionary effects of devaluation via the current account can explain the magnitude and ferocity

of some economic contractions following devaluation (see Bird and Rajan 2003 and Chapters 4 and 7 of this volume).

16. Although devaluation may have inflationary effects, I assume that the indirect deflationary effects via output exceed the direct inflationary effects via pass-through. This assumption appears valid for the East Asian countries, except Indonesia, which was not faced by price pressures during the 1997–1998 financial crisis (Boorman et al. 2000). Admittedly, this assumption may not be valid for other developing regions, especially those with a history of price instability.
17. This has come to be referred to as the "Laffer curve" effects of monetary policy (Furman and Stiglitz 1998). See Chapter 7 of this volume for a discussion of the Laffer curve and its macroeconomic implications.
18. Implicit in this statement is that the PPP holds.
19. Another indication of monetary policy laxity in Indonesia was the sharply negative real interest rates on offer in that country in 1997 and 1998 (Boorman et al. 2000).
20. To be sure, the country was also faced with severe sociopolitical instabilities that undoubtedly contributed to its economic collapse.
21. Indonesia and Thailand also imposed restraints on offshore trading of their currencies (Ishii, Otker-Obe and Cui 2001).
22. See Bartolini and Drazen (1997) for a theoretical model in which capital restraints can convey information about a policymaker's preferences to the market. There has been an active discussion of the costs and benefits of capital account liberalization. Interested readers are directed to some of the following key references: Arteta et al. (2001), Eichengreen (2002), Eichengreen and Leblang (2003), Klein (2003), Mathieson (1993), Obstfeld (1998) and Rodrik (1998)."
23. "This has come to be referred to as the "original sin" hypothesis, a term attributed to Hausmann et al. (2002). See Chapters 6 and 7 for a discussion of this issue in the context of currency crisis and management."

References

Aghion, P., P. Bacchetta, and A. Banerjee (2000). "A Simple Model of Monetary Policy and Currency Crises," *European Economic Review*, 44, 728–738.

Ariyoshi, A. K. Habermeier, B. Laurens, I. Itker-Robe, J. Canales-Kriljenko, and A. Kirilenko (2000). "Capital Controls: Country Experiences with Their Use and Liberalization," Occasional Paper No. 190, IMF.

Arteta, C., B. Eichengreen and C. Wyplosz (2001). "When Does Capital Account Liberalization Help More than it Hurts?" Working Paper No. 8414, NBER.

Asian Development Bank (ADB) (2000). *Asia Recovery Report 2000*. Manila, Philippines: ADB.

Bank for International Settlements (BIS) (1999). *69th Annual Report 1999*, Basle: BIS.

Bank of Thailand (BOT) (1998). "Focus on the Thai Crisis," *Quarterly Review of Thailand's Economic Issues*, 2, April–June.

Bartolini, L. and A. Drazen (1997). "Capital Liberalization as a Signal," *American Economic Review*, 87, 138–154.

Berg, A. (1999). "The Asia Crisis: Causes, Policy Responses, and Outcomes," Working Paper No. 99/138, IMF.

Bird, G. and R.S. Rajan (2000). "Restraining International Capital Flows: What does it Mean?" *Global Economic Quarterly*, 1, 57–80.

Bird, G. and R.S. Rajan (2002). "Optimal Currency Baskets and The Third Currency Phenomenon: Exchange Rate Policy In Southeast Asia," *Journal of International Development*, 14, 1053–1073.

Bird, G. and R. Rajan (2003). "Does Devaluation Lead to Economic Recovery or Economic Contraction?: Examining the Analytical Issues with Reference to Thailand," *Journal of International Development*, 15, 1–16.

Boorman, J., T. Lane, M. Schultze-Ghattas, A. Bulir, A. Ghosh, J. Hamann, A. Mourmouras, and S. Phillips (2000). "Managing Financial Crises: The Experience in East Asia," Working Paper No. 00/107, IMF.

Calvo, G. and R. Reinhart, "Fear of Floating," Quarterly Journal of Economics, 117, 379-408.

Corsetti, G., P. Pesenti and N. Roubini (1999). "What Caused the Asian Currency and Financial Crisis? Part I: Macroeconomic Overview," *Japan and The World Economy*, 11, 305–373.

Edison, H. and C. Reinhart (2001). "Stopping Hot Money," *Journal of Development Economics*, 55, 533–553.

Eichengreen, B. (2002). "Capital Account Liberalization: What do Cross-Country Studies Tell Us?" *World Bank Economic Review*, 15, 341–365.

Eichengreen, B. and D. Leblang (2003). "Capital Account Liberalization and Growth: Was Mahathir Right?" *International Journal of Finance and Economics*, 8, 205–224.

Fraga, A., I. Goldfajn, and A. Minella. (2003). "Inflation Targeting in Emerging Market Economies," Working Paper No. 10019, NBER.

Furman, J. and J. Stiglitz (1998). "Economic Crises: Evidence and Insights from East Asia." *Brookings Papers on Economic Activity*, 2, 1–114.

Glick, R. and M. Hutchison (2000). "Banking and Currency Crises: How Common Are Twins?" in R. Glick, R. Moreno and M. Spiegel (eds), *Financial Crises in Emerging Markets*. Cambridge, UK: Cambridge University Press.

Hausmann, R., U. Panizza, and E. Stein (2002). "Original Sin, Passthrough, and Fear of Floating," in M.I. Blejer and M. Skreb (eds), *Financial Policies in Emerging Markets*, Cambridge: MIT Press.

Hubbard. G. (2005). *Money, the Financial System, and the Economy*. New Jersey Addison-Wesley, 4th edition.

Ishii, S., I. Otker-Obe, and L. Cui (2001). "Measures to Limit the Offshore Use of Currencies—Pros and Cons," Working Paper No. 01/43, IMF.

Kaminsky, G. and C. Reinhart (1999). "The Twin Crises: The Causes of Banking and Balance-of-Payments Problems," *American Economic Review*, 89, 473–500.

Kaplan, E. and D. Rodrik (2001). "Did the Malaysian Capital Controls Work?" Working Paper No. 8142, NBER.

Klein, M. (2003). "Capital Account Openness and the Varieties of Growth Experiences," mimeo (January).

Krugman, P. (1979). "A Model of Balance of Payments Crises," *Journal of Money Credit and Banking*, 11, 311–328.

MacIntyre, A. (1999). "Political Institutions and the Economic Crisis in Thailand and Indonesia," in T. Pempel (ed.), *The Politics of the Asian Financial Crisis*. Ithaca: Cornell University Press.

Masson, P. (1998). "Contagion: Monsoonal Effects, Spillovers, and Jumps between Multiple Equilibria," Working Paper No. 98/142, IMF.
Mathieson, D. and C. Rojas-Suarez (1993). "Liberalization of the Capital Account," Occasional Paper No. 10, IMF.
Mishkin, F. (2003). *The Economics of Money, Banking and Financial Markets*. New Jersey: Addsion-Lesley, 6th edition.
Obstfeld, M. (1998). "The Global Capital Market: Benefactor or Menace?" *Journal of Economic Perspectives*, 12, 9–30.
Rajan, R.S. (1999). "Economic Collapse in Southeast Asia," *Policy Study*. The Lowe Institute of Political Economy, Claremont, California.
Rajan, R.S. (2001). "(Ir)relevance of Currency Crises Theory to the Devaluation and Collapse of the Thai Baht," *Princeton Studies in International Economics No. 88*, International Economics Section, Princeton University.
Rajan, R.S. (2002). "International Financial Liberalisation in Developing Countries: Lessons from Recent Experiences," *Economic and Political Weekly*, 37, 3017–30121.
Rajan, R.S. and R. Siregar (2003). "Centralized Reserve Pooling for the ASEAN Plus Three (APT) Countries," in *Monetary and Financial Cooperation in East Asia*, McMillan Press for the Asian Development Bank.
Rodrik, D. (1992). "Political Economy and Development Policy," *European Economic Review, Papers and Proceedings*, 36, 329–336.
Rodrik, D. (1998). "Who Needs Capital Account Convertibility? In Should The IMF Pursue Capital-Account Convertibility?" Essays in International Finance No. 207, International Economics Section, Princeton University.

6

Understanding Currency Crises and Monetary Policy Responses in Emerging Economies[1]

(Co-authored with Makarand Parulkar)

6.1 Introduction

When analyzing the appropriate monetary policy response during a currency crisis, it is important to keep in mind two distinct channels: (a) the impact of changing interest rates on exchange rates; and (b) the direct impact of exchange rate changes on output. The first pertains to the monetary side of the economy as given by the interest parity condition, while the second deals with the real side of the economy. The interaction between these two legs of the economy derives the equilibrium output and exchange rate changes in the economy. Thus, the net effect of monetary policy on output and exchange rate requires consideration of both dimensions of the economy.

With regard to the monetary side of the economy, the "orthodox" IMF view about the relationship between monetary policy and the exchange rate is that tight monetary policy strengthens the exchange rate by sending a signal that the authorities are committed to maintaining a fixed rate, as well as by providing the financial incentive for capital to remain in the country. Nevertheless, many doubts have been expressed about the direct exchange rate impact of a tight monetary policy stance during a crisis period. For instance, Stiglitz (1998) has noted:

> Although countries confronted with an exchange rate crisis have sometimes viewed themselves as facing a trade-off between the adverse effect of exchange rate depreciation and interest rate increases, if increases in interest rates lead to a decreased capital flow, there is no trade-off: higher interest rates weaken the economy directly and actually exacerbate the decline in the exchange rate.

But why might there be this perverse asset market response of an interest rate hike on exchange rates? As the East Asian crisis of 1997–1998 made apparent, there are balance sheet effects at work, given the large proportion of unhedged foreign currency debt that was accumulated (Bird and Rajan 2004; Krugman 1999; Montiel 2003 and especially Chapters 4 and 7 of this volume). In such a case a tight monetary policy could raise the probability that a country will be unable to service its debt (the so-called "Laffer curve" effects of monetary policy), further swelling the share of non-performing loans (NPLs) held by financial institutions. Thus, where tight monetary policy leads to increased concerns regarding "riskiness and destruction of collateral associated with the balance sheet effects of the crisis itself" (Boorman et al. 2000) it may prove to be counterproductive. Rather than domestic monetary policy neutralizing the recessionary effects of devaluation it may lead to additional capital outflows that intensify them.[2]

There has been a large and growing body of literature that has examined the exchange rate impact of interest rate changes, particularly following the East Asian crisis of 1997–1998. Conclusions remain mixed at best. For instance, applying daily data to a bivariate VAR model for the five countries most heavily affected by the Asian financial crisis, viz. Thailand, South Korea, Malaysia, Indonesia and Philippines, Caporale, Cipollini and Demetraides (2000) find that tight monetary policy does not help to stabilize the currencies under investigation. Using a standard monetary model of exchange rate determination, Basurto and Ghosh (2001) find that tighter monetary policy was associated with an appreciation of the currencies in Indonesia, Korea and Thailand. According to them there is little evidence of a "perverse" effect of a monetary tightening on the exchange rate. *A priori* this is not surprising in view of the fact that even if the direct impact of interest rate changes on the exchange rate is unambiguous, the net effect, which is what is implicitly measured by these studies, is far from apparent. Gould and Kamin (2000) find that monetary policy has no effect on the exchange rate after controlling for credit spreads and other factors. A number of other studies have concluded that tighter monetary policy leads to a weaker currency (for instance, see Furman and Stiglitz, 1998 and Goderis and Ioannidou, 2006). Montiel (2003) reviews some of the empirical work relating exchange rate and interest rate changes during a crisis period (especially the Asian crisis of 1997–1998).[3]

With regard to the real side of the economy there is further ambiguity as to how interest rate changes impact output. For instance, even if tight monetary policy does help to stabilize the exchange rate it may not necessarily be optimal if it curtails domestic output sharply. Conversely, failure to stem exchange rate declines could itself negatively impact output for various reasons (see Chapters 4 and 7 of this volume).

Overall, therefore, when considering the appropriate monetary policy stance it is critical to consider the interaction between both the real and the monetary sides of the economy simultaneously. Aghion, Bacchetta and Banerjee (2000) (henceforth A-B-B) develop a monetary model with nominal rigidities and foreign currency debt to examine the interaction between the real and monetary sides of the economy, hence allowing a determination of the net effects of monetary policy. As will be discussed, a significant advantage of A-B-B's model is that it lends itself naturally to graphical analysis encompassing both the monetary and the real sides of the economy.

The remainder of the chapter is organized as follows. Section 6.2 lays out and extends the basic A-B-B model to draw out the possible links between interest rates, exchange rates and output. Section 6.3 demonstrates the possibility of various equilibria situations (given by the intersection of the real and monetary sides of the economy) and goes on to analyze the impact of monetary policy on the real economy. To preview the main conclusion, we find that the impact of monetary policy on exchange rate and output is theoretically ambiguous. This in turn suggests that the appropriate monetary policy response could vary between countries at any point in time, or for a particular country between two different periods. The final section offers a few concluding remarks on policy issues.

6.2 The basic model

6.2.1 Assumptions

The basic framework and assumptions closely follow A-B-B. We consider a two-period small open economy model. Goods prices are determined at the beginning of each period and remain fixed for the entire period. There is a single good and purchasing power parity (PPP) holds *ex ante*, i.e., $P_t = E_t^e$ for each t, where P_t is the domestic price (which is preset at the beginning of the period) and E_t^e is the expected nominal exchange rate (domestic currency per unit of foreign currency at the beginning of period t). In period 1 the nominal exchange rate and the nominal interest rate will adjust, while there may be *ex-post* deviations from PPP because of unanticipated shocks.

6.2.2 The monetary sector

Assume the existence of the usual uncovered interest parity (UIP) condition:

$$(1+i_t)=(1+i^*)\frac{E^e_{t+1}}{E_t}+rp(i_t) \tag{1}$$

where i_t is domestic interest rates, i^* is the foreign interest rate, which is assumed constant. E_t and E^e_{t+1} are respectively the current exchange rate and expected future exchange rate (in terms of foreign currency), and rp_t is the risk premium which is assumed to rise with interest rates. As we will discuss later, this is a simple way of capturing the possible existence of Laffer curve effects of interest rates.[4]

Assume a standard real money demand function, $m^d_t = L(Y_t, i_t)$. The function $L(Y_t, i_t)$ has the usual properties, viz. of $L_1(.) > 0$ and $L_2(.) < 0$. Assume $L(0, i_t) > 0$. The money market equilibrium is given as usual:

$$M^s_t = P_t \cdot L(Y_t, i_t) \tag{2}$$

where M^s_t and P_t are the nominal money supply and price level at time t.

Combining Eqs. (1) and (2), along with the assumptions that the second period interest rate is exogenously fixed and the PPP assumption ($P_2 = E_2$), derives:

$$E_1 = \frac{1+i^*}{(1+i_1-rp(i_1))}\frac{M^s_2}{L(Y_2,i_2)} \tag{3}$$

Equation (3) reveals a negative relationship between E_1 and Y_2 and is represented graphically in (E_1, Y_2) space (Figure 6.1). As noted, A-B-B refer to this curve as the "IPLM curve" (interest parity-LM) and it is negatively sloped.[5] The IPLM curve may be shifted by changes in monetary policy in each period. For instance, an increase in M^s_2 will lead to a rise in E_2 via PPP which in turn leads to a depreciation in the current period (rise in E_1). Similarly, a rise in M^s_1 leads to a decline in i_1—and, ignoring the risk premium term in the first instance—this necessitates a currency depreciation in the current period (E_1 rises) for a given output level. This implies a rightward shift of the IPLM.

However, if Laffer curve effects exist, there is the strong perverse effect, whereby a rise in M^s_1 could lead to an exchange rate appreciation.

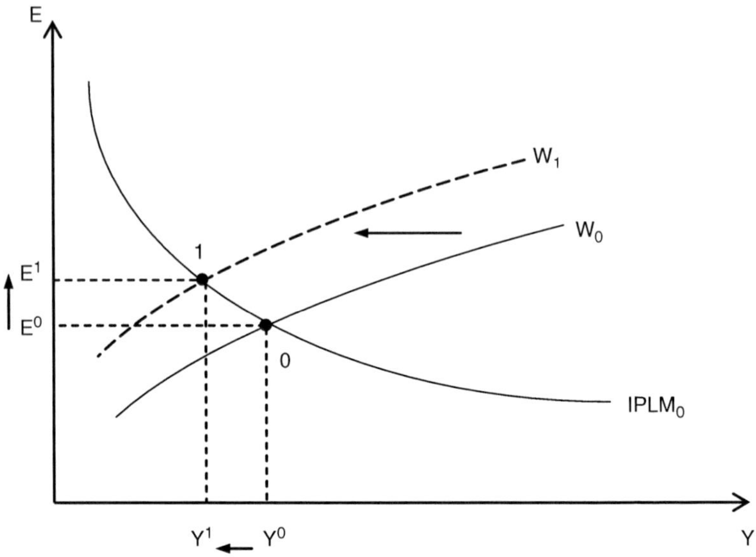

Figure 6.1 Real sector shock with positively sloped W curve
Source: Authors.

Radelet and Sachs (1998) explain these perverse effects as follows:

> (In) the unique conditions of the midst of a financial panic, raising interest rates could have the perverse effect of weakening the currency...Creditors understood that highly leveraged borrowers could quickly be pushed to insolvency as a result of several months of high interest rates. Moreover many kinds of interest-sensitive market participants, such as bond traders, are simply not active in Asia's limited financial markets. The key participants were the existing holders of short term debt, and the important question was whether they would or not roll over their claims. High interest rates did not feed directly into these existing claims...It is possible, however, that by undermining the profitability of their corporate customers, higher interest rates discouraged foreign investors from rolling over their loans.

However, the existence of "strong" Laffer curve effects must be questioned as they imply logically that a fall in interest rate will appreciate a currency. More likely to exist—if at all—are "weak" Laffer curve effects, i.e. there is little or no discernible change in the exchange rate for a given change in interest rates and thus no significant shift in the IPLM for a change in money supply. Indeed, while on the one hand a sharp interest rate hike may increase the probability of default, hence leading to a rise in risk premium, on the other hand an interest rate decline (particularly during a crisis) could be interpreted as policy laxity, leading to loss of confidence and capital flight. Thus, on balance the impact of interest rates on the risk premium is unclear.

6.2.3 The real sector: output and entrepreneurs' debt

Following A-B-B, assume the existence of credit constraints such that entrepreneurs can at most borrow an amount D_t that is proportional to their cash flow, W_t. In other words, $D_t = \mu_t W_t$ where μ is the "proportionality" or leverage factor. Entrepreneurs' capital stock is $K_t = W_t + D_t$. Assume a linear production technology as follows:

$$Y_t = \sigma K_t + \chi\left(\frac{E_{t-1}}{P_{t-1}}\right) \tag{4}$$

where σ is productivity parameter and $\chi(i_{t-1}, E_{t-1}/P_{t-1})$ denotes current exports which is a function of lagged interest rate and exchange rate. In other words, while sustainable output of the economy is given by the production function (capital stock and technology), unlike A-B-B we assume that the economy could be hit by an export shock which could alter output temporarily.[6] We further assume that exports are positively impacted by a lagged real depreciation (to account for J-curve and other inertial effects). In other words, $\chi'(E_{t-1}/P_{t-1}) > 0$. We denote this as the "pro-competitive effects" of exchange rate depreciation.

Current output thus becomes a linear function of current entrepreneurs' wealth:

$$Y_t = \sigma\left(1 + \mu_t(\bullet)\right)W_t + \chi\left(i_{t-1}, \frac{E_{t-1}}{P_{t-1}}\right) \tag{5}$$

Assume that the proportionality or leverage factor is as follows: $\mu_t = \mu(i_{t-1}, E_{t-1})$ where $\mu_1 < 0$ and $\mu_2 < 0$. The intuition is straightforward. The first term essentially captures the possibility that an interest rate hike worsens the state of the domestic financial and corporate sector, making banks more risk averse (the banking sector is not explicitly modelled here), hence reducing the extent of leverage of entrepreneurs. The second term captures the impact of balance sheet effects on the domestic financial sector, i.e. currency depreciation worsens the state of the financial sector, hence reducing the extent of leverage available to entrepreneurs, resulting in a curtailment of investment and output.[7]

We further assume that domestic consumers are unwilling to lend more than a real amount, D^c, in domestic currency to domestic firms in period 1. The remainder of the funding, $D_t - D_c$, is externally financed in foreign currency which is assumed to be unhedged.[8] The entire debt (principal plus interest) must be repaid by the end of period 2. Assume the cost of borrowing in domestic currency is i_t (i.e. floating rate), while that of foreign borrowing is i^* (which is assumed fixed).[9] Assuming debt costs are the only cost incurred, the aggregate nominal profits at the end of any period t can be expressed as:

$$\Pi_t = P_t Y_t - (1+i_t) P_t D^c - (1+i^*) P_t (D_t - D^c) \frac{E_t}{E_{t-1}} \tag{6}$$

When profits are positive, entrepreneurs use a proportion $(1 - \alpha)$ of these profits, for production in the following period (a proportion α of profits is distributed or consumed). Total net wealth available for next period production is thus either equal to zero, when net profits are not positive, or otherwise equal to retained earnings (which is some constant proportion of profits):

$$W_{t+1} = (1-\alpha) \frac{\Pi_t}{P_t} \tag{7}$$

Substituting eq. (6) into eq. (7) derives:

$$W_2 = (1-\alpha) \left[Y_1 - (1+i_1) D^c \frac{P_2}{P_1} - (1+i^*)(D_1 - D^c) \frac{E_1}{E_0} \right] \tag{8}$$

Focusing on the second-period output Y_2 derives:

$$Y_2 = \sigma(1+\mu(.))(1-\alpha) \left[Y_1 - (1+i_1) D^c - (1+i^*)(D_1 - D^c) \frac{E_1}{P_1} \right] + \chi\left(i_1, \frac{E_1}{P_1} \right)^{10} \tag{9}$$

Equation (9), which depicts the nexus between Y_2 and E_1, is referred to as the W-curve. For now we abstract from the possibility of even weak Laffer curve effects on interest rate—i.e. $(\partial i_1/\partial E_1) < 0$. In other words we assume that a depreciation accompanies monetary relaxation. Note that $(\partial Y_2/\partial E_1)$ cannot be signed *a priori*.

More to the point, there are four distinct channels:

a. The *competitiveness channel*: $\mathcal{X}'(E_{t-1}/P_{t-1})$. This is straightforward. A depreciation boosts exports and thus output.
b. The *leverage or credit channel*: $\mu_t = (i_{t-1}/E_{t-1})$, which has two subeffects:
   i. The first subeffect is $\mu_t(.) < 0$, i.e. a depreciation allows for a monetary relaxation, which in turn eases credit availability for entrepreneurs. This stimulates capital investment and growth.
   ii. The second sub-effect is $\mu_2 < 0$, i.e. depreciation worsens the net worth of the financial system, leading to reduced leverage.
c. The *debt cost channel*: $D^c(\partial i_1/\partial E_1)$. As interest rates are reduced, the interest burden on debt decreases, thus increasing profits, retained earnings and next period output.
d. The *balance sheet channel*: $(1 + i^*)(D_1 - D^c)$. A devaluation raises the domestic value of foreign debt, hence reducing the firm's net worth and future output.

Overall, therefore, we are unable to determine the shape of slope linking the exchange rate and output (so-called "W curve"). In what follows we undertake some simple comparative statics and discuss appropriate monetary policy responses in the event of a negative real sector shock assuming both positively sloped W curve (Case 1) and a negatively sloped W curve (Case 2).[11]

6.3 Equilibrium and comparative statics

6.3.1 Real sector shocks

Consider Case 1 with a positively sloped W curve and assume that $Y > 0$ in the first instance so as to allow for simple comparative statics (Figure 6.1). It is apparent that a negative real sector shock (productivity of export) in period 1 leads to a leftward shift of the W curve, causing a fall in output and currency depreciation (point 0 to 1). Consider Case 2 with a negatively sloped W curve and assume that there is a unique equilibrium with $Y > 0$ (Figure 6.2). Once again a negative real sector shock (productivity of export) leads to a leftward shift of the W curve with an output decline and currency depreciation. However, in this case there is a possibility of multiple equilibra, whereby output contraction and exchange rate depreciation could be "moderate" (point 1) or "sharp" (point 1^1).

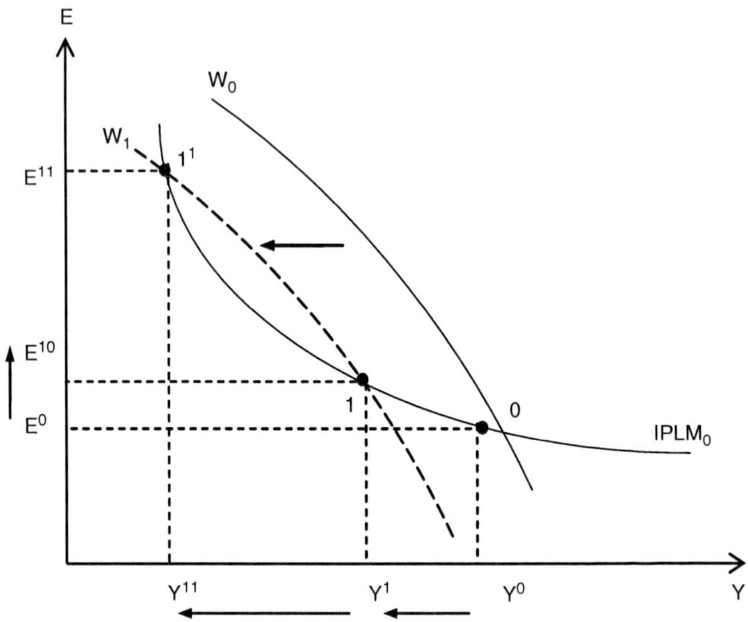

Figure 6.2 Real sector shock with negatively sloped W curve

Source: Authors.

6.3.2 Monetary policy response

What would be the appropriate monetary policy response in the event of a negative real sector shock? Abstracting from even the weak Laffer curve effects, an expansionary/contraction monetary policy in period 1 (M_t^s) leads to a decline in i_1 and a rise in the exchange rate and an upward/downward shift of the IPLM curve. An expansionary monetary policy in period 1 shifts the W curve rightwards as the interest rate decline raises output via the leverage channel (i.e. credit availability is eased) and domestic interest debt cost channel (*vice versa* for the case of contractionary monetary policy).

Consider Case 1 with an upward sloping W curve. In response to a negative real sector shock, a policy of *monetary contraction* would lead to a further fall in output, but the impact on the exchange rate is ambiguous (point 2) (Figure 6.3). The important point here is that a monetary contraction, while exacerbating the domestic output contraction, may not necessarily be successful in stabilizing the currency.

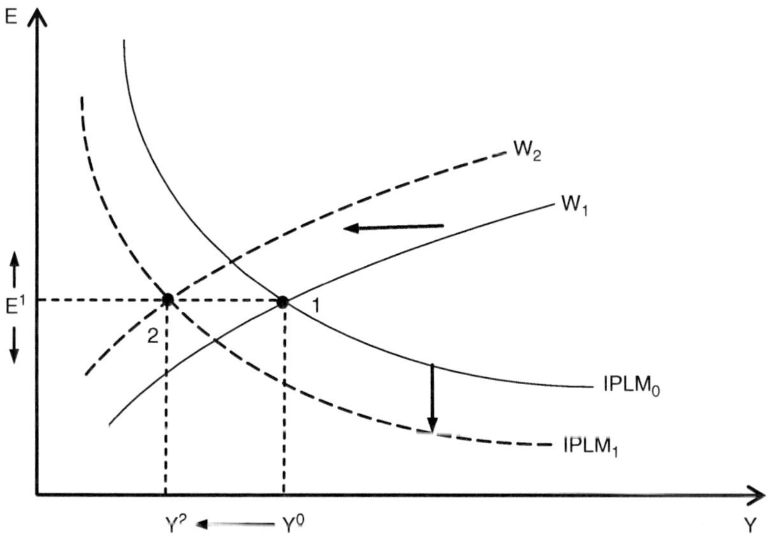

Figure 6.3 Monetary policy contraction with upward sloping W curve
Source: Authors.

In contrast, a policy of *monetary expansion* would unambiguously stabilize output but the impact on the exchange rate is once again ambiguous (Figure 6.4). There is a possibility that monetary expansion could be especially beneficial in the sense of raising output while also stabilizing the currency. This is more likely to be the case if the IPLM curve is less responsive to changes in interest rates compared with the W curve, which in turn may happen if one allows for the possibility of weak Laffer curve effects.[12]

Consider Case 2 with a downward sloping W curve. In order to focus on the comparative statics we assume unique equilibrium. *Monetary contraction* in this case leads to ambiguous results with regard to both output and exchange rates (Figures 6.5a,b). The same is true for *monetary expansion*. For instance, while there is a possibility of a "good equilibrium" of both currency and output stabilization (Figure 6.6a), there is a possibility of a "bad equilibrium" of both sharp output contraction and currency weakness (Figure 6.6b). In the presence of weak Laffer curve effects, the more likely scenario is one of output expansion and exchange rate weakness in the case of monetary expansion; and output contraction and exchange rate weakness in the case of monetary contraction.

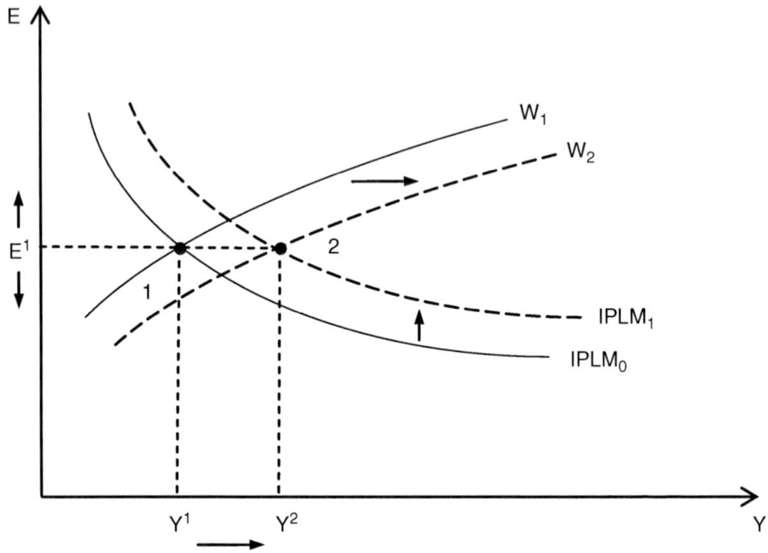

Figure 6.4 Monetary policy expansion with upward sloping W curve
Source: Authors.

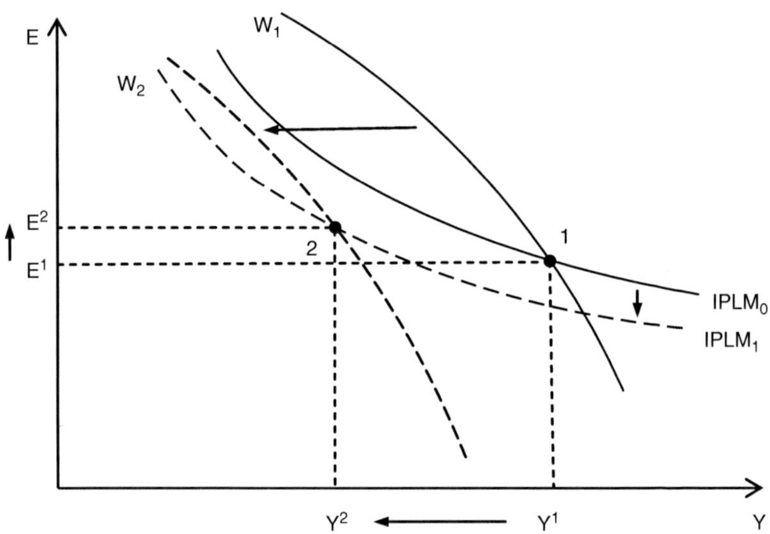

Figure 6.5a Monetary policy contraction with downward sloping W curve
Source: Authors.

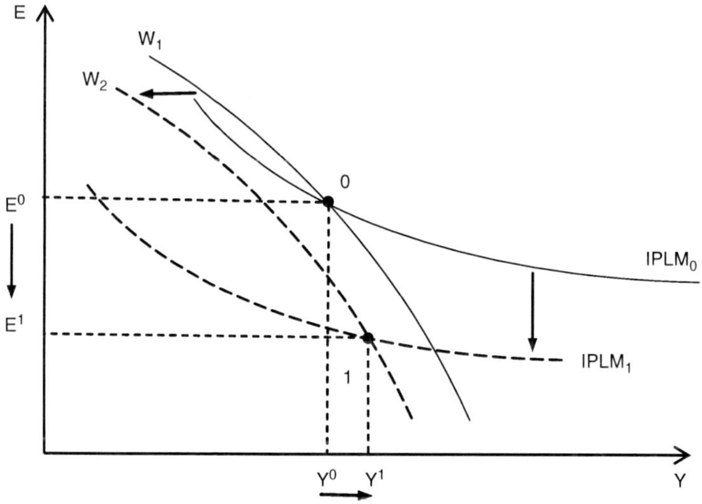

Figure 6.5b Monetary policy contraction with downward sloping W curve

Source: Authors.

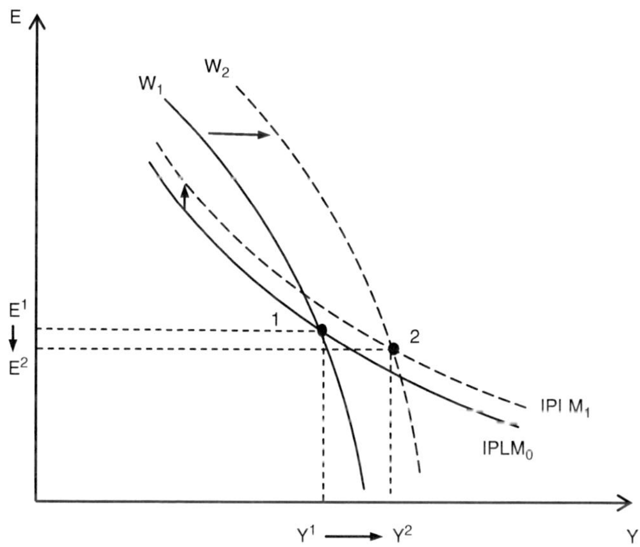

Figure 6.6a Monetary policy expansion with downward sloping W curve

Source: Authors.

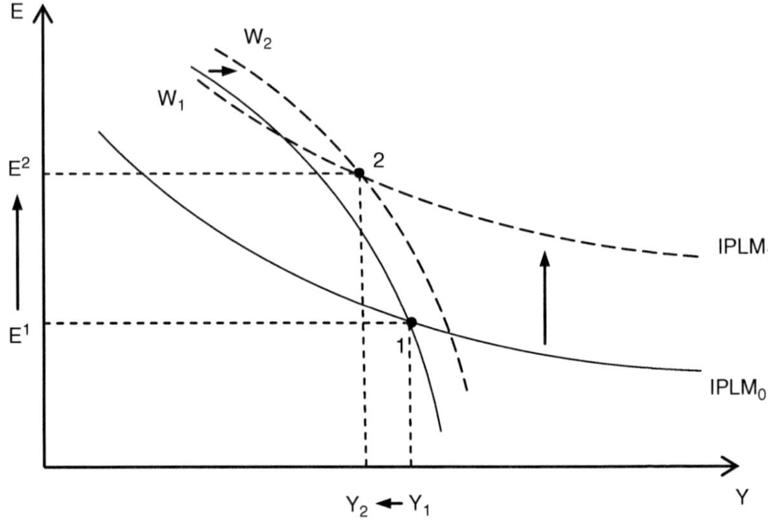

Figure 6.6b Monetary policy expansion with downward sloping W curve

Source: Authors.

Box 6.1 Summary of appropriate monetary policy responses

Shape of W Curve	**Monetary expansion**	**Monetary contraction**
No Laffer curve effects		
Case 1: Upward sloping	*E* uncertain *Y* rises	*E* uncertain *Y* declines
Case 2: Downward sloping	*E* uncertain *Y* uncertain	*E* uncertain *Y* uncertain
Weak Laffer curve effects		
Case 1: Upward sloping	*E* declines *Y* rises	*E* rises *Y* declines
Case 2: Downward sloping	*E* declines *Y* rises	*E* rises *Y* declines

Note: Rise in *E* implies currency depreciation.

Source: Authors.

Box 6.1 summarizes the preceding discussion. Some interesting conclusions emerge from this. One, in the absence of the weak Laffer curve effects, regardless of whether the W curve is upward or downward sloping, and, regardless of whether there is a monetary expansion or contraction, the impact on the exchange rate is uncertain. This may partly explain the mixed results obtained in the empirical literature to date that have examined the nexus between interest rates and exchange rates noted in Section 6.2.[13]

Two, in the absence of the weak Laffer curve effects, when the W curve is upward sloping, the impact of monetary contraction (expansion) is to unambiguously reduce (increase) output, as would be expected *a priori*. However, in the event of a downward sloping W curve the impact of output is ambiguous regardless of monetary policy stance.

Three, in the presence of weak Laffer curve effects, regardless of the slope of the W curve, the impact of monetary policy stance on output is entirely consistent with received orthodoxy, viz. it rises with a monetary loosening and falls with a monetary tightening.

Four, in the presence of weak Laffer curve effects the currency will always weaken with a monetary policy contraction and always appreciate with a monetary expansion. This is inconsistent with received wisdom but is more likely the case during a crisis period.

6.4 Conclusion

As is apparent, the issue of optimal monetary policy is particularly dependent on the presence of weak Laffer curve effects as well as the shape of the W curve. While it is generally acknowledged that weak Laffer curve effects are more likely to occur during a crisis period (see Chapter 7 of this volume), there has been much less attention paid to or awareness of the shape of the W curve which deals with the real side of the economy. Of course, as noted previously, there is a feedback effect in that the W curve is itself more likely to be downward sloping in the presence of the Laffer curve effects. Beyond this, the analysis above highlights three main factors that impact the shape of the W curve.

First, the greater the size of unhedged foreign currency debt the more likely the W curve is downward sloping. This follows directly from the discussion of the balance sheet effects noted previously and is consistent with recent empirical analysis by Eijffinger and Goderis (2006) and Goderis and Ioannidou (2006).

Second, the greater the size of the exportables sector and the more responsive exports are to devaluation, the more likely the W curve is upward sloping. This too is intuitive.

Third, the weaker or less developed the domestic banking system the more susceptible it is to sharp exchange rate depreciations (due to its exposure to uncovered liabilities directly, i.e. currency mismatch risk, or indirectly, i.e. credit risk). Thus, a given currency depreciation could significantly compromise the ability or willingness of banks to lend to domestic corporates, effectively making them more credit constrained and consequently making the W curve more likely to be downward sloping.

For instance, most East Asian economies in 1997–1998 were bank based, their financial institutions were relatively weak, and their corporates were highly leveraged with high unhedged external debt. And, while they were highly export-oriented economies, the simultaneous sharp devaluation by regional economies negated the competitive advantage any individual East Asian country might have enjoyed.[14] This suggests that the regional economies may well have had negatively sloped W curves. Assuming a negatively sloped W curve, if there are no Laffer curve effects, returning to Box 6.1, both expansionary and contractionary monetary policy stances have ambiguous effects on the exchange rate. If, however, weak Laffer curve effects are present, a monetary expansion is more likely to stabilize the currency as well as prevent an output contraction. This runs counter to IMF orthodoxy.

In the final analysis, when determining appropriate monetary policy stance during a crisis, policy makers need to be cognizant of (a) the potential perverse effects of capital flows in response to interest rate changes; (b) the extent of leverage of the corporate sector (in terms of aggregate size, currency denomination and maturity structure); (c) the extent of financial sector vulnerabilities; and (d) the possible influences of exchange rate and interest rate changes on the corporate and financial sectors and their repercussions on the overall economy.

Notes

1. This chapter draws on an article originally published in *Emerging Markets Trade and Finance*, 44 (3), 2008, 21–33 (M.E. Sharpe). Reprinted with permission.
2. There could be other reasons for this perverse asset market response of exchange rates to a change in monetary policy stance, including the role of signals *a la* Drazen and Hubrich (2003). For a nontechnical discussion of this and other channels, see Montiel (2003). Also see Chapter 7 of this volume.
3. Also see Eijffinger and Goderis (2006), Gould and Kamin (2000) and Chapter 7 of this volume.
4. For an alternative—more precise—way of modelling the Laffer curve effects, see Goldfajn and Baig (1998). The benefit of incorporating risk premium in this manner is that it allows for the interpretation of Laffer curve effects as either an erosion of investments due to probability of default or decline in investor expectations leading to outright capital flight.
5. Note that as with A-B-B we have assumed concavity of the IPLM. This requires that $L_1(\cdot) > 2[L_1(\cdot)]^2 / L(\cdot)$.

6 Another way of incorporating these effects might be to have export shocks impacting the technology parameter, i.e. there may be positive externalities from exporting.
7. A-B-B incorporate the first term, not the second.
8. The inability of many emerging economies to borrow externally in domestic currency terms has come to be referred to as the "original sin" hypothesis; see Hausmann et al. (2002). Also see discussion in Chapter 7 of this volume.
9. A-B-B assume that domestic currency borrowing is in fixed rates.
10. Note that $E_0 = P_1 = P_0$.
11. Note that the presence of weak Laffer curve effects makes it more likely that Case 2 holds as the debt cost and first subeffect of the credit channel become less significant.
12. This said, as noted, the presence of the Laffer curve effects makes it more likely that the W curve will be downward sloping. We return to this point later on.
13. However, it can be shown that this ambiguity in exchange rate movements disappears if the real sector is relatively interest rate inelastic. To be sure, low interest elasticity effectively leaves just the export competitiveness and balance sheet channels which work in opposite directions to impact the slope of the W curve.
14. Duttagupta and Spilimbergo (2004) find that there is high intraregional price elasticity in East Asia, but limited elasticity of substitution between goods from East Asia as a whole and the rest of the world, such that a regional real devaluation did not significantly increase East Asian global exports.

References

Aghion, P., P. Bacchetta and A. Banerjee (2000). "A Simple Model of Monetary Policy and Currency Crises," *European Economic Review*, 44, 728–738.

Basurto, G. and A. Ghosh (2001). "The Interest Rate-Exchange Rate Nexus in Currency Crises," *IMF Staff Papers*, 47, 99–120.

Bird, G. and R.S. Rajan (2004). "Does Devaluation Lead to Economic Recovery or Economic Contraction?: Examining the Analytical Issues with Reference to Thailand," *Journal of International Development*, 16, 141–156.

Boorman J., T. Lane, M. Schultze-Ghattas, A. Bulir, A. Ghosh, J. Hamann, A. Mourmouras and S. Phillips (2000). "Managing Financial Crises: The Experience in East Asia," Working Paper No. 00/107, IMF.

Caporale, G.M., A. Cipollini and P. Demetriades (2000). "Monetary Policy and the Exchange Rate During the Asian Crisis Identification Through Heteroscedasticity," Discussion Papers in Economics 00/11, University of Leicester.

Drazen, A. and S. Hubrich (2003). "Mixed Signals in Defending The Exchange Rate: What Do the Data Say?," mimeo (June).

Duttagupta, R. and A. Spilimbergo (2004). "What Happened to Asian Exports during the Crisis?," *IMF Staff Papers*, 51, 72–95.

Eijffinger, S.C.W. and B. Goderis (2006). "The Effect of Monetary Policy on Exchange Rates during Currency Crises: The Role of Short-term Debt and Institutions," mimeo (April).

Furman J. and J. Stiglitz (1998). "Economic Crises: Evidence and Insights from East Asia," *Brookings Papers on Economic Activity*, 2, 1–114.

Goderis, B. and V.P. Ioannidou (2006). "Do High Interest Rates Defend Currencies During Speculative Attacks? New Evidence," Working Paper No. 2006-11, CSAE, Oxford University.

Goldfajn I. and T. Baig (1998). "Monetary Policy in the Aftermath of Currency Crises: The Case of Asia," Working Paper No. 98/170, IMF.

Gould, D. and S.B. Kamin (2000). "The Impact of Monetary Policy on Exchange Rates During Financial Crises," International Finance Working Paper No. 669, Board of Governors of the Federal Reserve.

Hausmann, R., U. Panizza and E. Stein (2002). "Original Sin, Passthrough, and Fear of Floating," in M.I. Blejer and M. Skreb (eds.), *Financial Policies in Emerging Markets*, Cambridge: MIT Press.

Krugman, P. (1999). "Balance Sheets, the Transfer Problem, and Financial Crisis," in P. Isard, A. Razin, and A. Rose A (eds.), *International Finance and Financial Crises*, Boston: Kluwer Academic Press.

Montiel, P. (2003). "Tight Money in a Post-crisis Defense of the Exchange Rate: What have we Learned?," *The World Bank Research Observer*, 18, 1–23.

Radelet, S. and J. Sachs (1998). "The East Asian Financial Crisis: Diagnosis, Remedies, Prospects," *Brookings Papers on Economic Activity*, 1, 1–74.

Stiglitz, J. (1998). "Knowledge for Development: Economic Science, Economic Policy and Economic Advice," Annual Bank Conference on Development Economics, The World Bank.

7
How Best to Manage New-Style Currency Crises?[1]

Ramkishen S. Rajan

7.1 Introduction

The intensity and suddenness of recent currency crises has inspired a "third generation" crisis literature that focuses on: (a) sharp increases in the domestic value of foreign currency debt (so-called "balance sheet effects") which adversely affect a country's *solvency* position and (b) "sudden stops" in capital inflows (including outright reversals) which negatively influence a country's *liquidity* position.[2] As Dornbusch (2001) notes:

> A new-style crisis involves doubt about creditworthiness of the balance sheet of a significant part of the economy...and the exchange rate...(W)hen there is a question about one, the implied capital flight makes it immediately a question about both...(The) central part of the new-style crisis is the focus on balance sheets and capital flight...(T)hey involve a far more dramatic impact on economic activity than mere current account disturbances...both in terms of magnitude of the financial shock as well as disorganization effects stemming from illiquidity or bankruptcy.

Using a sample of 49 middle and larger income countries over the period 1992–1999, Stone and Weeks (2001) find that the curtailment of private capital flows and adverse balance sheet effects are among the most important factors determining the intensity of currency crises (defined as loss of real GDP relative to pre-crisis trend, conditional on the occurrence of a crisis). Using a sample of 24 developing and emerging economies over the period 1975–1997, Hutchison and Noy (2002) find that, while currency crises are associated with declines in investments and overall output in the short run, the real sector contractions are particularly marked in cases where currency crises occur simultaneously with current account reversals (Hutchison and Noy 2002). These current account reversals could be because of either a cessation of private capital flows *per se* (liquidity crunch) or adverse balance sheet effects (solvency crunch).[3]

Distinguishing between the *probability or warning signs of a crisis*, on the one hand, and the *intensity or depth of a crisis*, on the other, is consistent with Calvo and Mendoza (1996) and Rajan (2001), who suggest that new-style crises in developing and emerging economies ought to be seen as involving two stages: (a) an initial currency crisis/speculative attack which can either be self-fulfilling or fundamentals based and (b) the post-crisis output dynamics. While the first two generations of crisis models are well-equipped to handle the first issue (i.e. why does a crisis occur in the first instance?), the third generation crisis models are more pertinent to examining the second issue (i.e. what happens after the actual speculative attack?).[4]

Given the potential high costs of these new-style or "capital account" crises, there remains an ongoing debate on how they might best be *managed* when they do arise. While some popular International Economics textbooks continue to include brief discussions of the age-old Swan diagram, they have not used it to discuss new-style crises and appropriate crisis management policies.[5] An obvious limitation of the Swan diagram—as it is conventionally presented—is the lack of good microfoundations. This in turn may partly explain why its popularity has dwindled substantially over the last few decades.

The objective of this chapter is to contribute to resuscitating the use of the Swan diagram in the classroom and in policy discussions on crisis management. The next section briefly reviews the traditional framework of internal and external balance. Section 7.3 revisits the external balance (EB) schedule and shows how it might be reinterpreted as the financial side of the economy. Section 7.4 revisits the internal balance (IB) schedule and offers a simple model of the real side of the economy to explain why real devaluations might be *contractionary* rather than *expansionary*. Focus is on the open economy balance sheet approach—i.e. corporate leverage in unhedged foreign currency terms—which is taking on increasing significance in the IMF's policy analysis and prescriptions (for instance, see Allen et al. 2002 and IMF 2003a).[6] The penultimate section discusses the desirable policy mix in response to stylized shocks and different scenarios. The final section concludes the chapter with a brief discussion of how a country might reduce its vulnerability to adverse balance sheet effects.

7.2 Internal balance (IB) versus external balance (EB): conventional theory

The typical Swan diagram plots real exchange rates against real income or absorption. Policies to affect real absorption can be either fiscal or monetary. For instance, Krugman (1998) focuses on fiscal policy as the sole absorption or expenditure-reducing tool. The Swan diagram is also sometimes discussed in the context of monetary policy vis-à-vis fiscal policy, with the implicit assumption of a fixed exchange rate (e.g. Salvatore (2003), chapter 18, 640–642). The approach used in this chapter—in part inspired by Frankel (2001)—considers a "modified" Swan Diagram with real interest rates (i_t) on the vertical axis and real exchange rates (e_t) on the horizontal axis. We ignore fiscal policy altogether. Why?

The issue of appropriate fiscal policy stance during a crisis broadly involves conflicting pressures and tradeoffs. On the one hand, given the implicit or quasi deficits of the government (because of their blanket guarantees on banks, sterilization costs, etc), there is inevitably a need for considerable fiscal consolidation by the crisis-hit country. In addition, tight fiscal policy might be seen as a positive signal to international capital markets. On the other hand, the social damage of the crisis necessitates looser fiscal policy.[7] More importantly, fiscal policy is generally not a very flexible instrument to influence economic activity in the short run. This was made apparent during the Asian crisis of 1997–1998 (see Boorman and Associates 2000).

The External Balance (EB) schedule, which assumes that the balance of payments is in "equilibrium," is downward sloping. This is because, other things being equal, a fall in the real exchange rate (a real appreciation) leads to a loss of export competitiveness and a consequent worsening of the current account. This requires a rise in real interest rates to improve the capital account balance so as to ensure that the balance of payments regains "equilibrium," i.e. $\Delta R_t = k$ (where R_t international reserves and k is some target reserve level).[8] Points above and below the EB line depict balance of payments surplus and deficit, respectively.

The IB schedule, which assumes that the economy is operating at full employment ($y_t = y^*$), is upward sloping. This is because a fall in the real exchange rate leads to a loss of export competitiveness and consequent decline in output below full employment, hence requiring lower real interest rates to stimulate domestic demand (investment and interest sensitive consumption). Points above and below the IB schedule indicate recessionary conditions and overheating, respectively.

The EB and IB schedules thus divide the diagram into four zones or quadrants (Figure 7.1a). The Swan diagram nicely illustrates that one needs two instruments (interest rates and exchange rates) in order to attain both internal and external balance simultaneously (i.e. "Tinbergen's Targets instruments approach").

Two criticisms of the Swan diagram come to mind immediately. First, in the presence of an open capital account, does not the assumption of exchange rates and interest rates as independent policy instruments violate the "Impossible Trinity" hypothesis? Second, even ignoring the impossible Trinity, *at the time of a crisis*, how much control does a country really have on its exchange rate as an independent policy instrument? In particular, while encouraging or engineering a currency depreciation (over and above a freely functioning market rate) is easy enough to do (via either verbal interventions, i.e. talking down the currency, or stockpiling of reserves), what about a currency appreciation?[9]

The first question is easily answered either by assuming away perfect asset substitutability (Bansal and Dahlquist 2000)[10] or by recognizing

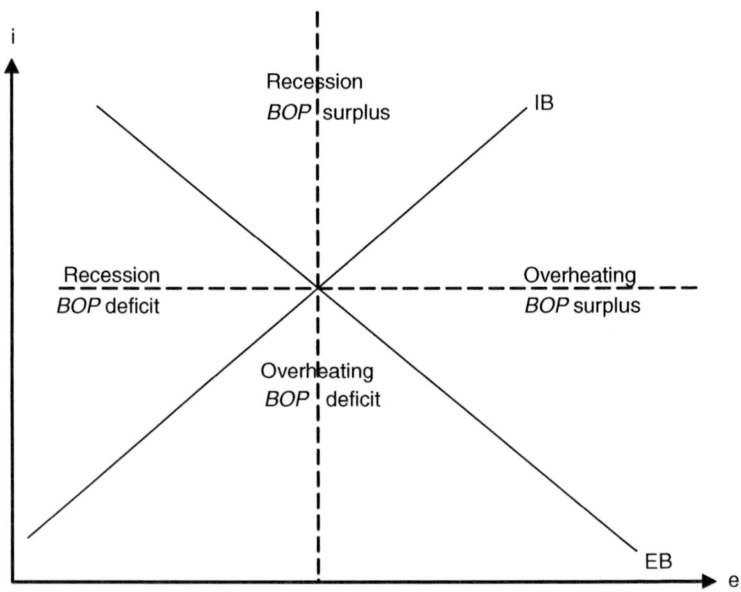

Figure 7.1a Four quadrants of the conventional Swan diagram
Source: Authors.

that the Impossible Trinity does not on its own imply that an intermediate regime is unviable. A country could pursue a policy of a managed float and retain a degree of monetary policy autonomy (Frankel 1999; Rajan 2002; Rajan 2003, chapter 4).[11]

With regard to the second criticism, in the context of crisis management, apart from affecting the exchange rate via varying the interest rate, anther way of thinking about appreciating versus depreciating a currency during a crisis would be in terms of adjustment versus financing. Specifically, while currency depreciation can be seen as a type of adjustment policy, attempting to maintain the strength of the currency can be brought about via regional or multilateral financing (that is sterilized so as not to undermine the underlying monetary policy stance). Thus, the Swan diagram is not only able to aid in the discussion of the issue of *expenditure switching* versus *expenditure reducing* (two forms of adjustment); it also implicitly provides some insights into the *adjustment* versus *financing* debate in the event of a crisis.[12] It is reasonable to expect that an external crisis that is permanent or intense—especially a terms of trade one—requires a real devaluation to regain competitiveness. In such an event, the following discussion (Section 7.5) can be viewed as pertaining to what happens postdevaluation, i.e. does one attempt to regain currency stability or allow it to decline even further?

7.3 Revisiting the EB schedule: the financial side

In view of the importance of sudden stops in new-style crises (the balance sheet effects are discussed in Section 7.4), the first obvious modification to the Swan diagram would be to interpret the EB schedule as solely depicting the *nonofficial* or private capital account balance. Indeed, it is the capital account that tends nowadays to be the focus of crisis management policy. The reason for considering only the nonofficial component of capital flows is that it allows us to keep the liquidity effects of official financing distinct from the movements of the EB schedule. From a policy perspective this can be justified by assuming that appropriate adjustment policies must be seen as being independent of financing (i.e. preventing moral hazard problems).

By separating the financial and the real sides of the economy (EB versus IB, respectively), one is able to isolate the effects of distinct shocks. For instance, while an export shock would have affected both the EB and IB schedules conventionally defined, in the current framework it has no direct influence on the EB, which is capital account driven; only the IB schedule is affected (see Section 7.5).

7.3.1 Simple theory

In the context of a small and highly open economy, the EB schedule might be reinterpreted in terms of the modified risk-adjusted, uncovered real interest parity (UIP) condition:

$$\rho(i_t)(1+i_t)=\left(1+i^*\right)\left(\frac{e^e_{t+1}}{e_t}\right)rp(i_t) \quad (1)$$

where: i^* = foreign real interest rates, $rp(i_t)$ = currency risk premium and $\rho(i_t)$ = probability of no default risk. Equation (1) incorporates perverse feedback or Laffer curve effects, i.e. $\rho' < 0$. In other words, a rise in real interest rates could worsen anticipated net returns by lowering the probability of repayment.[13] In addition, assuming risk aversion, $rp > 0$ and $rp' > 0$.[14] Thus, eq. (1) is an interest arbitrage condition that incorporates both default and currency risk (as discussed in Chapter 6 of this volume).[15]

However, Drazen (2003) questions the direct interest rate effects (perverse or otherwise) on exchange rates during a crisis period. As he notes:

> If the horizon over which a devaluation is expected is extremely short, interest rates must be raised to extraordinarily high levels to deter speculation when there is even a small expected devaluation. For example, even if foreign currency assets bore no interest, an expected overnight devaluation of 0.5 percent would require an annual interest rate of over 500% (1.005^{365} – 1)*100 = 517 to make speculation unprofitable... Though the "arithmetic problem" suggests why spectacular defenses may have only limited effects, this reasoning leaves other questions unanswered. First, why...might an interest rate defense..lead to even greater spectacular pressures against the currency? That is, why would there be *perverse* feedback from raising interest rates to speculative pressures? Second, even in the absence of perverse feedback effects, the "arithmetic problem" raises the question of why they ever work. How can an effectively minor change in the cost of speculation have such significant, and one might say, *disproportional* effects?

Drazen (2003) further argues that the impact of short term interest rate changes on the exchange rate may be due more to their informational content (i.e. "signals") than simply the costs of borrowing or investing (also see Drazen 2000). In particular, on the one hand, a rise in real interest rates could be a positive signal to market participants who infer that the monetary authority is willing and able to make tough decisions, as well as highlighting the authority's degree of commitment to the peg. On the other hand, poor fundamentals could signal a loss of reserves or desperation of policy makers in the face of persistent speculative attacks or the unsustainability of the high interest rate policy (given its high costs on the overall economy).

There are other reasons why the risk premium term may covary positively with interest rates. For instance, a tight interest rate policy could raise the government's contingent fiscal deficits (Flood and Jeanne 2000). This in turn might spook international capital markets, hence further weakening the currency. If the perverse effects are significant, the EB schedule—which now depicts the capital account balance more narrowly—becomes fairly steep.[16] While it is theoretically possible for the EB schedule to be upward sloping, it is generally acknowledged that this is highly unlikely (Frankel 2001).[17]

There is a burgeoning empirical literature on the exchange rate—interest rate nexus with conflicting/inconclusive results (see the recent literature review by Montiel 2003; also see Boorman and Associates 2000). This is not surprising in view of the different model specifications, methodologies, sample frequencies and country coverage of the studies. A more promising line of research appears to involve concentrating on a narrower set of issues in relation to Eq. 1 rather than the general nexus between exchange rates and interest rates. For instance, Basuro and Ghosh (2000) find little evidence that higher real interest rates lead to increased estimated risk premia in the crisis-hit East Asian economies of Indonesia, Korea and Thailand. Similarly, with regard to signalling effects, empirical analysis suggests that these effects are generally positive in the short term but perverse if persistent (Drazen and Hubrich 2003).

In any event, since the reformulation of the EB schedule is based on the interest parity condition, points off the EB schedule arise due to a wedge between exchange rates and interest rates (Ω_t). Specifically, points above the EB schedule could denote either persistent reserve accumulation (which is assumed to be sterilized) or the fact that controls on reserve flows are in place. So high interest rates could be sustained at a given exchange rate if capital controls on inflows are stiffened or reserves are accumulated. Points below the EB conversely denote reserve depletion (which, of course, cannot be sustained) or controls of capital outflows that can be fairly effectively maintained (Figure 7.1b).

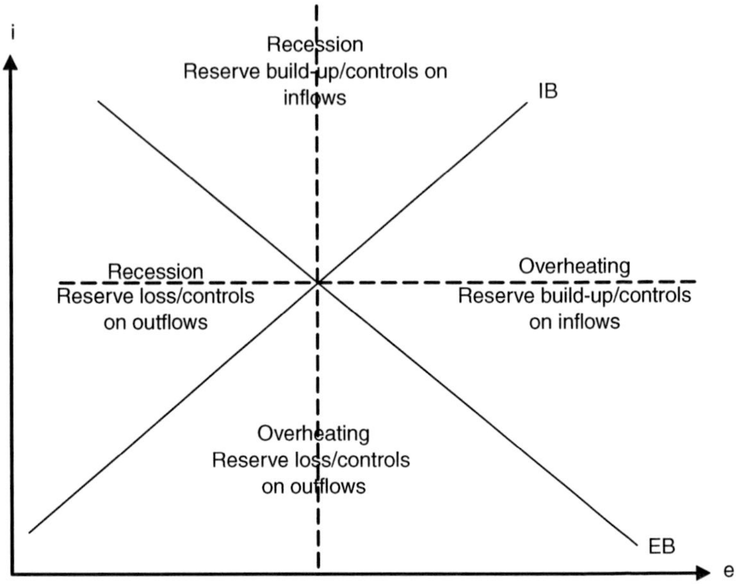

Figure 7.1b Four quadrants of the new-style Swan diagram[a]

Note: [a] The assumption here is that the IB schedule is upward sloping. As noted, the IB schedule could also be downward sloping. However, the general conclusion, viz. points above the IB schedule denote recession and points below denote overheating, remain valid.

Source: Authors.

7.4 Revisiting the IB schedule: the real side

As discussed above, while the EB schedule characterizes the financial side of the economy, the IB depicts the real side of the economy. The IB schedule (d*i*/d*e*) can be rewritten as follows:

$$\frac{di}{de} = -\left[\frac{(\partial y/\partial e)}{(\partial y/\partial i)}\right] \Big| y = y^* \qquad (2)^{18}$$

where y^* = full employment. In other words, as noted, the EB schedule denotes all combinations of *i* and *e* such that output remains at its full employment level. There is little controversy about the denominator in eq. 2, which is negative. What about the numerator?

The conventional view is that the numerator is unambiguously positive (due to the procompetitiveness effects). Thus, if real interest rates rise, real exchange rates must rise as well to maintain internal balance, hence deriving an upward sloping IB schedule. "New Structuralists" challenged both this analysis and the policy prescription that followed on from it (Taylor 1981). They argued that devaluation would be contractionary and that IMF programs were stagflationary. The New Structuralists have outlined various routes via which devaluation may, in principle, have a contractionary effect spanning both aggregate demand and aggregate supply. These contractionary channels have been extensively discussed elsewhere and will therefore not be detailed here (for instance, see Agenor and Montiel 1999; Bird and Rajan 2004; Caves, Frankel and Jones 2003, chapter 24; Lizondo and Montiel 1989). Suffice it to note that, by and large, the New Structuralist literature has focused on the demand side and the "real sector" (see Chapter 4 of this volume). However, as indicated by the Dornbusch quote in Section 7.1, the emphasis of new-style or capital account crises is on the financial or balance sheet side of the economy Indeed, it is unlikely that the "conventional" contractionary effects of devaluation via the current account can explain the *magnitude* and *ferocity* of some economic contractions following devaluation.

7.4.1 Basic model structure of real side of economy

In view of the importance of the balance sheet effect in recent crises in developing economies, it would be useful to consider a simple formalization of the issue based on a variant of the framework initially outlined by Aghion, Bacchetta and Banerjee (2000) and extended upon in Chapter 6 of this volume. In its simplest form the model extends over two periods, assumes a single tradable good, and the economy is made up of identical entrepreneurs/firms which are credit constrained *a la* Bernanke and Gertler (1989) and Bernanke, Gertler and Gilchrist (1998). Prices in each period are fixed/preset at the beginning of the period (assumed to equal to 1) such that monetary policy does have temporary real effects.[19] Purchasing power parity (PPP) holds in the second period (*ex-post* deviations are allowed in the first period when there is an external disturbance). In other words, the effects of external shocks disappear in the second period. Risk adjusted UIP holds imperfectly (for reasons discussed previously, we ignore the perverse effects here).

$$y_t = \sigma k_t + x(e_{t-1}) \text{ and } x'(.) > 0 \tag{3}$$

$$K_t = w_t + d_t \tag{4}$$

$$d_t = \eta_t w_t \tag{5}$$

$$\eta_t = \eta(i_{t-1}, e_{t-1}) \text{ and } \eta_1(.) < 0,\ \eta_2(.) < 0 \tag{6}$$

$$\pi_t = y_t - c_t \tag{7}$$

$$c_t = (1+i_t)d^c + (1+i^*)\left(\frac{e_t}{e_{t-1}}\right)\left(\frac{d_t}{d^c}\right) \tag{8}$$

where: y_t = real output; k_t = real capital stock; x_t = export function; w_t = domestic wealth in real terms; π_t = profit function in real terms; c_t = costs in real terms; d_t = total debt in real terms; d^c = domestic debt in real terms (assumed to be fixed); $(d_t - d^c)$= unhedged foreign debt in real terms.

Equation (3) states that in the long run sustainable output is characterized by linear production technology with capital as the sole input. However, output in the short run could deviate from the sustainable level in the case of export demand shocks. Exports in turn are positively related to real exchange rate variations (i.e. real depreciation boosts exports and output).[20]

Equation (4) states that the capital stock is financed by available wealth ("entrepreneurship") as well as by debt/borrowing. Capital stock is assumed to depreciate fully in one period. Equation (5) states that the amount of borrowing to finance capital spending is proportional to available wealth (η_t). In other words, financial markets are imperfect; firms are credit constrained and the total amount of borrowing is limited by available collateral.[21]

Equation (6) state that η_t falls with domestic interest rate hikes or currency depreciations, i.e. $\eta_1(.) < 0$ and $\eta_2 < 0$.[22] Intuitively, as interest rates in the economy increase or the currency devalues, other things being equal, the greater is the probability of corporate bankruptcies and a consequent worsening of the credit position of the banks (i.e. a rise in the share of nonperforming loans). This could lead to an outright banking crisis and an economy-wide credit crunch.[23] Using a sample of 19 developing and emerging economies in the 1990s, Mulder, Perrelli and Rocha (2002) find that corporate balance sheet variables (such as leveraged financing and high short term debt to working capital) affect the depth of a crisis (measured as the weighted loss of exchange rates and reserves), particularly when they interact with the total size of bank credit. This suggests that crises tend to be most intense when "corporate weaknesses are transmitted through the banking system" (p. 15).[24]

Equation (7) is simply the profit function (revenues less costs) for the typical firm; and eq. (8) is the firm's cost function. The only cost considered here is that on interest incurred on borrowing. Specifically, the first term on the right hand side (r.h.s.) of eq. (8) is the real interest cost on domestic debt, while the second term on the r.h.s. is the real interest cost on foreign debt that is accumulated in the beginning of the period or at the end of the previous period. While foreign interest rates are assumed to be fixed, the interest on domestic debt is assumed to be floating or variable.[25] We do not concern ourselves here with how and why firms might choose the mix between domestic and foreign currency debt (see Section 7.6).

With appropriate substitutions we have:

$$\pi_t = y_t - \left[(1+i_t)d^c + (1+i^*)\left(\frac{e_t}{e_{t-1}}\right)\left(\frac{d_t}{d^c}\right)\right]. \tag{9}$$

Assume α is a proportion of profits that is retained by the firm (assume they are consumed or distributed for simplicity).[26] Thus, wealth holdings (which act as collateral) can be written as follows:

$$w_{t+1} = (1-\alpha)\pi_t + w_t \tag{10}$$

The question we are interested in here is: what is the impact of a change in e_1 on y_2? From eq. (10), we have:

$$w_2 = (1-\alpha)\pi_1 \qquad (11)^{27}$$

So,

$$\begin{aligned} y_2 &= \sigma(1+\eta(.))w_2 + x(.) \\ &= \sigma(1+\eta(.))(1-\alpha)[y_1 - (1+i_1)d^c - (1+i^*)e_1(d_1 - d^c)] + x(.) \end{aligned} \qquad (12)^{28}$$

Note that

$$\frac{dy_2}{de_1} = \left(\frac{\partial y_2}{\partial e_1}\right) + \left(\frac{\partial y_2}{\partial i_1}\right)\left(\frac{\partial i_1}{\partial e_1}\right) \tag{13}$$

(a) (b) (c)

7.4.2 Output effects of real devaluation: theory

Referring to eq. (13), (a) and (b) essentially denote the IB schedule (see eq. 2); (c) is the EB schedule (see eq. 1) which is unambiguously negative (ignoring strong perverse Laffer curve or signaling effects). Our focus here is on the IB schedule.

a. (b) is unambiguously negative. Why? First is the "credit easing" channel: $\eta_1(\cdot) < 0$. Second is the "lower interest burden" channel: $(1 + i_1)d^c < 0$.[29]
b. (a) cannot be signed *a priori*. Why? There are three channels that need to be considered. First is the "procompetitiveness" channel, which is positive: $x'(.) > 0$. Second is the "banking crisis" / "credit crunch" or "illiquidity" channel, which is negative: $\eta_2(.) < 0$. Third is the balance sheet or "insolvency" channel: $-[(1 + i^*)(d_1 - d^c)]$, which is also negative, i.e. a real depreciation leads to a rise in the domestic value of existing unhedged foreign debt due to currency depreciation and reduced profits (we explore this issue in Section 7.6).[30]

This simple model highlights a number of channels via which devaluation may affect output and provides the microfoundations for the IB schedule. If the procompetiveness channel outweighs the other two channels we have the conventional effect, viz. $\partial y_2/\partial e_1 > 0$ and an upward sloping IB schedule[31]; else the IB schedule is downward sloping.[32] Regardless of the slope of the IB schedule, as discussed, points above the schedule denote recession or output operating below capacity, while points below denote overheating or output running above capacity (Figure 7.1b).

7.4.3 Output effects of real devaluation: empirics

There has been a large and growing empirical literature testing the output effects of real devaluation. The analysis in Chapter 4 of this volume suggests that there exists a difference between crisis and non-crisis periods, i.e. "state contingent" devaluation. Using annual data from twenty-four countries over the period from 1981 to 1999, they find that real devaluation in "normal" times is *not* contractionary. Only "crisis-induced" devaluations appear to be contractionary.[33] While there are a number of possible factors driving this result (including concerns about spurious correlation and reverse causality), one reason for this might have to do with the size of depreciations. Specifically, with "small" exchange rate changes (i.e. during "normal" periods) the procompetitiveness effect might dominate, while for "large" ones (i.e. during "crisis" periods) the balance sheet and banking crisis channels may dominate (Aghion, Bacchetta and Banerjee 2000 and Krugman 2003).[34] Graphically this corresponds to an IB schedule that is positively sloped but backward bending for large devaluations (discussed in Section 7.5). Lahiri and Vegh

(2001) suggest a nonlinear or "fear of floating" rule, whereby authorities should allow the currency to float in response to a "small shock" but should try to avoid any large real exchange rate changes.

Given the possible difference between crises and non-crisis periods, Gupta, Mishra and Sahay (2003) focus specifically on 195 crisis episodes across ninety-one developing countries between 1970 and 1998.[35] They find that the size of the export sector is positively associated with short run growth, while short term debt to reserves and nominal debt burdens are both negatively associated with growth, though the latter is statistically insignificant. The study also finds that output contractions post-crisis are more likely the greater the initial (i.e. pre-crisis) capital inflows into the country and the more liberal the country's capital and current account transactions. In addition, contractions are more likely if trade competitors devalue, as this negates the procompetitiveness effects of any single country.

There is a small but growing literature investigating the effect of sharp devaluations on individual firms rather than aggregate macro variables. For instance, Forbes (2002) uses a database from Worldscope covering over 13,500 nonfinancial companies in 42 countries between 1997 and 2000. On examining events of large depreciations in 12 countries (with the other 30 countries used as a control group),[36] she found that, in the year after the depreciation, firms generally experience a rise in market capitalization but a decline in growth in net income (in local currencies). This suggests to the author that depreciations in general lower immediate income but raise future expected profit. In other words, large or crisis-induced devaluations appear to be contractionary in the short run but not over time. Turning to firm characteristics, the findings indicate that firms with higher debt ratios tend to have lower income growth, while firms with greater foreign sales exposures performed notably better after depreciations. This is broadly consistent with the stylized model discussed above.

7.5 Implications for crisis management: stylized examples

What are the implications of the preceding discussion for crisis management? As a first step, it is useful to note that, as with the conventional Swan diagram, there are four distinct quadrants off the EB and IB schedules (Figure 7.1a). To return to internal and external balance simultaneously requires a combination of policies. Optimal policy combinations could differ depending on whether the IB is positively or negatively sloped, and, if the latter, whether it is steeper or flatter than the

EB schedule. Consider the conventional case where the EB schedule is negatively sloped and fairly elastic (i.e. highly interest sensitive) and the IB schedule is positively sloped. We refer to this as Case 1a (Figure 7.2). By contrast, if the banking crisis and balance sheet channels dominate the procompetitiveness effects, the IB schedule is downward sloping. Assuming that the EB schedule remains downward sloping but is fairly inelastic (due to the significance of perverse Laffer curve and signaling effects), there are two other possible cases. Case 1b (Figure 7.3) is where the IB schedule is steeper than the EB schedule. Case 1c (Figure 7.4) is where the EB schedule is steeper than the IB schedule.

Rather than examine *all* policy combinations for all quadrants for all cases, we instead focus on stylized cases when an economy is initially in equilibrium (internal and external balance) but is then hit by a (negative) external shock. This is justifiable by the fact that the reason for the reformulation of the Swan diagram in the first instance has been to examine optimal policy combinations in the event of a crisis. We consider two stylized shocks below, viz. risk premium shock and export shock, as well as a combination of both.

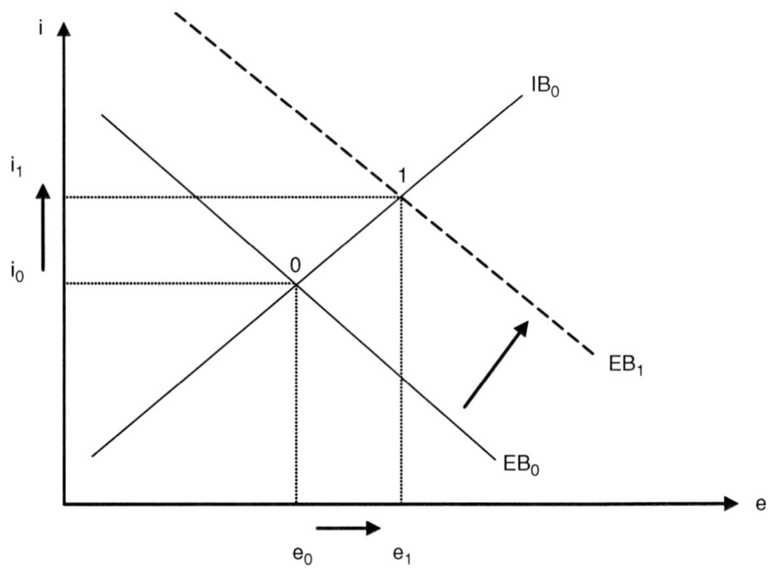

Figure 7.2 Crisis management following an adverse risk premium shock: *case 1a*

Source: Authors.

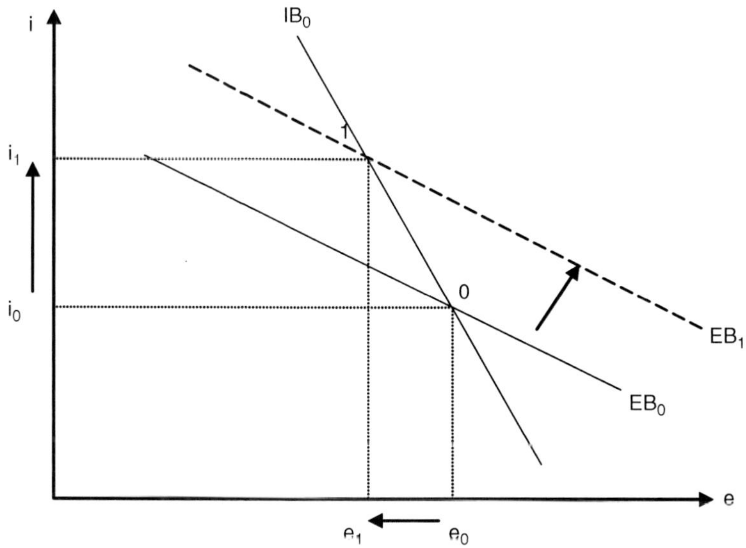

Figure 7.3 Crisis management following an adverse risk premium shock: *case 1b*

Source: Authors.

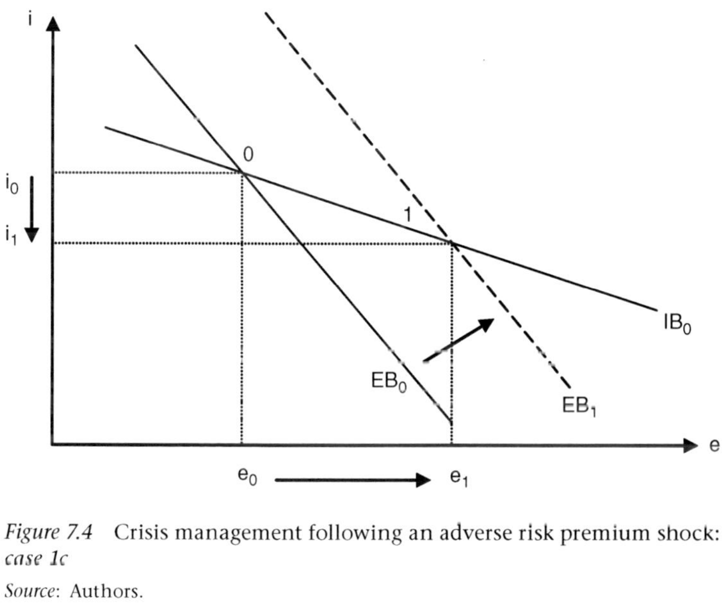

Figure 7.4 Crisis management following an adverse risk premium shock: *case 1c*

Source: Authors.

7.5.1 Adverse risk premium shock

Consider the case of a negative exogenous risk premium shock which leads to a sudden stop in capital flows. This can be depicted by a rightward shift of the EB schedule.[37] What mix of policies is needed to maintain both internal and external balance? In Case 1a there is a need for the IMF's conventional policy mix of real exchange rate depreciation and higher interest rates, i.e. expenditure reducing plus expenditure switching. In Case 1b the external shock requires tighter monetary policy but real exchange rate appreciation, i.e. expenditure reducing plus financing which is frontloaded. The intuition is straightforward. A rise in risk premium disturbs the capital account balance and requires a rise in interest rate to regain equilibrium. The rise in interest rates causes output to fall below full employment level, hence necessitating an exchange rate depreciation (adjustment) in Case 1a and an appreciation (financing) in Case 1b. In Case 1c the external shock requires a combination of real depreciation and looser monetary policy, i.e. expenditure increasing plus expenditure switching policies. The intuition here is as follows. Given that the EB schedule is more interest elastic than the IB schedule, the principle of effective classification suggests that the external balance is best regained via currency devaluation. This in turn leads to a domestic contraction, hence requiring a monetary expansion.

7.5.2 Adverse export shock

A similar exercise can be carried out in the event of a negative export shock. In such a case the IB schedule shifts down. Once again we have three cases (2a–c) (Figures 7.5–7). In Case 2a, if the IB schedule is positively sloped (the EB is always assumed negatively sloped), the policy mix to regain internal and external balance would be to lower interest rates and a depreciated currency (Figure 7.5). In Case 2b, with a negatively sloped IB schedule, and as long as it is steeper than the EB schedule, the appropriate policy combination is tighter interest rates and a stronger currency. In Case 2c, where the EB schedule is steeper than the IB schedule, the policy mix to simultaneously regain internal and external balance would be to loosen monetary policy and permit the currency to depreciate, just as in Case 2a. Table 7.1 summarizes the foregoing analysis.

7.5.3 Combination of shocks and policy complexities

What if the economy were to be hit by a combination of adverse risk premium and export shocks? It is easy to see that in the case of a conventionally sloped upward sloping IB schedule (Cases 1a–2a) the appropriate

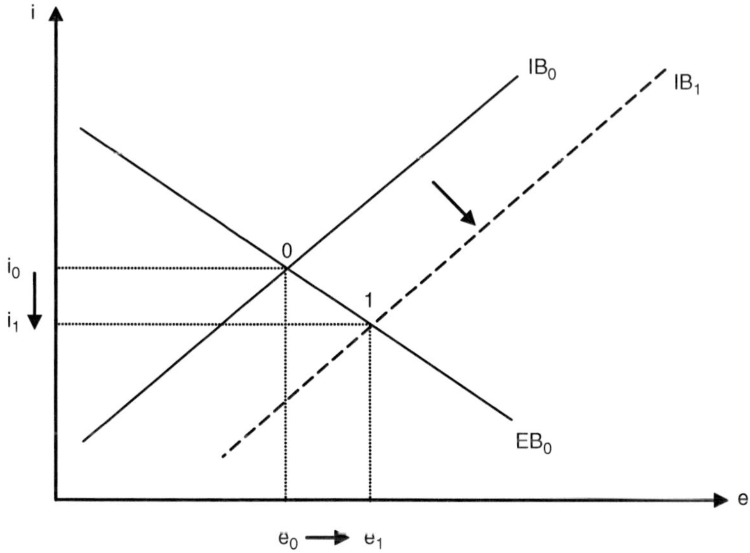

Figure 7.5 Crisis management following an adverse export shock: *case 2a*
Source: Authors.

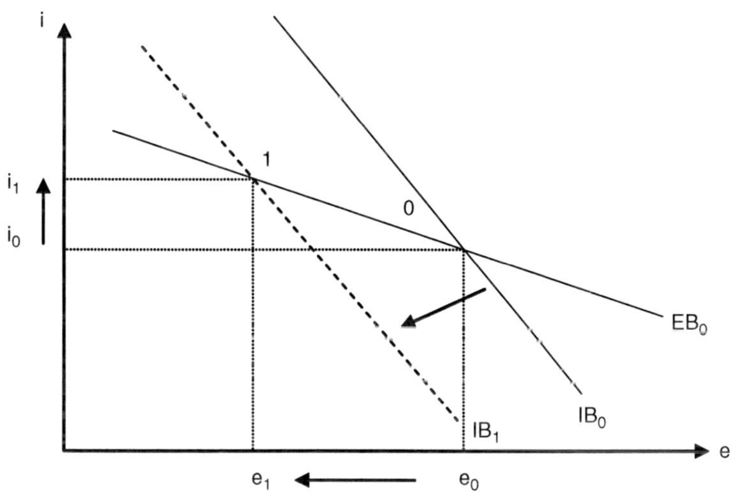

Figure 7.6 Crisis management following an adverse export shock: *case 2b*
Source: Authors.

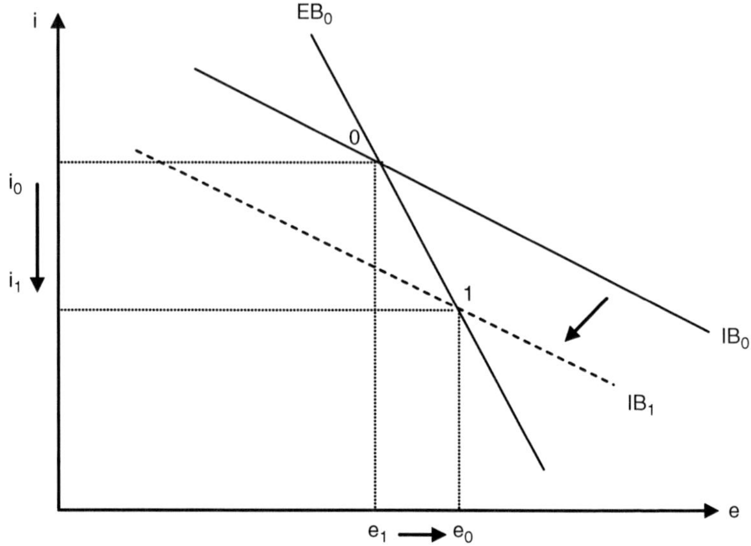

Figure 7.7 Crisis management following an adverse export shock: *case 2c*
Source: Authors.

Table 7.1 Optimal monetary and exchange rate policy mix

	Adverse risk premium shock	**Adverse export shock**
Upward sloping IB schedule	Case 1a higher interest rate (*expenditure reducing*) and real exchange rate depreciation (*expenditure switching*)	Case 2a lower interest rate (*expenditure increasing*) and real exchange rate depreciation (*expenditure switching*)
Downward sloping IB but steeper than EB	Case 1b higher interest rate (*expenditure reducing*) and real exchange rate appreciation (*financing*)	Case 2b higher interest rate (*expenditure reducing*) and real exchange rate appreciation (*financing*)
Downward sloping IB but flatter than EB	Case 1c lower interest rate (*expenditure increasing*) and real exchange rate depreciation (*expenditure switching*)	Case 2c lower interest rate (*expenditure increasing*) and real exchange rate depreciation (*expenditure switching*)

Source: Authors.

policy response is to allow the currency to depreciate, though the direction of interest rate policy is ambiguous. However, in the other two cases (i.e. Cases 1b–2b and Case 1c–2c) the crisis management policies remain unchanged.

Appropriate policy combinations could become especially complicated if one assumes that the slope of the EB schedule is generally upward sloping but then switches to being downward sloping in the event of sharp depreciations. As Figure 7.8 shows, in the event of an adverse risk premium shock, it is unclear what the optimal combination of adjustment versus financing policies would be (points 1^0 and 1^2). Indeed, there could also be circumstances where there is a nonintersection of the EB and IB schedules such that there would be no combination of policies that attain external and internal balance simultaneously (point 1^1).[38] Note that in such an event there is a need for a third instrument, such as fiscal policy (which will shift the IB schedule up), if both internal and external balance is to be regained. Intuitively, *ceteris paribus*, expansionary fiscal policy requires tighter interest rates to keep output at full employment, hence shifting the IB schedule upwards (also see Krugman 1998).

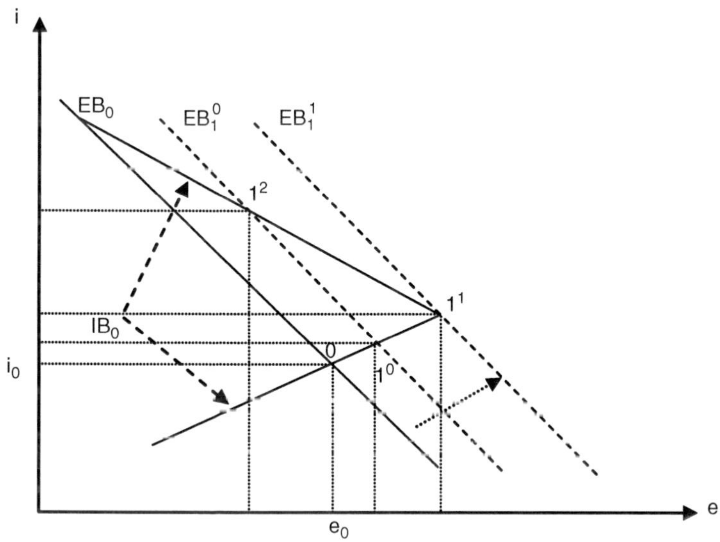

Figure 7.8 Crisis management following adverse risk premium shock: multiple equilibria case

Source: Authors.

As the preceding analysis emphasizes, the optimal combination of policies is subject to a lot of "ifs and buts" depending on the type of external shock and the exchange and interest rate elasticities of internal and external balance curves. This ambiguity nicely captures the policy debate that has been rife at the IMF and elsewhere on dealing with new-style crises.[39] For instance, consider the following description of the internal debate within various IMF departments on the appropriate monetary policy stance to deal with the crisis in Indonesia (the three departments involved were the PDR or Policy Development Review, MAE or Monetary and Exchange Affairs Department and RES or Research Department):

> The...PDR...and MAE argued for tight monetary policy with high interest rates. PDR argued that the corporate and banking sectors could not bear the added costs from any further depreciation...On the other hand,...(the research RES and APD argued against further tightening monetary policy and raising interest rates. RES was concerned that an interest rate defense was not feasible with a weak banking system and a vulnerable corporate sector. It pointed out that if confidence remained low...higher interest rates would damage the corporate and banking sectors, thereby further eroding confidence. (IMF-IEO 2003)

This example is as good a reminder as any that in most cases the appropriate answer to many a macroeconomic question is "it depends on the circumstances at hand". When determining appropriate crisis management policies, policy makers need to be cognizant of (a) the potential perverse effects of capital flows in response to interest rate changes; (b) the extent of leverage of the corporate sector (in terms of aggregate size, currency denomination and maturity structure); (c) the extent of financial sector vulnerabilities; and (d) the possible influences of exchange rate and interest rate changes on the corporate and financial sectors and their repercussions on the overall economy also see Chapter 6 of this volume.

7.6 Conclusion

The new-style currency crises that have afflicted a number of developing and emerging economies of late are characterized by sudden stops in capital inflows (flow issue) and adverse balance sheet effects (stock issue). This chapter has argued that the age-old Swan diagram, appropriately modified, is able to provide quite useful insights into how a country might manage the crisis via a combination of expenditure switching and reducing polices (adjustment) and financing.

Given the uncertainties with regard to management of new-style crisis noted above (also see Boorman and Associates 2000), it is all the more important to try to minimize the chances of such crises occurring in the first instance. While a detailed elaboration on steps to strengthen crisis prevention is well beyond the scope of this chapter (see Bird and Rajan 2002 and Rajan 2003, chapter 3), the issue of liability dollarization warrants exploring. After all, it is this factor that plays a significant role in determining the slope of the Internal Balance schedule and accordingly raises challenges and uncertainties with regard to what constitutes an optimal policy mix.

What steps need to be taken to reduce vulnerability due to uncovered foreign currency borrowing? There are two closely related questions. Why are emerging economies *unable* to borrow overseas in their own currencies, especially long term, and therefore unable to hedge, i.e. the "original sin" phenomenon (Eichengreen, Hausmann and Panizza 2003)? As Hausmann (1999) notes:

> if a country cannot borrow in its own currency, it cannot hedge the exposure to its foreign debt. To do so, foreigners would have to take a long position in pesos, and that is equivalent to assuming that the country can borrow abroad in pesos. (p. 144)[40]

Of course, there is always a price at which lenders will be willing to lend in a foreign currency, i.e. at an interest premium.[41] Insofar as the premium that is generated in emerging market interest rates reflects currency and country risk perceptions, a closely related question is: why are domestic borrowers (in the emerging economy) *unwilling* to pay that premium and instead choose to borrow in foreign currency despite the inherent riskiness of these actions? At least two possible reasons come to mind.

One, there could be an asymmetry in the risk perception of the domestic agents (potential borrowers) and foreign creditors, with the former's risk perceptions being less than the latter's. This could arise because of different information sets or the domestic agents expecting a bailout by the government in the event of an adverse shock. If this is the case, the only willing borrowers at high interest rates will be those least likely to repay the loans. This adverse selection problem in turn raises the risk premium levied by foreign lenders, which could become prohibitively high.

Two, if domestic agents in the emerging economy are concerned about the possibility of being hit by random real shocks which might affect their cash flow and thus their ability to repay the high interest, on the one hand, and if there are nontrivial costs of defaulting interest payments during downturns, on the other, rational cost-benefit calculus may lead domestic agents to opt for "cheaper" foreign currency borrowing. This point is formalized by Jeanne (2002).

How might a country overcome the original sin phenomenon short of imposing outright restrictions on foreign borrowing (quantitative or otherwise)? Returning to the reason for the risk premium required to induce foreign creditors to hold the emerging economy's currency at the margin, while part of *default* risk premium has to do with concerns about creditworthiness of the country (i.e. risk of nonpayment), part of the *currency* risk premium has to do with the lack of credibility of the monetary authorities.

The *default risk* premium could possibly be reduced if the government or international agencies (such as the World Bank) act as guarantors for at least a portion of the country's debt, though this could lead to concerns about moral hazard. With regard to the *currency risk* premium, the concern about investing in the country's currency is that there is the possibility that the monetary authority may choose to opportunistically inflate the economy / devalue the currency. Thus, the argument has recently been made that a precondition for foreigners to be willing to hold the emerging economy's assets is that they be widely held by domestic agents. The rationale is that with a wide holding of the domestic assets by domestic residents it is much less likely that the government will be tempted to erode the real value of the debt.[42] In this regard, countries should actively foster the development of well-functioning and vibrant domestic and regional bond markets, a policy recommendation that many developing countries in Asia and Latin America appear to have taken on board.

Notes

1. This chapter draws on an article originally published in *Journal of International Development*, 44 (3), 2008, 21–33 (John Wiley & Sons Limited). Reprinted with permission.
2. For a discussion of the economic consequences of sudden stops in capital inflows, see Calvo and Reinhart (2000).
3. While Hutchison and Noy (2002) opine that the coincidence of current account reversals and currency crises are due only to a curtailment in capital flows ("sudden stops"), these current account reversals may occur if there are significant domestic insolvencies, leading to a curtailment of imports, for instance.

4. Also see Mulder, Perrelli and Rocha (2002). For recent literature reviews on the first and second generation crises models, see Flood and Marion (1999), Jeanne (2000) and Rajan (2001) in the context of the Thai crisis of 1997–1998. Caves, Frankel and Jones (2003, chapter 24) describe third generation models as being moral hazard driven at the national level *a la* Dooley (2000). However, the Dooley "insurance" model is more appropriately seen as being part of the first generation family pioneered by Krugman (1979).
5. For instance, there is an interesting but rather general and wide-ranging discussion of crises in developing and emerging economies in chapter 24 of Caves, Frankel and Jones (2003). However, the authors make little attempt to relate the discussion to the analytics of the Swan diagram introduced in chapter 18 of their book. Also see Salvatore (2003, chapter 18).
6. Recent theoretical contributions in this area are by Aghion, Bacchetta and Banerjee (2000, 2003), Cespedes, Chang and Velasco (2000) and Krugman (2003), among others.
7. See Kopits (2000) for a detailed discussion of the role of fiscal policy during a crisis and Heller (1997) for a more general discussion of fiscal policy management under open capital regimes. Heller (2002) offers an overview of the IMF's perspective on "sound fiscal policy".
8. Recall that in the typical Keynesian setting—which is the implicit assumption behind the Swan diagram—prices are sticky, such that real exchange rate changes are largely due to nominal exchange rate changes (i.e. we abstract from the deflationary effects). We return to this issue later.
9. The implicit assumption here is that the country has a very limited stock of reserves. Of course, this may be one of the reasons why many countries in Asia have recently begun to stockpile reserves after having gone through the regional crisis of 1997–1998 (Aizenman and Marion 2003; IMF 2003b; and Chapters 1 and 9 of this volume and references cited within).
10. Indeed, there is evidence suggesting that sterilization *is* effective in many developing and emerging economies. For instance, see Ouyang et al. (2007) in the case of China and Chapter 1 of this volume for other emerging Asian economies.
11. In any event, as will be discussed below, the risk adjusted uncovered interest parity is never violated.
12. As Krugman (1998) notes, more effective would be a combination of large-scale official financing (which should be front-loaded), combined with roll-overs, standstills and other sorts of coordinated private sector involvement to reduce moral hazard effects (i.e. "bailing in" versus "bailing out"). We do not delve into these issues here. See for instance, Boorman and Associates (2000), IMF-IEO (2003), Roubini (2001) and Willett (2002).
13. Default can be defined generally as including partial or delayed payments. In addition, $\rho'' < 0$. Note that this is not the only type of Laffer curve mechanism in international finance. For instance, see Krugman (1989) for a discussion of the debt relief Laffer curve.
14. Two points should be noted. One, it is also possible that expected exchange rates could change, i.e. "elastic expectations of change" *a la* Charles Kindelberger (2001). Also see Montiel (2003). Ignoring the Laffer curve effects, Fama (1984) has shown that a necessary condition for there to be

a perverse relationship between i_t and e^e_{t+1} is that there is a negative correlation between risk premia and expected exchange rate changes. Two, the focus here is on risk *perceptions*. The actual impact of interest rate hikes on the real economy pertains to the EB schedule, which is explored in Section 7.4.

15. The last term in E=eq. (1) (Ω_t) denotes a wedge that might prevent risk adjusted interest arbitrage from holding perfectly. We elaborate on this at a later stage below. Suffice it to note here that the EB schedule is defined as eq. (1) *without* the wedge term.
16. Thus, any point above the EB schedule implies a nonofficial capital account surplus, while that below implies a capital account deficit. If one assumes that the current account adjustments are relatively sluggish, this corresponds to a BOP surplus and deficit, respectively.
17. Krugman (1999) has noted:

    I have heard some people propose what amounts to a sort of foreign exchange-interest rate Laffer curve: if you cut interest rates this will strengthen the economy, and the currency will actually rise. This is as silly as it sounds.
18. Equation (2) is easily derived as follows:

$$dy = \left(\frac{\partial y}{\partial e}\right)de + \left(\frac{\partial y}{\partial i}\right)di = 0.$$

19. This could arise because of menu costs or other frictions. Empirical analysis of currency crises in developing and emerging economies suggests that the impact of devaluations is deflationary rather than stagflationary, i.e. inflation does not rise following a large devaluation (for instance, see Burstein, Eichenbaum and Rebelo 2002 Goldfajn and Werlang 2000).
20. We abstract from the New Structuralist reasons as to why devaluation might be contractionary. Aghion–Bacchetta–Banerjee do not incorporate the export demand effect. Neither do they allow for the banking crisis channel.
21. Claessens, Djankov and Xu (2000) summarize available evidence on the extent of leverage of Asian corporations prior to the 1997–1998 crisis.
22. Aghion, Bacchetta and Banerjee (2003) implicitly assume that $\eta_2(\cdot) = 0$.
23. An obvious limitation of the above framework is the absence of a banking sector. Aghion, Bacchetta and Banerjee (2003) extend their original (2000) model to incorporate a competitive banking sector. Kiyotaki and Moore (1997) investigate the transmission of shocks following declines in asset prices and falls in collateral values (leading to bankruptcies and credit crunches). Also see Krugman (2003), who refers to the incorporation of asset prices and balance sheet effects as "fourth generation" crisis model.
24. Eichengreen and Arteta (2002, Table 1) succinctly summarize the principal empirical studies on banking crises. Their comprehensive empirical investigation finds rapid domestic credit growth to be one of the few robust causes of banking crises.
25. Aghion–Bacchetta–Banerjee assume that the interest rate on domestic debt is on fixed terms, thus ignoring this interest rate channel.
26. In a fuller general equilibrium model this would need to be modeled explicitly.

27. Note that $w_1 = 0$.
28. Note that $p_1 = e_0 = 1$.
29. While not discussed in this simple supply-side model, there is the possibility of the conventional Keynesian demand channel which works in the same direction.
30. Some might question why the valuation effects involve *real* rather than *nominal* depreciation. While the assumption of price rigidity makes this distinction irrelevant here, more importantly, the appropriate comparison is not nominal devaluation versus doing nothing. If a real depreciation is called for and nominal exchange rates are rigid, the result will be domestic deflation and a rise in the country's risk premium in anticipation of expected devaluation at a later stage. This in turn will raise the country's level of indebtedness even without a nominal devaluation (Cespedes, Chang and Velasco 2000).
31. For instance, Goldstein (1998) has noted:

    When market participants lose confidence in a currency and attach a high probability to further falls, it is difficult to induce them to hold the currency without higher interest rates... Moreover, halting a free fall of the currency takes on added importance when banks or corporations in the crisis country have large foreign currency obligations coming due in the short term.
32. Cespedes, Chang and Velasco (2000) present a dynamic stochastic model that allows for the default risk premium (the ρ term in eq. 1) to be endogenously determined by the net worth of the corporate sectors. One could also assume that risk premium is procyclical for various reasons. For instance, risk perceptions could rise with dimming export growth prospects. Conversely, one could assume that changes in *rp* directly influence the size of external debt ($d_t - d^c$). Either of these complicates the analysis as it implies dynamic interlinkages between the EB and IB schedules, which can no longer be seen as independent.
33. Their definition of currency crisis and output is based on Goldstein, Kaminsky and Reinhart (2000). They consider actual devaluations as well as exchange market pressure that does not lead to an actual devaluation. They measure output as deviations from a trend.
34. Two other reasons for this may be the sharp curtailment of private capital inflows during a crisis period (captured by the EB schedule), or contagion which limits the procompetitiveness effects of devaluation in any single country.
35. The authors use a number of standard definitions of crisis, including that based on Goldstein, Kaminsky and Reinhart (2000). They measure output as the difference in average growth in the crisis and the first post-crisis periods and the average growth in three pre-crisis tranquil periods.
36. The twelve events are: Thailand (July 1997), Philippines (July 1997), Indonesia (August 1997 and January 1999), Malaysia (September 1997), South Korea (November 1997), Czech Republic (February 1998), Greece (March 1998), South Africa (June 1998), Mexico (August 1998), Pakistan (August 1998), Israel (October 1998) and Brazil (January 1999).
37. Of course, as noted in Section 7.4, risk perceptions might not be entirely exogenous, e.g. they could be procyclical.

38. This could also occur if the EB and IB schedules are more or less parallel and hence do not intersect (Frankel 2001).
39. Indonesia was the worst impacted by the Asian crisis of 1997–1998, experiencing an output contraction of almost 30 percent of GDP.
40. Slavov (2003) explores the issue of hedging in emerging economies in some detail with particular reference to Asia.
41. For bank-based explanations of the persistent interest premia offered by emerging economies, see Bird and Rajan (2001).
42. Closely related to this risk-of-inflation (i.e. expropriation) argument, McLean and Shrestha (2001) have suggested that the development of a euro bond market is also a means of overcoming the original sin phenomenon. They find evidence that this was the case in Australia, New Zealand and South Africa, none of which appear to be plagued by the original sin problem. Mehl and Reynud (2005) explore the reasons behind the original sin problem and suggest it is a combination of factors including high inflation, high debt-service-to-GDP ratio, inverted slope of yield curve and, probably most pertinent for developing East Asia, narrow investor base.

References

Agenor, P. and P. Montiel (1999). *Development Macroeconomics*, Princeton: Princeton University Press.

Aghion, P., P. Bacchetta and A. Banerjee (2000). "A Simple Model of Monetary Policy and Currency Crises," *European Economic Review*, 44, 728–738.

Aghion, P., P. Bacchetta, and A. Banerjee (2003). "A Corporate Balance-Sheet Approach to Currency Crises," mimeo (April).

Aizenman, J. and N. Marion (2003). "The High Demand for International Reserves in the Far East: What is Going On?," *Journal of Japanese and International Economics*, 17, 370–400.

Allen, M., C. Rosenberg, C. Keller, B. Setser and N. Roubini (2002). "A Balance Sheet Approach to Financial Crisis," Working Paper No. 02/210, IMF.

Bansal, R. and M. Dahlquist (2000). "The Forward Premium Puzzle: Different Tales from Developed and Emerging Economies," *Journal of International Economics*, 51, 115–144.

Basuro, G. and A. Ghosh (2000). "The Interest Rate-Exchange Rate Nexus in the Asian Crisis Countries," Working Paper No. 00/19, IMF.

Bernanke, B. and M. Gertler (1989). "Agency Costs, Net Worth, and Business Fluctuations," *American Economic Review*, 79, 14–31.

Bernanke, B., M. Gertler, and S. Gilchrist (1998). "The Financial Accelerator in a Quantitative Business Cycle Framework," Working Paper No. 6455, NBER.

Bird, G. and R.S. Rajan (2001). "Banks Financial Liberalisation and Financial Crises in Emerging Markets," *The World* Economy, 24, 889–910.

Bird, G. and R.S. Rajan (2002). The Evolving Asian Financial Architecture, *Princeton Essays in International Economics No. 226*, International Economics Section, Princeton University.

Bird, G. and R.S. Rajan (2004). "Does Devaluation Lead to Economic Recovery or Economic Contraction?: Examining the Analytical Issues with Reference to Thailand," *Journal of International Development*, 16, 41–56.

Boorman, J., T. Lane, M. Schulze-Ghattas, A. Bulir, A. Ghosh, J. Hamann, A. Mourmouras, and S. Phillips (2000). "Managing Financial Crises: The Experience in East Asia," Working Paper No. 00/107, IMF.
Calvo, G. and E. Mendoza (1996). Mexico's Balance-of-Payments Crisis: A Chronicle of a Death Foretold, *Journal of International Economics*, 41, 235–264.
Calvo, G. and C. Reinhart (2000). "When Capital Inflows Come to a Sudden Stop: Consequences and Policy Options," in P. Kenen and A. Swoboda (eds), *Reforming the International Monetary and Financial System*, Washington DC: IMF.
Caves, R.J. Frankel and R. Jones (2003). *World Trade and Payments*, New Jersey Pearson Addison Wesley, 9th Edition.
Cespedes, L., R. Chang, and A. Velasco (2000). "Balance Sheets and Exchange Rates," Working Paper No. 7840, NBER.
Claessens, S., S. Djankov, and L.C. Xu (2000). "Corporate Performance in the East Asian Financial Crisis," *The World Bank Research Observer*, 15, 23–46.
Dooley, M. (2000). "A Model of Crises in Emerging Markets," *The Economic Journal*, 110, 256–272.
Dornbusch, R. (2001). "A Primer on Emerging Market Crises," Working Paper No. 8326, NBER.
Drazen, A. (2000). "Interest Rate and Borrowing Defense Against Speculative Attack," *Carnegie-Rochester Conference Series on Public Policy*, 53, 303–348.
Drazen, A. (2003). "Interest Rate Defense Against Speculative Attack as a Signal: A Primer," in M. Dooley and J. Frankel (eds), *Managing Currency Crises in Emerging Markets*, Chicago: University of Chicago.
Drazen, A. and S. Hubrich (2003). "Mixed Signals in Defending the Exchange Rate: What do the Data Say?," mimeo (June).
Eichengreen, B. and C. Arteta (2002). "Banking Crises in Emerging Markets: Presumptions and Evidence," in M. Blejer and M. Skreb (eds), *Financial Policies in Emerging Markets*, Cambridge, MA: MIT Press.
Eichengreen, B., R. Hausmann and U. Panizza (2003). "Currency Mismatches, Debt Intolerance and Original Sin: Why are They Not the Same and Why it Matters," Working Paper No. 10036, NBER.
Fama, E. (1984). "Forward and Spot Exchange Rates," *Journal of Monetary Economics*, 14, 319–338.
Flood, R. and N. Marion (1999). "Perspectives on the Recent Currency Crisis Literature," *International Journal of Finance and Economics*, 4, 1–26.
Flood, R. and O. Jeanne (2000). "An Interest Rate Defense of a Fixed Exchange Rate," Working Paper No. 00/159, IMF.
Forbes, K. (2002). "How do Large Depreciations Affect Firm Performance", *IMF Staff Papers*, 49, 214–238.
Frankel, J. (1999). No Single Currency Regime is Right for All Countries or at All Times, *Princeton Essays in International Economics No. 215*, International Economic Section, Princeton University.
Frankel, J. (2001). "Coping with Crises in Emerging Markets: Adjustment Versus Financing," in P. Kenen and A. Swoboda (eds), *Key Issues in Reform of the International Monetary System*, Washington, DC: International Monetary Fund.
Goldfajn, I. and S. Werlang (2000). "The Pass-through from Depreciation to Inflation: A Panel Study," mimeo (April).

Goldstein, M. (1998). *The Asian Financial Crisis: Causes, Cures, and Systemic Implications*, Washington, DC: IMF.

Goldstein, M., G. Kaminsky, and C. Reinhart (2000). *Assessing Financial Vulnerability: An Early Warning System for Emerging Markets*, Washington, DC: Institute of International Economics.

Gupta, P., D. Mishra, and R. Sahay (2003). "Output Response to Currency Crises," IMF Working Paper No. 03/230, IMF.

Hausmann, R. (1999). "Discussion," in *Capital Flows and the International Financial System*, Sydney: Reserve Bank of Australia.

Heller, P. (1997). "Fiscal Policy Management in an Open Capital Regime," Working Paper No. 97/20, IMF.

Heller, P. (2002). "Considering the IMF's Perspective on a 'Sound Fiscal Policy'," Policy Discussion Paper No. 02/8, IMF.

Hutchison, M. and I. Noy (2002). "Sudden Stops and the Mexican Wave: Currency Crises, Capital Flow Reversals and Output Loss in Emerging Markets," Pacific Basin Working Paper Series No. 02–03, Federal Reserve Bank of San Francisco.

International Monetary Fund (IMF) (2003a). The Balance Sheet Approach and its Applications at the Fund, prepared by the Policy Development and Review Department (June 30).

International Monetary Fund (IMF) (2003b). *World Economic Outlook 2003*, Washington, DC: IMF (September).

IMF-Independent Evaluation Office (IEO) (2003). *The IMF and Recent Capital Account Crises: Indonesia, Korea, Brazil*, Washington, DC: IMF.

Jeanne, O. (2000). "Currency Crises: A Perspective on Recent Theoretical Developments," *Princeton Special Papers in International Economics No. 20*, International Economics Section, Princeton University.

Jeanne, O. (2002). "Why Do Emerging Markets Borrow in Foreign Currency?," mimeo (November).

Kindelberger, C. (2001). *Manias, Panics, and Crashes: A History of Financial Crises*, Wiley Investment Classics.

Kiyotaki, N. and J. Moore (1997). "Credit Cycles," *Journal of Political Economy*, 105, 211–248.

Kopits, G. (2000). "How Can Fiscal Policy Help Avert Currency Crises," Working Paper No. 00/185, IMF.

Krugman, P. (1979). "A Model of Balance of Payments Crises," *Journal of Money, Credit and Banking*, 11, 311–325.

Krugman, P. (1989). "Market-based Debt Reduction Schemes and Welfare," in J. Frenkel, M. Dooley and P. Wickam (eds), *Analytical Issues in Debt*, Washington, DC: IMF.

Krugman, P. (1998). "Latin America's Swan Song," mimeo (undated).

Krugman, P. (1999). "Will Asia Bounce Back?," in. R. Sato, R. Ramachandran and K. Mino (eds), *Global Competition and Integration*, Boston: Kluwer Publishers.

Krugman, P. (2003). "Crises: The Next Generation," in E. Helpman and E. Sadka (eds), *Economic Policy in the International Economy: Essays in Honor of Assaf Razin*, Cambridge, UK: Cambridge University Press.

Lahiri, A. and C. Vegh (2001). "Living with the Fear of Floating: An Optimal Policy Perspective," Working Paper No. 8391, NBER.

Lizondo, S. and P. Montiel (1989). "Contractionary Devaluation in Developing Countries," *IMF Staff Papers*, 36, 182–227.
McLean, B. and S. Shrestha (2001). "International Borrowing in Domestic Currency: What Does it Take?," Reserve Bank of Australia, mimeo (January)
Mehl, A. and J. Reynud (2005). "The Determinants of 'Domestic' Original Sin in Emerging Market Economies," Working Paper No. 560, European Central Bank.
Montiel, P. (2003). "Tight Money in a Post-crisis Defense of the Exchange Rate: What Have We Learned?," *The World Bank Research Observer*, 18, 1–23.
Mulder, C., R. Perrelli, and M. Rocha (2002). "The Role of Corporate, Legal and Macroeconomic Balance Sheet Indicators in Crisis Detection and Prevention," Working Paper No. 02/59, IMF.
Ouyang, A.Y., R.S. Rajan, and T.D. Willett (2007). "China as a Reserve Sink: The Evidence from Offset and Sterilization Coefficients," Working Paper No. 10/2007, Hong Kong Institute for Monetary Research.
Rajan, R.S. (2001). "(Ir)relevance of Currency-Crisis Theory to the Devaluation and Collapse of the Thai Baht," *Princeton Studies in International Economics No. 88*, International Economics Section, Princeton University.
Rajan, R.S. (2002). "Exchange Rate Policy Options for Post-crisis Southeast Asia: Is There a Case for Currency Baskets?," *The World Economy*, 25, 137–163.
Rajan, R.S. (2003). *Economic Globalization and Asia: Essays on Finance, Trade and Taxation*, Singapore: World Scientific Publishing.
Roubini, N. (2001). "Bail-ins, Bailouts, Burden Sharing and Private Sector Involvement in Crisis Resolution: The G-7 Framework and Some Suggestions on the Open Unresolved Issues," mimeo (July).
Salvatore, D. (2003). *International Economics*, Wiley Publishers, 8th Edition.
Slavov, S. (2003). "But Can't they Hedge??? Managing Foreign Exchange Risk under 'Original Sin'," Working Paper No. 177, CREDPR, Stanford University.
Stone, M. and M. Weeks (2001). "Systemic Financial Crises, Balance Sheets, and Model Uncertainty," Working Paper No. 01/162, IMF.
Taylor, L. (1981). "IS/LM in the Tropics: Diagrammatics of the New Structuralist Macro Critique," in W. Cline and S. Weintraub (eds), *Economic Stabilization in Developing Countries*, Washington, DC: The Brookings Institution.
Willett, T.D (2002). "Why is there So Much Disagreement about the IMF and Reform of the International Financial Architecture?," mimeo (August).

8

Can High Reserves Offset Weak Fundamentals?[1]

(Co-authored with Jie Li)

8.1 Introduction

An important element of the ongoing global macroeconomic imbalances is the large and growing stockpile of international reserves by Asian economies. To be sure, between end 1990 and 2004 international reserves (excluding gold) in Asia rose from US$ 400 billion to US$ 2,600 billion (Figure 8.1; also see Chapters 1 and 9 of this volume).[2] Part of the motivation for the reserve accumulation may derive from a deep-rooted mercantilist desire by Asian governments to maintain undervalued exchange rates and bolster domestic employment, as well as a general reluctance to forsake hard or soft US dollar pegged regimes (Cavoli and Rajan 2009, chapter 1).[3] Apart from these exchange rate objectives, which have resulted in rapid reserve accumulation as a side effect, Asian countries have chosen explicitly to build up reserves for precautionary or insurance motives (Bird and Rajan 2003). For instance, Aizenman and Marion (2003) have noted that the "behavior has changed since the Asian financial crisis," and go on to suggest that the "recent build-up of large international reserve holdings in a number of Asian emerging markets may represent precautionary holdings" (p. 11).

Precautionary motives for accumulating reserves encompass both crisis management and crisis prevention. The former refers to the role of reserves in reducing the extent of exchange rate (and output) adjustment if a crisis does happen. This in turn could refer to the ability to either (a) finance underlying payments imbalances or (b) provide liquidity in the face of runs on the currency. Crisis prevention refers broadly to a reduction in the incidence of a crisis. The argument here is simply that, other things equal, high reserves may be viewed as a sign of strength of an economy, thus reducing the chances of a run against the currency. Indeed, many studies have confirmed that

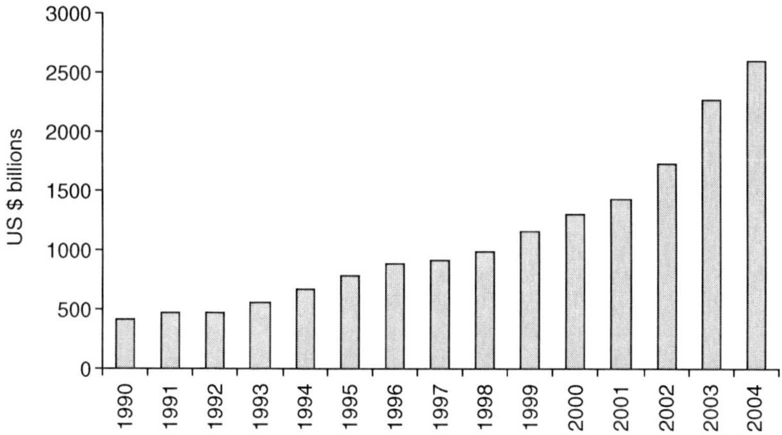

Figure 8.1 International reserves in Asia, 1990–2004
Source: Based on data from International Financial Statistics.

high reserves to short term debt or money supply ratios have consistently stood out as being robust predictors of a crisis (Bird and Rajan 2003; De Beaufort Wijnholds and Kapteyn 2001 and Willett et al. 2004). Some have even suggested that sufficiently high levels of reserves can fully offset weak fundamentals (Sachs et al. 1996). Counterbalancing these precautionary motives for holding reserves are their high opportunity costs, which arise from substituting high yielding domestic assets for lower yielding foreign ones. These costs can be proxied as the difference between the domestic marginal product of capital and the returns obtained on the reserve assets (usually US Treasuries).[4]

This chapter has a rather modest objective. It attempts to develop a simple optimizing model to determine the optimal reserve holdings by a country looking to minimize the net costs of holding reserves. In so doing the chapter also attempts to determine the validity of the Sachs et al. (1996) assertion that sufficiently high levels of reserves can compensate for weak fundamentals.

The remainder of this chapter is organized as follows. The next section outlines the basic structure of the model and solution. Section 8.3 discusses the nexus between weak fundamentals and optimal reserve size. Section 8.4 offers some concluding observations.

8.2 The model

8.2.1 Basic structure and assumptions

The basic model structure is fairly simple and intuitive. We assume a risk averse central bank's aim is to minimize the expected total costs to the economy from holding international reserves (*R*), which is its choice variable.[5]

As noted, the major precautionary benefits from holding reserves are twofold. One, a stockpile of reserves may reduce the probability of a crisis occurring in the first instance, i.e. crisis prevention role. Two, reserves help reduce the adjustment costs if a crisis does occur, i.e. crisis management role.

In other words:

$$TC = PC_C + RC_R \tag{1}$$

TC: expected total costs.
R: level of international reserves.
C_C: unit cost associated with the crisis, measured as the output loss, viz. the difference of the output levels between normal times and crises.
C_R: unit opportunity cost of holding reserves. We assume this to be constant.
P: probability of crises which is a function of *R* as well as a vector of weak fundamentals (*X*). In addition, $P_X > 0$ and $P_R < 0$.

The output loss (C_C) is assumed to be the difference of the output levels between normal times and crisis.

$$C_C = Y_N - Y_C \tag{2}$$

Y_N: the output level in normal times; and Y_C: the output level in crisis times.

We assume, for simplicity, that the only input of production is capital (*K*):

$$Y = F(K) \tag{3}$$

where: $\frac{\partial F}{\partial K} > 0, \quad \frac{\partial^2 F}{\partial K^2} < 0$.

We need to make explicit the costs of a crisis. Assume that during normal times $K = \bar{K}$. To maintain a degree of generality, we assume that a crisis—bad state of nature—acts as a negative supply shock in the sense that either the extent of capital stock deteriorates or the average productivity of capital declines (A).[6] However, for a given crisis, the bad state of nature is inversely related to the amount of reserves. In other words, the higher the stock of reserves, the lower the extent of impact of the bad state of nature. So:

$$K = \begin{cases} \bar{K}, & \text{in normal times} \\ A(R)\bar{K}, & \text{in crises} \end{cases} \tag{4}$$

where, $0 < A(R) < 1$ and $A(R) > 0$.[7]

Plugging eqs. (3) and (4) into (2), we can express the output loss as a function of reserves:

$$C_C = Y_N - Y_C = F(\bar{K}) - F[A(R)\bar{K}] \tag{5}$$

From eq. (5) we have:

$$\frac{\partial C_C}{\partial R} = -F'[A(R)\bar{K}] * \bar{K} * \frac{\partial A}{\partial R} < 0. \tag{6}$$

Equation (6) reveals a negative relationship between the reserve holding and output loss during a crisis.

8.2.2 Model solution

The central bank minimizes the loss function (eq. 1) so as to choose the optimal reserve. The first order condition of this minimization problem is:

$$\frac{\partial P}{\partial R} * C_C + \frac{\partial C_C}{\partial R} * P + C_R = 0. \tag{7}$$

For concreteness, we make use of some specific functional forms. Let the probability function of crisis be:

$$\begin{aligned} P &= P(X;R) \\ &= \exp[-R/X]. \end{aligned} \tag{8}$$

Following Sachs et al. (1996), X usually consists of at least four variables, viz. current account deficit (CAD), lending boom (LB), real exchange rate appreciation (RER), and the size of external debt (STD).[8] The probability function reveals that with the accumulation of higher levels of reserves (R) the probability of crisis will converge to 0. If the level of reserves is close to 0, the probability of crisis will increase, peaking at 1. Meanwhile, if the weak fundamentals (X) are close to 0, the probability of crisis will decrease to 1; and if the weak fundamentals (X) are significantly high, the probability of a crisis will increase to 1.

From eq. 8 we have:

$$\frac{\partial P}{\partial R}=\left(-\frac{1}{X}\right)\left[\exp\left(-\frac{R}{X}\right)\right]=-\frac{P}{X} \tag{9}$$

Plugging eq. 9 into eq. 7 and solving for P derives:

$$P=\frac{C_R}{((C_C/X)-\lambda)}, \quad \text{while } \lambda=\frac{\partial C_C}{\partial R} \tag{10}$$

From eqs 7 and 10 we have:

$$\exp\left(-\frac{R}{X}\right)=\frac{C_R}{((C_C/X)-\lambda)} \tag{10'}$$

In order to solve for R^*, assume

$Y = K^a$ and $A(R) = 1 - \text{expt}(-R)$

Note that when $R \rightarrow 0$, $A(R) = [1 - \text{expt}(-R)] \rightarrow 0$; when $R \rightarrow \infty$, $A(R) \rightarrow 1$.

$$C_c = Y_N - Y_C = F(\bar{K}) - F[A(R)\bar{K}] = \bar{K}^a[1 - (1 - e^{-R})^a] \tag{11}$$

$$\lambda=\frac{\partial C_C}{\partial R}=-a\bar{K}^a e^{-R}(1-e^{-R})^{a-1} \tag{12}$$

Plugging eqs 11 and 12 into eq. 10 and rearranging derives:

$$\frac{e^{-R/X}\bar{K}^a[1-(1-e^{-R})^a]}{X}+a\bar{K}^a e^{-R-(R/X)}(1-e^{-R})^{a-1}=C_R \tag{13}$$

The left hand side of eq. 13 can be interpreted as the marginal benefit of holding reserves, while the right hand side is the marginal cost of reserves. In other words, an optimizing central bank will continue to build up reserves as long as the marginal benefits of so doing exceed the marginal costs (opportunity costs). While this result is intuitive, the contribution of the simple model is to flesh out the factors that impact the marginal benefits which in turn allow us to analyze the nexus between weak fundamentals and reserve holdings. We elaborate on this issue in the next section.

8.3 Findings and implications

While the right hand side of eq. 13 is assumed constant, the left hand side is decreasing in R.[9] Given this, we have the following proposition: *the sufficient condition for the existence of R* is* $X \leq (\bar{K}^a/C_R)$. Why?

We can set the domain of the left hand side as $[0, \infty)$. If we set the initial R as 0, then, the output loss $C_C = \bar{K}^a$, and the marginal output loss, $\lambda = 0$. Thus, the left hand side of eq. 13 is reduced to $(\bar{K}^a/X)$. Therefore, the condition that $X \leq (\bar{K}^a/C_R)$ can ensure there is at least one level of R such that the left hand side is greater than or equal to the right hand side of eq. 13.

The proposition can be reinterpreted as follows. If the fundamentals (X) are sufficiently weak or the opportunity costs of holding reserves are sufficiently high, such that $X > (\bar{K}^a/C_R)$, there may not be any interior solution to R*. In other words, for extremely weak fundamentals no amount of reserves can help prevent a crisis from occurring (Figure 8.2).

For the case where $X < (\bar{K}^a/C_R)$, there is an interior solution for R*. Worsening fundamentals (i.e. rising X) will lead to higher probability of crisis. This in turn increases the marginal benefit of reserve holdings at any given reserve level. Therefore, the MB schedule will shift up from R* to R** (see Figure 8.3).[10] So generally, as fundamentals get

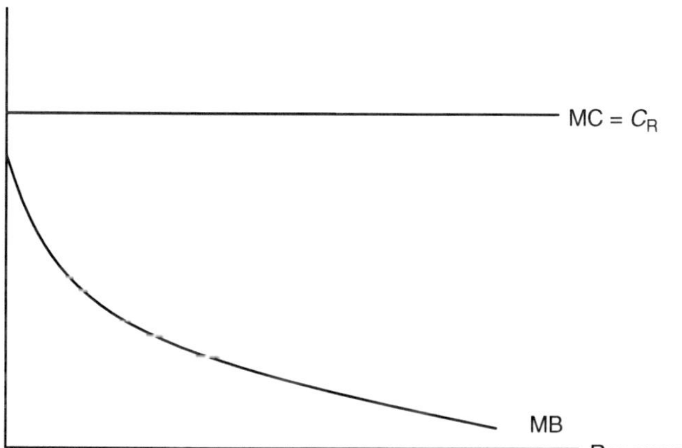

Figure 8.2 Reserves insufficient to offset weak fundamentals
Source: Authors.

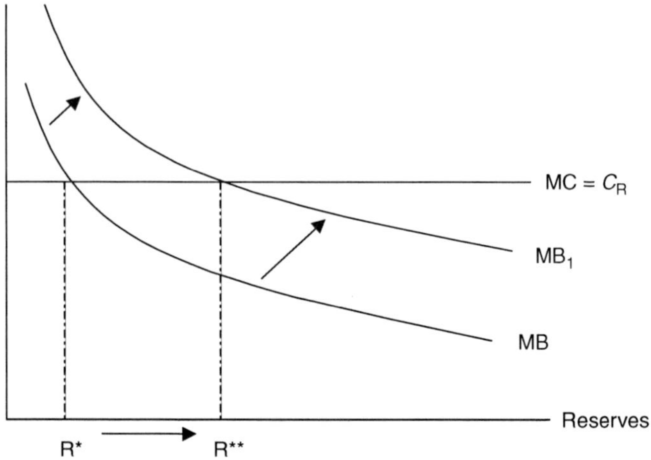

Figure 8.3 Worsening fundamentals compensated for by higher reserves

Source: Authors.

weaker, countries need to hold correspondingly more reserves, and high reserves can offset weak fundamentals only if the fundamentals are not "too weak."

8.4 Conclusion

This chapter has explored the issue of optimal reserve holdings by a central bank within a context of a simple analytical model. An important limitation of the model arises from the assumption of a constant opportunity cost of reserves. More realistically, insofar as these costs can be proxied as the opportunity cost, it is important to consider the impact of changes in the capital stock and production on the marginal costs of reserve holdings. This notwithstanding, the model suggests that, in general, high reserves can help offset weak fundamentals. However, if fundamentals are sufficiently weak no level of reserves will be able to offset the weak fundamentals. In other words, for "hopelessly weak" fundamentals, a crisis is inevitable and reserves cannot act as a substitute for domestic policy reforms and adjustments.[11] Conversely, if fundamentals are "sufficiently strong", a crisis will never occur. However, if fundamentals are within a certain range—zone of vulnerability—other things equal, higher levels of reserves may help offset the negative impact of weak fundamentals. With fundamentals in the vulnerable zone, high reserves could have a powerful effect in protecting against crises. This also suggests that reserve needs should be related to the state of fundamentals in a nonlinear manner. While this may contradict the conclusion of Sachs et al. (1996), it is broadly in line with the critique by Willett et al. (2004), and is also consistent with the escape clause based second-generation models of currency crisis (Obstfeld 1986, 1994 and Rajan 2001).

We return to the issue of reserve stockpiling in Asia. The fact that a number of Asian countries are consciously looking to use part of their accumulated reserves to finance physical infrastructure (e.g. India and Thailand) or strengthen their financial institutions (e.g. Korea and China) seems to indicate that they have reached a level at which their perceived marginal benefits have been outweighed by their marginal costs. This in turn suggests that the recent buildup of reserves in Asia has been due more to exchange rate motivations (i.e. mercantilism or general commitment to pegged regimes which are undervalued) than to a conscious attempt to buy "insurance cover".

Annex 8.1

This Annex derives the conditions under which the Marginal benefit (*MB*) curve rises with *X*.[12] Taking the first derivative of the left hand side of eq. 13 w.r.t. *X* derives:

$$MB = e^{-R/X}\left\{\frac{\bar{K}^a[1-(1-e^{-R})^a]}{X} + a\bar{K}^a e^{-R}(1-e^{-R})^{a-1}\right\}$$

To simplify the notations, let $y = \bar{K}^a[1 - (1 - e^{-R})^a$ and $z = a\bar{K}^a e^{-R}(1 - e^{-R})^{a-1}$

$$\frac{\partial MB}{\partial X} = \frac{Re^{-R/X}}{X^2}\left(\frac{y}{X} + z\right) - e^{-R/X}\left(\frac{y}{X^2}\right)$$

$$= e^{-R/X}\left(\frac{Ry}{X^3} + \frac{Rz}{X^2}\right) - e^{-R/X}\left(\frac{y}{X^2}\right)$$

$$= e^{-R/X}\left(\frac{yR + XRz - yX}{X^3}\right)$$

$$= e^{-R/X}\left[\frac{y(R-X)}{X^3} + \frac{Rz}{X^2}\right]$$

If $R > (yX/(y + Xz))$, then, $y(R - X) + XRz > 0$, and $(\partial MB/\partial X) > 0$.

Notes

1. This chapter draws on an article originally published in *Economia Internazionale*, 59 (3), 2006, 317–332 (Camera di Commercio Genova). Reprinted with permission.
2. Asia's share of global reserves correspondingly rose from about 40 percent in 1990 to 65 percent by 2004.
3. This aside, it is also possible that countries that have loosened their pegged regimes still choose to hold high reserve levels as they are viewed as a sign of creditworthiness, hence reducing the degree of exchange rate volatility. Some evidence of this thesis is offered by Hviding et al. (2004).
4. Two caveats are in order. One, it is sometimes noted that reserves could be used to pay down external debt. The difference between the interest rate paid on the external debt and that earned on reserve assets could be a proxy for opportunity cost of holding reserves. Two, another set of costs of persistent reserve accumulation arises due to the inflationary consequences of excess liquidity and/or the costs of mopping up the liquidity, i.e. sterilization (for instance, see Kletzer and Spiegel 2004).
5. For an early cost-benefit analysis on the issue of optimal reserves, see Ben-Bassatand Gottlieb (1992).
6. Alternatively, one could define a crisis as something that reduces the extent of capital reversal (Kim et al. 2005).
7. If we interpret the shock in terms of capital reversals (*CR*), viz. the difference of capital flows in crisis and previous inflows, then $CR = K_C - \bar{K} = [A(R) - 1]\bar{K}$.
8. For instance, $X = \alpha\text{CAD} + \beta\text{LB} + \gamma\text{RER} + \eta\text{STD}$. However, in view of the possible tradeoffs between the various variables, there is not yet a clear indication of the best way of interacting them to come up with a suitable vector of weak fundamentals (Willett et al. 2004).
9. Taking the partial derivative w.r.t. *R* we see that the more *R* rises, the lower are $(e^{-R/X}\bar{K}^a/X)$, $[1 - (1 - e^{-R})^a]$, $e\bar{K}^a e^{-R-(R/X)}$, and $(1 - e^{-R})^{a-1}$. All these terms are positive. Therefore, with the increase of *R*, all the terms on the left hand side of eq. 13 decrease. In other words, the left hand side is a decreasing function of *R*.
10. Annex 1 derives the specific conditions under which the *MB* curve rises with *X*.
11. Indeed, first generation crisis models imply that if fundamentals are sufficiently weak that a crisis is inevitable, reserve levels should only influence the timing of crises, not whether they occur.
12. While not shown here, the impact of a change of X on the slope of the MB curve (i.e. $\partial(\partial MB/\partial R)/\partial X$) is ambiguous.

References

Aizenman, J. and N. Marion (2003). "The High Demand for International Reserves in the Far East: What's Going On?," *Journal of Japanese and International Economics*, 17, 370–400.

Ben-Bassat, A. and D. Gottlieb (1992). "Optimal International Reserves and Sovereign Risk," *Journal of International Economics*, 33, 345–362.

Bird, G. and R.S. Rajan (2003). "Adequacy of Reserves in the Aftermath of Crises," *The World Economy*, 26, 873–891.

de Beaufort Wijnholds, J.O. and A. Kapteyn (2001). "Reserve Adequacy in Emerging Market Economics," Working Paper No. WP/01/143, IMF.

Cavoli, T. and R.S. Rajan (2008). *Exchange Rate Regimes and Macroeconomic Management in Asia*, Hong Kong: Hong Kong University Press, forthcoming.

Hviding, K., M. Nowak, and L. Antonio Ricci (2004). "Can Higher Reserves Help Reduce Exchange Rate Volatility?: An Empirical Investigation," mimeo (IMF).

Kim, J.S., J. Li, O. Sula, R.S. Rajan, and T.D. Willett (2005). "Reserve Adequacy in Asia Revisited: New Benchmarks Based on the Size and Composition of Capital Flows," Conference Proceedings, in *Monetary and Exchange Rate Arrangement in East Asia*, Seoul: Korea Institute for Economic Policy.

Kletzer, K. and M. Spiegel (2004). "Sterilization Costs and Exchange Rate Targeting," *Journal of International Money and Finance*, 23, 897–915.

Obstfeld, M. (1986). "Rational and Self-fulfilling Balance of Payments," *American Economic Review*, 76, 72–81.

Obstfeld, M. (1994). "The Logic of Currency Crises," *Cahiers Économiques et Monetaries*, 43, 189–213.

Rajan, R.S. (2001). "(Ir)relevance of Currency-Crisis Theory to the Devaluation and Collapse of the Thai Baht," *Princeton Studies in International Economics 88*, International Economics Section, Princeton University.

Sachs, J., A. Tornell, and A.Velasco (1996). "Financial Crises in Emerging Markets: the Lessons from 1995," *Brookings Papers on Economic Activity*, 1, Brookings Institution, 147–215.

Willett, T.D., E. Nitithanprapas, I. Nitithanprapas, and S. Rongala (2004). "The Asian Crises Reexamined," *Asian Economic Papers*, 3, 32–87.

Part III

Monetary and Financial Cooperation in Asia

9

Examining the Case for an Asian Reserve Pool[1]

(Co-authored with Reza Siregar, Graham Bird)

9.1 Introduction

There are at least two important dimensions to the current macroeconomic imbalances plaguing the global economy. First is the rapid stockpiling of reserves by a number of Asian economies since the late 1990s. While Japan and China together account for about half of Asia's reserve holdings (which stood at well over US$ 2,000 billion), South Korea, Taiwan, Hong Kong, India and Singapore each also hold over US$ 100 billion of reserves (Kim et al. 2005). Second is the issue of the sustainability of the US current account deficit and its resulting implications for the US dollar (Bernanke 2005).

There is, in fact, a school of thought that argues that the global macroeconomic situation—whereby the US current account deficit is partly financed by the reserves accumulated by Asian countries which have maintained undervalued exchange rates—is a perfectly normal state of affairs (for instance, see Dooley et al. 2003, 2004a,b). Proponents of such a view point to the Bretton Woods system of fixed exchange rates that was initiated in 1944 with an agreement between the war-ravaged Western European countries and the US that the latter would keep its borders open for exports from the former. Thus, while the US acted as the "importer of last resort," the Western European countries pegged their respective currencies at undervalued levels to the US dollar to remain cost-competitive. The currency undervaluation and resulting foreign exchange market intervention allowed Western Europe to acquire reserves which were in turn used to finance the US current account deficit at a low cost. There was no immediate or obvious pressure on the US to check its excessive spending. This system of global fixed exchange rates pegged to the US dollar lasted until 1973.

This US–Western Europe axis between 1944 and 1973 (with Japan joining in the 1960s) seems to bear an uncanny resemblance to the current relationship between the US and vendor financing by Asia, leading some to suggest that a New Bretton Woods system has emerged since the 1990s. Proponents of this point of view argue that the current arrangement of international settlements ought to be able to persist for a long time to come, as many developing Asian countries (China in particular, but also others in Southeast Asia, India and Korea) are attempting to grow rapidly by exporting to the US by maintaining an undervalued currency. The Asian central banks are in turn perfectly happy to hold US sovereign paper as a necessary condition to sustain the export led growth.

According to proponents of this view, Asia will not stop financing the US on a large scale as that will lead to a marked rise in US long-term interest rates, which in turn might trigger a collapse in the US property and equity prices and a concomitant fall in US consumer spending on all goods and services, including those from Asia. According to this logic, the current global macroeconomic imbalances are structural and inherently stable; fears of global instability are grossly overstated.[2]

While the suggestion that a New Bretton Woods system has emerged is rather intriguing, it runs into some major problems when matched against the facts (also see Eichengreen 2004). The rapid buildup in reserves in Asia began in earnest only after the Asian crisis of 1997–1998 and escalated from 2000 onwards largely because of capital account surpluses (as foreign investors have been anticipating Asian currency revaluations and resulting capital gains). Pre-1997 many developing countries in Asia actually ran current account deficits. The conventional wisdom then was that Asian economies were growing and industrializing rapidly and needed high levels of foreign capital to spur their development, and the current account deficits would eventually be self-correcting. This was, after all, the experience of a number of other developed countries in Asia, such as Singapore.

Thus, unless there has been a significant and conscious change in the growth strategies in Asia post-crisis, one would be hard pressed to argue that the ongoing imbalances are part of some sort of grand bargain or implicit global understanding which can persist *ad infinitum*. More likely, at least in the case of Southeast Asia and Korea, the current account adjustments (from deficit to surplus) were forced on the region by the crisis and it has persisted partly because domestic demand—investment demand in particular—has not fully recovered from the shock of 1997–1998. As such, while many Southeast Asian countries continue to be high savers, they no longer maintain investment rates as high as they used to be in the 1980s and 1990s. The resulting surpluses in the private sector financial balances in Asia have in turn been recycled to the US to finance that country's national dissavings.

In addition, while the official sector dominated capital flows in the pre-1970s period, international private portfolio flows are much more significant nowadays. Thus, even if there were some grand Bretton Woods-type bargain between the US and Asian central banks, there is no reason to expect the private sector's assessment of the relative attractiveness of US assets to be influenced by any such global understanding among national governments.

Having argued against the New Bretton Woods thesis, this chapter focuses on one aspect of the global macroeconomic imbalance, viz. reserve management in Asia. While others have discussed the mercantilist rationale and consequences of such reserve stockpiling (for instance, see Rajan 2004), this chapter focuses on the precautionary demand for reserves in Asia in the broader context of monetary cooperation in East Asia.[3] Section 9.2 briefly reviews the factors that go into the determination of "optimal reserves" in general, and specifically in the case of East Asia. Section 9.3 investigates the gains, if any, to be reaped if East Asian economies were to pool their reserves. Section 9.4 concludes with a summary and brief discussion of how the proposed reserve pool would fit into the larger context of evolving East Asian monetary regionalism.[4]

9.2 Cost-benefit calculus determining optimal reserve holdings

9.2.1 Some analytical background

Reserves are held because they act as a buffer against a balance of payments (bop) shock. Owned reserves represent a guaranteed and an unconditional source of liquidity. However, there is a significant opportunity cost of stockpiling reserves as the country effectively swaps high yielding domestic assets for lower yielding foreign ones.[5] We briefly outline below a simple theory of the demand for international reserves based on a cost-benefit calculus (Bird 1978).

The bottom-right quadrant of Figure 9.1 illustrates a negative relationship between the quantity of reserves held and the speed of adjustment. In other words, the fewer reserves held, the faster the speed of adjustment needed to adjust to a balance of payments shock. The bottom-left quadrant illustrates a positive association between the

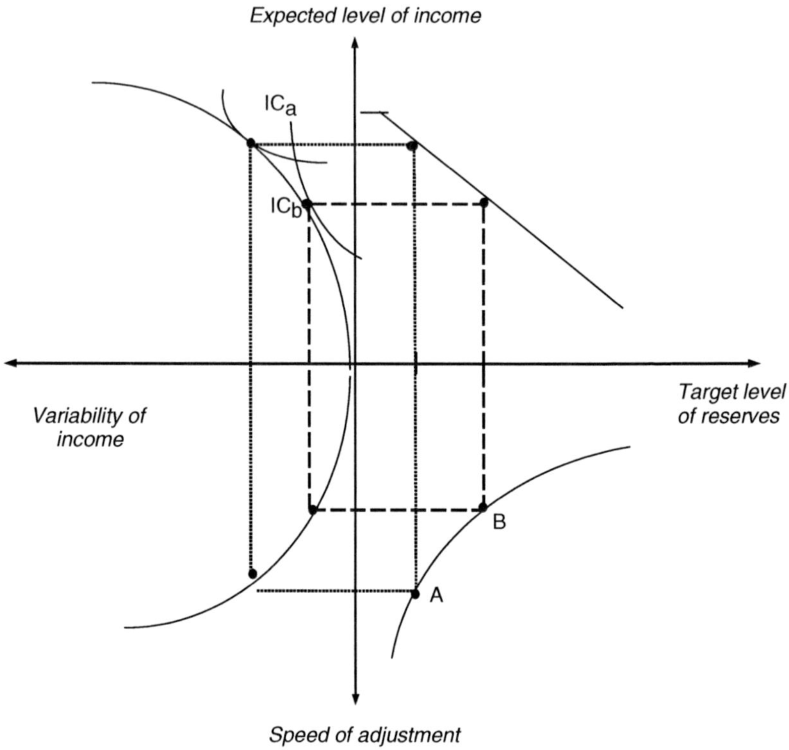

Figure 9.1 Determining the optimal reserve holdings
Source: Adapted from Clark (1970).

speed of adjustment to a BOP shock and the variability of income. The quicker is adjustment, the more variable is income. The top-left quadrant reveals a negative nexus between (expected) income levels and the quantity of reserves held. This essentially represents the opportunity costs of holding reserves, i.e. the larger the reserves held, the lower the amount of capital investment that may be undertaken.[6] Putting these three quadrants together derives the top-right quadrant, which shows a positive association between expected income levels and the variability of income. Thus, other things equal, the greater the demand for reserves, the slower the speed of adjustment and the lower the variability of income, though this benefit comes at a cost of lower income levels. The demand for reserves will be determined at the point of tangency between the central bank's indifference curve (IC_A) and the curve showing the trade-off between expected income and variability of income (point A).

The preceding framework can be thought of as a generalization and graphical representation of the buffer stock model developed by Frenkel and Jovanovic (1981). Under certain assumptions, Frenkel–Jovanovic derives the optimal reserve holdings to be as follows:

$$R_0 = (c\sigma/r^{0.5})^{1/2} \tag{1}$$

where R_0 = desired reserves; c = country-specific nominal constant; σ = standard deviation of reserve movements; and r = opportunity cost of holding reserves. Equation 1 reveals desired reserve holdings to be a positive function of volatility and a negative function of the opportunity costs of maintaining reserves.

9.2.2 Reserve holdings in East Asia: are they optimal?

While Flood and Marion (2001) discuss how the Frenkel–Jovanovic model has performed empirically and proceed to outline useful theoretical and empirical extensions to it, Aizenman and Marion (2003) have recently estimated the following generalized reserve equation using a panel of 122 developing countries over the period 1980–1996:

$$\begin{aligned} \ln(R_{it}/P_{it}) = {} & \alpha_0 + \alpha_1\ln(pop_{it}) + \alpha_2\ln(gpc_{it}) + \alpha_3\ln(exa_{it}) \\ & + \alpha_4\ln(imy_{it}) + \alpha_5\ln(neer_{it}) + \varepsilon_t \end{aligned} \tag{2}$$

where: R is actual holdings of reserves minus gold (millions of US$ deflated by the US GDP deflator, P); *pop* is the total population of the country; *gpc* is real GDP per capita; *exa* is the volatility of real export receipts; *imy* is the share of imports of goods and services in GDP; and *neer* is the volatility of the nominal effective exchange rate.

The authors explain the choice of dependent variables as follows:

> Real reserve holdings should increase with the size of international transactions, so we would expect reserve holdings to be positively correlated with the country's population and standard of living. Reserve holdings should increase with the volatility of international receipts and payments if they are intended to help cushion the economy, so we would expect reserve holdings to be positively correlated with the volatility of a country's export receipts. Reserve holdings should also increase with the vulnerability to external shocks. We

> therefore expect reserve holdings to be positively correlated with the average propensity to import, a measure of the economy's openness and vulnerability to external shocks. Finally, since greater exchange-rate flexibility should reduce the demand for reserves because central banks no longer need a large reserve stockpile to manage a fixed exchange rate, reserve holdings should be negatively correlated with exchange-rate volatility. (p. 6)

In the case of East Asia, in-sample results largely confirm the authors' priors. Indeed, if anything, the estimated reserve equations systematically *overpredicted* reserve holdings (between one and two standard deviations from the average). This would be expected *a priori* as their estimating equation excludes any measure of the opportunity cost of holding reserves.[7] However, out-of-sample results for the crisis period in East Asia in 1997–1999 reveal a systematic *underprediction* of reserves in most of the East Asian countries (except Malaysia). Incorporating political variables does not alter these conclusions. Thus, the authors conclude that "behavior has changed since the Asian financial crisis," and go on to suggest that the "recent build-up of large international reserve holdings in a number of Asian emerging markets may represent precautionary holdings" (p. 11). In terms of the general framework outlined in Section 9.2.1, this implies that the more risk averse a country's monetary authorities, the steeper is its indifference curve, and therefore the greater the desired reserve holdings (Point B in Figure 9.1).[8]

Stockpiling reserves by the East Asian economies implies more generally that, at the margin, the benefits of extra reserves are perceived as exceeding the costs. There may be a political premium placed on avoiding future crises and retaining the option of a slower speed of adjustment should the balance of payments position weaken and external assistance be found inadequate (see Chapters 1 and 8 of this volume on the precautionary motive for reserve accumulation).[9] However, this comes at a price, given the opportunity cost of holding reserves. Is there any way in which the liquidity yield from holding reserves may be generated without the need for individual countries to continually accumulate them? One way may be for regional economies to pool their reserves and derive the benefits of scale economies. But how might one judge the potential size of benefits from reserve pooling? Before attempting to estimate such gains (or lack thereof), we first need to estimate the level of reserves that members would have to hold independently.

9.3 Assessing the size and benefits of a reserve pool

9.3.1 Reserve-to-imports ratio revisited

Assume reserve pooling is undertaken as part of a broader policy of economic integration including trade integration.[10] In such a case, part of what was formerly external trade will become intraregional. Insofar as the reserve to imports (R/M) ratio is considered a reasonable, albeit highly imperfect, yardstick of reserve adequacy (Bird and Rajan 2003, and Table 9.1), the reclassification of a large part of formerly external trade will now imply that the region will be holding a substantial pool of "excess reserves." In the case of East Asia, how much would this excess be, and what would be the gains from reserve pooling?[11]

To ascertain the gains from reserve pooling we first compute the international reserves to imports ratio for the individual country (equation 3) and for the overall group (equation 4).

$$\text{Ratio}(i) = R_i/M_i \tag{3}$$

$$\text{Ratio} = \frac{\sum_i R_i}{\sum_i M_i}, \forall i = 1,\ldots,n \tag{4}$$

where: R_i and (ΣR_i) are the average level of reserves held by the individual country (i) and by the group countries during a specified period of time, respectively. M_i and (ΣM_i) are the average monthly level of imports for each country (i) and the group, respectively. (n) is the total number of countries joining the group.

If reserve pooling among the East Asian economies is part of a broader goal of trade integration, the arrangement implies that reserves will not be needed to cover the imports from other member countries.[12] Consequently, the same average level of individual country reserve holdings will correspond to a higher number of monthly import coverage. Conversely, to maintain the same import coverage, each member country and the region need only hold a lower amount of reserves. This may be formally stated as follows:

$$\text{Ratiopol}(i) = R_i/M_i - s.M_i \tag{5}$$

$$\text{Ratiopol} = \frac{\sum_i R_i}{\sum_i (M_i - s.M_i)}, \forall i = 1,\ldots,n \tag{6}$$

where: (s) is the share of intraregional imports.

Table 9.1 Reserves as proportion of imports (months), GDP (in percent) and average amount (in US$ millions) (1992–2004)

Country	1992	1995	1998	2001	2004
Indonesia					
Imports[a]	3.0	2.7	7.1	9.6	11.9
GDP	8	7	15.9	17.2	13.9
Average[b]	10,376.7	13,022.5	19,020.8	27,863.5	34,523.9
Malaysia					
Imports[a]	4.2	3.0	5.1	4.6	N/A
GDP	30	27	34	35	46.7
Average[b]	15,082.8	25,063.0	21,441.8	28,071.3	55,017.6
Philippines					
Imports[a]	2.8	2.1	3.6	4.8	3.5
GDP	8	9	13	19	15.5
Average[b]	3,941.9	6,199.4	8,771.2	12,771.5	13,068.97
Singapore					
Imports[a]	5.7	5.7	7.3	7.8	9.1
GDP	82	82	90	91	92.9
Average[b]	38,028.3	65,798.9	73,170.9	75,687.8	102,704.7
Thailand					
Imports[a]	4.9	4.9	6.2	6.4	6.1
GDP	18	22	23	28	25.7
Average[b]	19,574.5	33,455.7	27,020.1	31,734.4	43,355.9
Hong Kong					
Imports[a]	3.0	3.1	6.1	6.8	5.4
GDP	35	40	55	66	74.1
Average[b]	N/A	53,283.5	92,826.8	113,307	121,103.3
China					
Imports[a]	3.1	5.9	9.5	9.0	N/A
GDP	4.6	10.7	15.5	15.9	30
Average[b]	33,875.2	67,595.4	145,535.8	194,410.2	494,608.2
Korea					
Imports[a]	2.2	2.5	5.6	8.5	9.4
GDP	5.0	4.0	5.0	20.6	22.9
Average[b]	15,365.3	29,679.9	42,351.3	97,834.1	171,948.0
Japan					
Imports[a]	2.1	3.9	10.2	14.3	23.8
GDP	2.0	4.0	5.0	8.5	16.6
Average[b]	71,408.6	166,451.2	213,459.8	374,028.8	806,165

Notes: [a] Ratio to average monthly imports of merchandise goods; [b] Monthly average of total foreign exchange reserves minus gold.

Source: Based on data from IFS-CD ROM and ADB Database.

We now compute the "hypothetical reserve level"; the level of total international reserves that the individual country (HR(i)) and the non-pooling group (HR) would have to hold to have the same months of import coverage that it would have under the pooling arrangement.

$$\mathrm{HR}(i) = \mathrm{Ratiopol}(i) * M_i \tag{7}$$

$$\mathrm{HR} = \mathrm{Ratiopol} * \sum_i M_i, \forall i = 1, \ldots, n \tag{8}$$

The average excess gains from joining the pooling for each individual member (equation 9) and for the group (equation 10) are:

$$\mathrm{ER}(i) = \mathrm{HR}(i) - R_i \tag{9}$$

$$\mathrm{ER} = \mathrm{HR} - \sum_i R_i \tag{10}$$

where: (ER) is the excess reserve level during the specified period.

Tables 9.2a and 9.2b reports the findings for the ASEAN-5 (Indonesia, Malaysia, Philippines, Thailand and Singapore) plus China, Korea and Japan—commonly referred to as ASEAN plus Three (APT)—as well as

Table 9.2a Reserve–Import ratio with and without pooling (ASEAN-5) + Korea + China + Hong Kong + Japan (1990–1998)

Country	s (Share of intraregional imports in %)[a]	Average reserve–import ratio without pooling (months of imports)	Average reserve–import ratio with pooling (months of imports)
Indonesia	43.2%	5.08	8.94
Malaysia	52.9%	4.47	9.49
Philippines	43.8%	2.89	5.15
Thailand	47.8%	6.11	11.70
Singapore	52.3%	6.85	14.36
Korea	37.1%	2.93	4.67
China	45.6%	7.96	14.62
Hong Kong	66.4%	4.16	12.39
Japan	28.2%	6.63	9.23
Total of ASEAN-5 + Korea + China + Hong Kong + Japan	45.0%	5.62	10.10

Source: [a] Based on raw data obtained from East Asian economic perspectives, Vol. 11, February 2000, *The International Centre for the Study of East Asian Development*, Kitakyushu.

Hong Kong, for the pre-crisis and the crisis period of 1990–1998.[13] We obtain the foreign exchange reserve data from the *IFS CD-ROM* of the International Monetary Fund (IMF).

From our computation, we find that the average share of intraregional imports in the overall imports of the individual country ranges from the low of 28 percent for Japan to the high of 66 percent for Hong Kong. For the ASEAN-5, the range is narrower, between 43 percent and about 52 percent. As for the overall group of the economies, we find that the average *(s)* equals 0.45 for that group of East Asian economies during the specified period.

Based on the available information, we then calculate (Ratiopol(*i*)) and (Ratiopol). The results show that the number of months of import coverage for the ASEAN-5 should increase by as little as two months for the Philippines and as much as seven months for Singapore (Table 9.2a). As for the rest of the East Asian countries, Korea will gain the smallest increase in the import coverage by less than two months, while Hong Kong will gain the most (an extra coverage of eight months of import). Lastly, the East Asian countries as a group should enjoy an extra coverage of four months of import by committing themselves to the regional pooling.

Reflecting the variations in the reserve–import ratio, the average "excess" reserves from pooling for each individual are also very diverse (Table 9.2b). Korea appears to gain the least amount of excess reserves (US$ 15 billion), while Hong Kong stands to gain the most (US$ 105 billion). As a whole, East Asia stands to reap around US$ 330 billion of excess reserves for the period between 1990 and 1998.[14] This being the case, a logical question would be: what are the fiscal costs of failing to derive the reserve benefits from integration?

We compute the fiscal costs (FC) as follows:

$$FC(i) = (\text{int}^{i} - \text{int}^{USA}) * ER(i) \tag{11}$$

$$FC = (\text{int}^{EA} - \text{int}^{USA}) * ER \tag{12}$$

where: (FC(*i*)) and (FC) are the estimated fiscal costs for the individual country and for the group; (int^{EA}) is the average annual interest rate of the 3 to 6 months time deposit offered by East Asian commercial banks; and (int^{USA}) is the equivalent average deposit rate offered by US commercial banks. We obtain interest rate data from the IMF's *IFS CD-ROM*.[15]

The average interest rate in East Asia shows a 3.3 percentage point premium over the equivalent US rate, although there are significant

Table 9.2b Actual reserve, hypothetical reserve and fiscal cost (1990–1998)

Country	Average actual reserve (in US$ million) (A)	Average hypothetical reserve with pooling (in US$ million) (B)	Excess reserve (in US$ million) (B–A)	Fiscal cost (in US$ million)[a]
Indonesia	13,535.60	23,832.25	10,296.65	1,518.75
Malaysia	20,852.30	44,241.72	23,389.42	376.57
Philippines	5,795.63	10,303.50	4,507.87	326.82
Thailand	25,967.09	49,738.46	23,771.37	1,243.24
Singapore	55,562.61	116,478.26	60,915.65	−1,041.66
Korea	25,615.49	40,760.83	15,145.34	666.39
China	71,505.29	131,410.40	59,905.11	1,713.29
Hong Kong	53,605.23	159,584.19	105,978.96	−476.90
Japan	142,398.20	198,281.90	55,883.70	−1,832.99
Total of ASEAN-5 + Korea + China + Hong Kong + Japan	414,837.40	745,074.98	330,237.58	10,831.79

Note: [a] Positive number implies cost.

Source: Authors.

variations within East Asia. For the specified period, the commercial bank deposit rate in Indonesia averaged close to 15 percentage points higher than the US rate. The Philippines' and Thailand's commercial deposit rates were also significantly well above the US rates by about 7 and 5 percentage points, respectively. In contrast, the commercial banks in Singapore, Hong Kong and Japan offered lower deposit rates than the commercial banks in the US. From equations 11 and 12, we derive the fiscal cost of holding excess reserves to be well over US$ 10 billion for the period at hand for the group. China and Indonesia suffered the highest fiscal costs (about US$ 1.7 billion and US$ 1.5 billion, respectively). Malaysia and Philippines incurred average fiscal costs of around US$ 320–US$ 370 million, while those of Thailand and Korea were US$ 1.2 billion and US$ 670 million, respectively. Due to the negative interest rate spreads, Singapore, Hong Kong and Japan actually benefited from holding their excess reserves denominated in US dollars. The foregoing notwithstanding, it is important to note that the results highlighted in Table 9.2b are likely to underestimate the full fiscal cost of reserve hoarding as the cost of the financial capital in East Asia (reflected by the deposit interest rate) is likely to be far lower than the marginal cost of capital (which is the true opportunity cost of reserves).

9.3.2 Variability of reserves: coverage index

While the preceding measure of reserve gains from integration is intuitive, there are at least two problems with it.

First, there are limitations in using imports as a scaling factor for determining reserve adequacy. Crises during the 1990s and beyond have predominantly been crises of the capital account. Reserve adequacy benchmarks accordingly need to be modified to allow for both imports and capital outflows as potential drains on reserves (Bird and Rajan 2002; Fischer 2001 and Reddy 2002). For instance, the Reserve Bank of India (RBI) states:

> (W)ith the changing profile of capital flows, the traditional approach of assessing reserve adequacy in terms of import cover has been broadened to include a number of parameters which take into account the size, composition, and risk profiles of various types of capital flows as well as the types of external shocks to which the economy is vulnerable. (Reddy 2002, p. 6)

Second, the foregoing analysis assumes that reserve pooling is carried out in tandem with intensified trade and possibly even monetary integration. What if the region does not opt for economic integration? Is there any way of gauging the gains from reserve pooling? Since international reserve holdings have been found to be a theoretically and statistically significant determinant of creditworthiness, depleting them may induce capital outflows. If capital outflows reflect a perception within private capital markets that a country is illiquid, reducing international reserves is unlikely to be an effective strategy. The reversibility that makes reserve depletion credible in the context of trade deficits is often absent in the context of capital outflows.

In view of the foregoing, there seems to be a sound rationale for minimizing the variability of reserve holdings. How is this related to a reserve pool? Medhora (1992b) observes:

> By belonging to the reserve pool, the member countries have ... access to the others' reserves during times of need. At the same time, by pooling, each country is taking on the variability of the entire pool, rather than just the variability of its own reserves. (p. 213)

It has been argued that a more appropriate way of measuring international reserve adequacy is to compare average reserve holdings with their variability (Medhora 1992a,b and Williams et al. 2001). This so-called "reserve coverage index" encompasses two potential sources of gain from reserve pooling, viz. an increase in average effective holdings and a decrease in their variability.[16]

We define the coverage index in country i as:

$$C_i = \mathrm{PR}/Var(\mathrm{PR}) \tag{13}$$

where: PR is the average level of reserve holdings (or access to reserves), i.e. effective reserves during a particular time period, and Var(PR) is the variability of reserves during the same period.[17]

Each individual country may also consider a partial pool, whereby each can access its own reserves as well as the partially pooled reserves of all the other members. The coverage index for the partial pool is computed as follows:

$$C_i = \frac{R_i + \sum_{j \neq i} p.R_j}{Var\left[R_i + \sum_{j \neq i} p.R_j\right]} \tag{14}$$

where: p is the degree of pooling ($0 < p < 1$) and R_i and R_j are the total reserves of countries i and j (assumed to be the members of the pool).

From equations 13 and 14, the coverage under reserve pooling will be higher than in the independent situation if the variability of the pool is lower than that of each country's reserves separately, or if the increased access to the larger pool of reserves outweighs the higher variability of the pooled reserves.

The formulation of the pooled-coverage index assumes that each country has unrestricted access to the pool. If one country draws on the pool it reduces coverage for the other member countries. Hence, the pooled system is a zero sum game. The effects of pooling can be quantified by examining the hypothetical scenario in which "each country had wanted to maintain the level of coverage that it actually enjoyed, but did not belong to the pool" (Medhora 1992b, p. 217).

This hypothetical reserve level is calculated by using the following equation.

$$\mathrm{HR}_i = C_i * Var(R_i) \tag{15}$$

HR_i is the hypothetical reserve—the level of reserves that each country would have had to hold had it not belonged to the pool, but still wanted to maintain the same coverage afforded by the pool. C_i is the coverage index of country *i* under pooling, and $Var(R_i)$ is the variability of country *i* 's own reserves. The gains/losses from reserve pooling may be measured as follows:

$$G/L = \mathrm{HR} - \mathrm{PR} \qquad (16)$$

where: G/L is the gain (+) or loss (–) in international reserve levels and HR and PR are the hypothetical and actual average foreign exchange reserves, respectively.

Table 9.3 reports the average quarterly reserve holdings for each country and their variability from the last quarter of 1993 to the first quarter of 2002.[18] Based on this data, and for each country, we first compute the coverage index without pooling (0 percent) and then simulate the country's coverage index by imposing additional 10 percent increments in the level of pooling commitment (from 10 percent pooling to 100 percent pooling) (Table 9.4). The overall coverage index without pooling for the selected East Asian economies is well above 4. However the range runs from 1.76 for Korea to 8.02 for Thailand. We then simulate the coverage index *for every 10 percent* increment in pooling commitments. The highest overall average for the coverage index with pooling is found to be at a 10 percent commitment; it implies a significant gain from pooling.

Table 9.3 Average and variability of the foreign exchange reserves[a] (q4: 1993–q1: 2002)

	Average reserve (US$ million)	**Variability of reserve (US$ million)**
Indonesia	20,089.50	6,544.70
Malaysia	27,279.30	4,044.4
Philippines	9,730.20	3,007.50
Singapore	68,708.62	11,907.80
Thailand	31,356.30	3,908.80
Korea	52,018.60	29,593
China	123,447.80	55,142.30
Hong Kong	79,172.80	24,171.50
Japan	237,171.90	86,988.50

Note: [a] Variability computed using standard deviations.

Source: Computed from data from IFS-CD ROM and ADB database.

Table 9.4 Coverage with and without pooling for ASEAN-5, Korea, Japan, China and Hong Kong (q4:1993–q1:2002)[b]

	0 percent[a]	1 percent	10 percent	20 percent	30 percent	40 percent	50 percent	60 percent	70 percent	80 percent	90 percent	100 percent
Indonesia	3.07	3.128	3.150	3.152	3.148	3.147	3.146	3.145	3.144	3.144	3.143	3.143
Malaysia	6.75	6.741	4.080	3.585	3.406	3.313	3.257	3.219	3.192	3.172	3.156	3.143
Philippines	3.24	3.261	3.176	3.159	3.153	3.149	3.147	3.146	3.144	3.144	3.143	3.143
Singapore	6.19	7.559	4.752	3.982	3.661	3.486	3.376	3.300	3.245	3.203	3.169	3.143
Thailand	8.02	8.010	4.319	3.690	3.466	3.352	3.283	3.236	3.203	3.178	3.159	3.143
Korea	1.76	1.856	2.399	2.677	2.828	2.924	2.989	3.037	3.073	3.101	3.124	3.143
Japan	2.73	2.746	2.818	2.839	2.945	2.989	3.027	3.057	3.084	3.106	3.126	3.143
China	2.24	2.275	2.520	2.699	2.818	2.905	2.969	3.019	3.059	3.093	3.119	3.143
Hong Kong	3.28	3.281	3.264	3.231	3.207	3.189	3.176	3.166	3.159	3.152	3.147	3.143
Average	**4.142**	**4.317**	**3.386**	**3.229**	**3.181**	**3.164**	**3.153**	**3.147**	**3.145**	**3.144**	**3.143**	**3.143**

Notes: [a] Without pooling; [b] Data for the foreign exchange reserve of Hong Kong from the IFS, CD ROM is available only from quarter 1, 1993.

Source: Authors.

We estimate the coverage index for *every 1 percent from 0 to 10 percent and then from 10 to 20 percent* to locate the level of pooling that will most benefit the East Asian economies as a group. The results are again summarized in Table 9.4.

Several key findings emerge. Based on the highest overall average of coverage index, our results suggest that, as a group, the economies stand to benefit most by committing to a 1 percent pooling arrangement. However, looking at the individual countries, the pooling arrangement will not benefit all members equally; the optimal shares to be pooled may be different across countries. For instance, Indonesia will benefit most from 20 percent pooling, while the other two ASEAN economies (Philippines and Singapore) and Hong Kong enjoy the highest coverage index by pooling a mere 1 percent share of their respective reserves.[19] As for the larger North Asian economies, Japan, Korea and China gain most by committing all their respective reserves. Malaysia and Thailand are the only two countries that do not benefit by any level of pooling commitment.

Table 9.5 (Column 2) shows the hypothetical reserves within a pool, assuming each country participates according to its optimal shares as

Table 9.5 Reserve gains and losses with the pooling scheme (Q4: 1993–Q1: 2002)

	Actual average reserves (PR) (US$ million)	**Hypothetical reserves (HR) (US$ million)**	**Gain/Loss in reserves (HR–PR) (in US$ million)**	**Fiscal cost[d] (in US$ million)**
Indonesia	20,089.50	20,628.89[a]	539.40	76.81
Malaysia	27,279.30	27,263.30[b]	–16.00	– 0.098
Philippines	9,730.20	9,807.45[b]	77.26	3.44
Singapore	68,708.62	90,011.06[b]	21,302.4	–483.60[e]
Thailand	31,356.30	31,309.49[b]	–46.80	–1.30
Korea	52,018.60	93,010.8[c]	40,992.20	1,524.9
China	123,447.80	173,312.24[c]	49,864.44	605.4
Hong Kong	79,172.80	79,306.69[b]	133.89	–0.522[e]
Japan	237,171.90	273,404.85[c]	26,232.95	–1,062.4[e]
Total	651,067.50	894,404.26[b]	243,336.76	1,028.10

Notes: [a] with 20 percent pooling; [b] with 1 percent pooling; [c] with 100 percent pooling; [d] derived using interest rate differentials of average time deposit of 3–6 months for 1993–2001; [e] the negative fiscal costs for Singapore, Hong Kong and Japan are due to the negative interest rate spread (the US time deposit rate is higher than the domestic rates in these countries).

Source: Authors.

previously calculated. Two caveats need to be noted before proceeding. First, the optimal shares in Table 9.4 were computed on the assumption that all countries in the group contribute an identical proportion of their reserves to the regional pool. A 20 percent share may no longer be optimal for Indonesia when other countries are not pooling the same share of their own reserves. Second, we assume that Malaysia and Thailand participate at a 1 percent share (given the other benefits from being part of a regional reserve arrangement).

Keeping these caveats in mind, we find that, for the group as a whole, the aggregate reserve savings (i.e. hypothetical less actual reserves) are over US$ 240 billion. The corresponding fiscal gains to the region from pooling (or fiscal costs from not pooling) are about US$ 1 billion, with significant variations between individual countries. The fiscal costs for Malaysia and Thailand are negative, though relatively negligible since our calculations suggest that any pooling is suboptimal for them. Those for Japan and Singapore are negative as their respective interest rates are less than the US interest rates of an equivalent maturity. However, as noted, if we use the differential between the marginal cost of capital in these two countries and the US interest rate, the fiscal costs to these two countries are likely to be positive.

The coverage ratio estimated above is one of the first formal attempts to quantify the costs and benefits of regional reserve pooling. This said, its use as a measure of assessing the adequacy of reserve holdings is not without its limitations. Key among these is the fact that it is probably a more appropriate measure of the benefits from diversification. Reserve pooling in the Asian context largely focuses on the "insurance" motive, i.e. access to a liquidity pool at times of crisis in international capital markets. In relation to this, the very presence of a large shared liquidity pool of reserves may, *ceteris paribus*, reduce the probability of a crisis. Our analysis suggests that there are greater benefits to be had from *partial* as opposed to *complete* pooling.

9.4 Conclusion

The fact that the Asian economies maintain about two-thirds of the world's foreign exchange reserves suggests that, first, there is potential resource misallocation with significant opportunity costs and, second, the region has sufficient aggregate reserves to develop a large and credible common reserve pool arrangement. The reserves are reasonably evenly distributed across many strong currency countries including Japan, China, Korea and Singapore. This is important since, if the region had a balance of "weak currency" countries, creating sustainability by means of a common reserve pool would be difficult. It is highly unlikely that strong currency countries would allow their reserves to be constantly compromised by weaker currency countries.

From a systemic and individual country perspective it may be desirable to have "tiers of liquidity" (or concentric defense lines). The top tier would be owned reserves. From a government's perception an advantage associated with these is that they may be used quickly and without conditions. The second tier could take the form of regional liquidity arrangements. This tier could take the form of a regional reserve pool. In the West African Economic and Monetary Union (WAEMU)[20]:

> each central bank is obliged to maintain 65 percent of its official reserves in the operations account. In the first instance, each country draws down on its own account of pooled and unpooled reserves. Once these are fully drawn down, the other countries' pooled reserves may be used. In essence, there is no statutory limit on a member country's use of reserves. A crisis management scheme takes over when..(aggregate)..reserves fall below the prescribed threshold, not when the reserves of individual countries are exhausted. (Williams et al. 2001, p. 7)

The third tier would be conventional IMF lending, which in turn ought to be subdivided into liquidity-based lending and more conventional structural adjustment based lending. In the case of the former, it would be appropriate for the conditionality linked to liquidity-based lending to be closely aligned with financial and macro conditionality determined by the regional monetary facility (in conjunction with the IMF). All in all, with such a tiered structure, the degree of liquidity could be inversely related to the degree of conditionality. In the case of the second tier and a regional reserve pool in East Asia, a natural starting point would be the Chiang Mai Initiative (CMI), which is essentially a network of bilateral currency swaps and repurchase agreements as a "firewall" against future financial crises (see Chapter 10 of this volume).

If the CMI does evolve into a regional liquidity facility, it would be natural to ask whether effective financial cooperation can be pursued without regional exchange rate coordination. Certainly, any explicit form of exchange rate coordination would be helped by a reserve pooling arrangement. But it would also require the closer coordination of regional macroeconomic policies, which in turn may require some sort of constraining arrangement to ensure policy compliance and avoid moral hazard. Asia, in contrast, does not currently have the consensus or political will necessary to consider establishing a coordinated exchange rate regime (Eichengreen and Bayoumi 1999). Indeed, small but strong currency countries like Singapore are unlikely to be willing to forsake the discretion they have over their own macro policy and subordinate this to a regional monetary alliance that is untested and where their voice would be small.

Greater exchange rate coordination facilitates intraregional trade, and the optimal size of reserve holdings of the region as a whole might decline as intraregional trade replaces external trade.[21] In addition to this, the reduced need to stabilize intraregional exchange rates also implies a lower precautionary demand for reserves.[22] Furthermore, countries hold reserves as a war chest against adverse geopolitical developments and other "non-market considerations" (Reddy 2002). To the extent that closer monetary integration enhances intraregional security and reduces some of these intraregional geopolitical considerations, the region's aggregate demand for reserves may decline over time. The analysis in this chapter suggests that, while reserve accumulation in Asia may be understandable following the need to borrow from the IMF in 1997/1998, it may not be the best policy. There is a significant fiscal cost and the precautionary benefits may be better provided by an expanded system of partial reserve pooling. The selection of individual reserve accumulation therefore hints at the significant resistance to the dilution of national sovereignty to which reserve pooling would give rise and the political constraints on regional monetary cooperation.

Notes

1. This chapter draws on an article originally published in *Asia-Pacific Journal of Economics and Business*, 5 (12), 2005, 21–39 (Curtin University of Technology, Australia and Ryukoku University, Kyoto, Japan). Reprinted with permission.
2. "While the US and global economy did suffer a sharp slowdown from the second half of 2008, this was not due to the disorderly unwinding of the global imbalances which have persisted."
3. See Aizenman and Lee (2005) for an initial attempt to differentiate between the precautionary and mercantilist motives for reserve buildup in Asia.
4. Admittedly, it is not clear at this stage whether East Asia is necessarily the appropriate focal point of Asian regionalism. For instance, there is a strong case to be paid for the inclusion of India, Australia and New Zealand as well in an initial core group (for instance, see Rajan 2005). However, this chapter focuses on a subset of East Asian economies (see Section 9.3 and Chapter 10 of this volume).

5. Conversely, reserve holdings confer a benefit to nations that supply the reserve currency as they are effectively obtaining low interest loans (with no currency risk).
6. Of course, to the extent that reserve holdings are seen as a sign of strength, a larger level of reserves may encourage greater capital inflows. We ignore this possible effect in the analysis in this chapter.
7. Aizenman and Marion (2003) exclude the opportunity cost variable as they argue that it is not a significant explanatory factor, but more so because of the difficulty of obtaining consistent data series on interest rates for developing countries.
8. Unlike the more general framework, the Frenkel–Jovanovic model does not explicitly capture changes in loss aversion.
9. Apart from concerns about conditional access to fickle global capital markets (discussed in Bird and Rajan 2003; also see Willett 2001), Aizenman and Marion (2003) also suggest that this precautionary motive may arise from costly domestic tax collection and inelastic fiscal liabilities.
10. See Section 9.4 for a discussion of reserve pooling in the presence of regional exchange rate coordination.
11. This was one of the questions asked during the advent of the euro.
12. In other words, members can gain by economizing on reserve holdings (*a la* the European Union).
13. The shares of intraregional imports (s) are based on data from The East Asian Economic Perspectives of ICSEAD (2000).
14. Another way of seeing the gains from integration is to note that, if the region wanted to maintain the same average import coverage without pooling (i.e. 5.6 months), the amount of reserves saved would be about US$ 185 billion.
15. We assume for simplicity that the bulk of East Asian reserves are held in US dollar. This is probably not too far from reality. In 1999, 78 percent of global international reserves were in US dollar (D'Arista 2000). Eichengreen and Mathieson (2000) offer a recent discussion on the currency composition of international reserves.
16. See Medhora (1992b) for a discussion about concerns relating to reserve variability.
17. Variability of PR is represented by the standard deviation of the reserve during a specified time period.
18. The initial period of last quarter 1993 was selected due to the availability of the foreign exchange reserve holding data from the IFS CD-ROM, IMF.
19. While this is not shown in Table 4, we tried other shares such as 5 percent and 15 percent but the conclusions are unaltered.
20. The WAEMU, established in 1994, consists of eight countries (Benin, Burkina Faso, Cote d'Ivoire, Guinea-Bissau, Mali, Niger, Senegal and Togo). The WAEMU has a common central bank (BCEAO) and shares some other institutions. The WAEMU and the Central African Economic and Monetary Community (CAEMC) together comprise the CFA franc zone (Williams et al. (2001) discuss the institutional arrangements of these institutions).
21. Frankel and Rose (2002), Glick and Rose (2002) and Rose (2000) estimate gravity models using both cross-sectional and time series data and conclude that a common currency is especially trade stimulating intraregionally.

22. Offsetting these effects, with a full-fledged currency union, there will be an automatic decline in "international reserves" with the redefinition of regional currencies. However, this is of less relevance for Asia (compared with Europe, for instance) as the US dollar is the most important reserve asset in Asia.

References

Aizenman, J. and N. Marion (2003). "The High Demand for International Reserves in the Far East: What's Going On?," *Journal of Japanese and International Economics*, 17, 370–400.

Aizenman, J. and J. Lee (2005). "International Reserves: Precautionary Versus Mercantilist Views, Theory and Evidence," mimeo (May).

Bernanke, B. (2005). "The Global Saving Glut and the US Current Account Deficit," Homer Jones Lecture (St. Louis, Missouri, April 14).

Bird, G. (1978). *The International Monetary System and the Less Developed Countries*, London: Macmillan.

Bird, G. and R.S. Rajan (2002). "The Evolving Asian Financial Architecture," *Princeton Essays in International Economics No. 226*, International Economics Section, Princeton University.

Bird, G. and R.S. Rajan (2003). Too Much of a Good Thing?: The Adequacy of International Reserves in the Aftermath of Crises, *The Word Economy*, 26, 873–891.

Clark, P. (1970). "Demand for International Reserves: A Cross-Country Analysis," *Canadian Journal of Economics*, 3, 577–594.

D'Arista, J. (2000). "International Foreign Exchange Reserves: An Update," *Capital Flows Monitor*, June 23, Financial Markets Center.

Dooley, M., P. Garber, and D. Mathieson (2003). "An Essay on the Revived Bretton Woods System," Deutsche Bank Global Markets Research, September.

Dooley, M., P. Garber, and D. Mathieson (2004a). "A Map to the Revived Bretton Woods End Game: Direct Investment, Rising Real Wages and the Absorption of Excess Labor in the Periphery," Deutsche Bank Global Markets Research, June.

Dooley, M., P. Garber, and D. Mathieson (2004b). "The Revived Bretton Woods System: Alive and Well," Deutsche Bank Global Markets Research, December.

ICSEAD (2000). *East Asian Economic Perspectives*, Vol. 11, February.

Eichengreen, B. (2004). "Global Imbalances and the Lessons of Bretton Woods," Working Paper No. 10497, NBER.

Eichengreen, B. and T. Bayoumi (1999). "Is Asia an Optimum Currency Area?, Can it Become One? Regional, Global and Historical Perspectives on Asian Monetary Relations," in S. Collignon and J. Pisani-Ferri (eds), *Exchange Rate Policies in Asian Emerging Countries*, London: Routledge Press.

Eichengreen, B. and D. Mathieson (2000). "The Currency Composition of Foreign Exchange Reserves: Retrospect and Prospect," Working Paper No. 00/131, IMF.

Fischer, S. (2001). "Opening Remarks, IMF/World Bank International Reserves: Policy Issues Forum," Washington, DC, April 28.

Flood, R. and N. Marion (2001). "Holding International Reserves in an Era of High Capital Mobility," *Brookings Trade Forum 2001*, Washington, DC: Brookings Institution.

Frankel, J. and A. Rose (2002). "An Estimate of the Effect of Common Currencies on Trade and Income," *Quarterly Journal of Economics*, 117, 437–466.
Frenkel, J. and B. Jovanovic (1981). "Optimal International Reserves: A Stochastic Framework," *Economic Journal*, 91, 507–541.
Glick, R. and A. Rose (2002). "Does a Currency Union Affect Trade?: The Time Series Evidence," *European Economic Review*, 46, 1125–1151.
Kim, J.S., J. Li, O. Sula, R.S. Rajan and T.D. Willett (2005). "Reserve Adequacy in Asia Revisited: New Benchmarks Base on the Size and Composition of Capital Flows," in *Monetary and Exchange Rate Arrangement in East Asia*, Seoul, Korea Institute for International Economic Policy.
Medhora, R. (1992a). "The West African Monetary Union: Institutional Arrangements and the Link with France," *Canadian Journal of Development Studies*, 13, 409–425.
Medhora, R. (1992b). The Gain from Reserve Pooling in the West African Monetary Union, *Economia Internazionale*, 45, 209–222.
Rajan, R.S. (2004). "The US Current Account Deficit, Exchange Rate Flexibility and Asian Reserves," *RIS Policy Brief No. 11*, New Delhi, January.
Rajan, R.S. (2005). "Asian Economic Cooperation and Integration: Sequencing of Financial, Trade and Monetary Regionalism," in *Asian Economic Cooperation and Integration: Progress, Prospects and Challenges*, Manila: Asian Development Bank.
Reddy, Y.V. (2002). "India's Foreign Exchange Reserves: Policy, Status and Issues," lecture at the National Council of Applied Economic Research, New Delhi, May 10.
Rose, A. (2000). "One Money, One Market: Estimating the Effect of Common Currencies on Trade," *Economic Policy*, 15, 7–46.
Willett, T.D. (2001). "International Financial Markets as Sources of Crisis or Discipline: The Too Much, Too Late Hypothesis," *Essays in International Finance No. 208*, International Economics Section, Princeton University.
Williams, O., T. Pollius, and S. Hazel (2001). "Reserve Pooling in the Eastern Caribbean Currency Union and the CFA Franc Zone: A Comparative Analysis," Working Paper No. 01/104, IMF.

10
Taking Stock of Monetary and Financial Cooperation in Asia[1]

Ramkishen S. Rajan

10.1 Introduction

Ever since the currency crisis of 1997–1998 there has been a great deal of interest in enhancing regional economic cooperation in Asia. It is important to keep in mind that economic regionalism is multidimensional in nature. As noted by Kuroda (2005), economic regionalism can be broadly divided into four categories, viz. trade and investment; monetary and financial[2]; infrastructure development and related software; and cross-border public goods (cooperation with regard to contagious diseases such as avian flu and SARS, as well as cross-border pollution such as the haze fires in Indonesia which affected many of its Southeast Asian neighbours). This chapter concentrates on the issue of *de jure* (as opposed to *de facto*) monetary and financial regionalism in Asia. In other words, the focus here is on policy initiatives underway in Asia to enhance monetary and financial regionalism and the analytical bases for these initiatives rather than on examining the actual level of financial and monetary links that already exist (which may or may not have been facilitated via regional policy mechanisms).

There are a number of factors that have motivated monetary and financial regionalism in Asia. First have been the financial crisis of 1997–1998 and the perceived inadequate response to it from extra regional players. Second are the ongoing concerns about underrepresentation of Asia in International Monetary Fund (IMF) quota distribution and Asia's apparent lack of voice in international monetary affairs, along with the belief that Asia has ample resources for regional self-help.[3] Third have been external developments in regionalism, particularly the deepening and broadening of the European Union (EU). To be sure, many economists have remained circumspect about the potential benefits of deeper monetary integration in Asia (do the microeconomic benefits outweigh the macroeconomic costs arising from loss of monetary policy sovereignty?), and there are signs of emerging tensions within the EU regarding the net benefits of a single currency. Nevertheless, there is no doubting the inspiration that many Asian policymakers have drawn from the deepening and broadening of European regionalism, especially in the monetary and financial areas. Fourth has been the growing *de facto* economic interdependence (so-called "market driven regionalism") as well as the regional nature of spillovers ("contagion").[4]

There are many gradations of monetary and financial regionalism, ranging from the weak form involving regional policy dialogue and surveillance, on the one hand, to exchange rate and monetary coordination, on the other. To maintain focus, this chapter concentrates more narrowly on some "medium forms" of monetary and financial regionalism, broadly defined as the development of regional liquidity arrangements and regional financial markets. The specific rationale for such "medium forms" of monetary and financial regionalism arises directly from the "capital account nature" of crises. As will be discussed, beyond "sound" macro policies, these new-style crises have in turn made apparent the need to (a) ensure availability of sufficient liquidity in the event of a bust; (b) diversify sources of funding / channels of intermediation to minimize intensity of busts; and (c) minimize balance sheet mismatches (both maturity as well as currency mismatches) (Rajan 2003).

The remainder of this chapter is organized as follows. Section 10.2 takes stock of the recent ongoings in monetary regionalism in Asia, paying specific attention to the Chiang Mai initiative (CMI). Section 10.3 discusses recent ongoings in the area of financial regionalism in Asia, focusing specifically on bond market integration in the form of the Asian Bond Fund (ABF). The final section discusses next steps that might be taken to enhance monetary and financial regionalism in Asia.

10.2 Monetary regionalism in Asia: CMI

The CMI is a network of swap arrangements which was agreed among Asian plus Three (APT) countries in May 2000.[5] It is important to keep in mind that the CMI was not envisaged to be either a mechanism for inappropriate currency pegging in the region or a mechanism for managing a crisis after it erupts. Rather, it is primarily aimed at preventing a crisis from erupting in the first instance. But what is the analytical basis for pursuing such a regional liquidity arrangement? Stylized preventive steps in the event of crisis of confidence include: (a) some combination of raising interest rates to reduce capital outflows and a "calibrated" currency depreciation[6]; (b) talking up the market to try and instill confidence; and (c) ensuring availability of sufficient liquidity. The latter involves ensuring the availability of sufficient own resources (i.e. reserves) as well as organizing external liquidity arrangements that are automatically accessible when needed.

10.2.1 Importance of liquidity

It has long been recognized that inadequate liquidity can threaten the stability of international financial regimes (Bird and Rajan 2002). Illiquidity can create crises even when economic fundamentals are sound, or it can make a bad situation worse when the fundamentals are weak. Moreover, once it becomes a problem, illiquidity further undermines the confidence of international capital markets. Capital outflows increase, thereby reducing liquidity still further. The speed and intensity of economic adjustment following a crisis are largely dictated by the scarcity of liquidity; it is the extreme shortage of liquidity that called for rapid adjustment in East Asia in 1998. For instance, Eichengreen and Rose (2001) stress that the East Asian process of "V-shaped" adjustment was not very different from the stylized patterns of previous currency crisis episodes in developing countries. However, the degree of initial contraction and subsequent recovery was far greater in East Asia, attributable to the severe liquidity crisis that was triggered by investors' panic (Rajan and Siregar 2001).

Having appreciated the importance of ensuring adequate liquidity as a safeguard against future financial crises, many Asian countries consciously attempted to build up reserves immediately after the crisis partly as a precautionary motive (Aizenman and Marion 2003; also see Rajan and Siregar 2004 and Chapter 9 of this volume). Nonetheless, it is recognized that reserve accumulation (so-called "floating with a life-jacket") is costly on many fronts (as the country effectively swaps high yielding domestic assets for lower yielding foreign ones). In addition, there is the question of what the appropriate size of reserve holdings is; against what yardstick should reserve adequacy be measured (Bird and Rajan 2003 and Kim et al. 2005)? Since international reserve holdings have been found to be a theoretically and statistically significant determinant of creditworthiness (Bussiere and Mulder 1999; Disyatat 2001 and Haque et al. 1996), depleting them as a way of cushioning the effect of capital outflows on the exchange rate may make matters worse by inducing further capital outflows.

In view of this, it is recognized that countries need to buttress their own reserve holdings with external liquidity arrangements. The need to provide adequate liquidity to help forestall a crisis in a distressed economy and prevent its spread to other countries took center stage in the reform of the financial architecture immediately after the crisis. The IMF's response was to create the Contingent Credit Line (CCL). "The CCL was conceived as a precautionary line of defense to help protect countries pursuing strong policies in the event of a balance of payments need arising from the spread of financial crises" (IMF 2001, p. 37). The idea here was to establish a precautionary line of credit for countries with "sound" policies that might be affected by contagion from a crisis and to finance this from outside the Fund's quota-based resources by new arrangements to borrow (NAB). The negotiation of conditionality with potential users of the CCL would therefore take place before the country needed to draw on liquidity from the Fund. But no country negotiated a CCL. Consequently the facility underwent a major review and partial overhaul and was eventually shut down. The CCL has not been replaced by another similar liquidity facility and the international financial architecture has made limited progress in the area of liquidity enhancement as a financial safeguard.

Against this background, and in recognition that financial stability has the characteristics of a regional public good, it is understandable that Asian countries have been eager to promote regional monetary cooperation. The CMI has taken center stage in this regard.

10.2.2 Evaluating the CMI

The CMI has two components, viz. (a) ASEAN swap arrangement (ASA) which was expanded from five to ten countries, and from US$ 200 million to US$ 1 billion; and (b) networks of bilateral Swap arrangements (BSAs) among the three North Asian countries (Japan, China, Korea) and one of the three and one of the ASEAN countries (see http://www.mof.go.jp/english/if/CMI_0707.pdf 1).[7]

The expanded ASA is to be made available for two years and is renewable upon mutual agreement of the members. Each member is allowed to draw a maximum of twice its commitment from the facility for a period of up to six months with the possibility of a further extension of six more months at most. The basic characteristics of the BSAs are as follows. 20 percent of the liquidity can be drawn automatically without conditionality for 630 days (90 days, renewable seven times). Interest paid is LIBOR +1.5 percent for the first 180 days, rising by 50 basis points for each renewal to a maximum of LIBOR +3 percent. Importantly the swap providing countries form their own individual opinions on the potential swap recipient. Drawing of more than 20 percent regional liquidity requires the country to come under IMF conditionality.

While the CMI is an important step in Asian monetary regionalism, as it is the first time regional countries have precommitted resources as a means of regional financial safeguard, it clearly remains a work in progress. A number of important details remain to be worked out if the CMI is to be an effective liquidity enhancing measure.

First is the inadequate size, especially of the liquid component. For instance, the current aggregate size of US$ 83 billion among all 13 APT countries—while growing all the time—still pales in comparison to the crisis packages offered to Korea, Indonesia and Thailand in 1997–1998. Second is the issue of how coordination between potential creditor countries is to be done. For instance, is the bilateral arrangement subject to regional approval? How is borrowing/lending to be distributed? Both these questions lead on to the key issue of how to regionalize (though more commonly referred to as "multilateralize") the CMI, which is a series of bilateral and rather uncoordinated swaps. In fact, in the Joint Ministerial Statement of 8th APT's Finance Ministers' Meeting in Istanbul in May 2005 there was an agreement to reevaluate the process/possibility of regionalizing the arrangements.[8] As part of this there was an agreement to look into developing a collective mechanism to activate the swaps. There was also a recognition of the need to improve on and link surveillance more closely and effectively to the CMI. Overall, it would be fair to say that, until these issues are sorted out, the best thing that has happened to the CMI is that the region has not been faced by a crisis to test its effectiveness.

10.3 Financial regionalism in Asia: ABF

While the regional economies are taking noteworthy steps to strengthen, upgrade and integrate their financial systems, the contagious nature of the 1997–1998 crisis has led many observers and policymakers to the view that there are positive externalities from cooperating to strengthen their individual financial sectors, to develop regional financial markets, and to diversify their financial structures away from bank based systems to bond markets. What is wrong with Asia's continued heavy dependence on bank lending as a source of private market financing? Bond financing is considered a relatively more stable source of debt financing as bank loans are primarily illiquid, fixed-price assets in the sense that the interest rate—which is the price of the loan—does not vary much on the basis of changing market circumstances. Thus, almost all the adjustment has to take place via rises and falls in the quantity of bank lending, which in turn leads to sharp booms and busts in bank flows.[9] These sudden reversals in bank flows had calamitous and long-lasting effects on the domestic financial systems in the East Asian economies in 1997–1998. The World Bank (2004) has also acknowledged the importance of bond markets compared with bank lending, noting:

> (c)ompared to the bank market, bond markets offers some advantages in terms of longer maturities, tradability, and back-weighted repayment structures that help support equity returns. (p. 157)[10]

In this regard there have been two main initiatives underway in East Asia. One is the ABF established by the eleven members of the Executives' Meeting of East Asia-Pacific Central Bank (EMEAP),[11] and the other is the Asian Bond Market Initiative (ABMI) by Asian Plus Three (APT) economies.[12] The latter, which was endorsed at the ASEAN+3 Finance Ministers Meeting (AFMM) in Manila on August 2003, focuses primarily on developing efficient bond markets in Asia to enable the private and public sectors to raise and invest long-term capital. The activities of the ABMI are primarily concentrated on facilitating access to the market through a wider variety of issuers and enhancing market infrastructure to foster bond markets in Asia.

10.3.1 Evaluating the ABF schemes

The focus of the remainder of this section is specifically on the ABF, which was established on June 2, 2003. The first stage of the ABF essentially involved the regional governments voluntarily contributing about 1 percent each of their reserves to a fund dedicated to purchasing regional sovereign and semi-sovereign bonds denominated in US dollars. The initial size of the ABF was about US$ 1 billion and the fund has been passively managed by the investment management unit of the Swiss-based BIS. The mandate is to invest in bonds in eight of the eleven member countries of EMEAP, the developed countries of Australia, New Zealand and Japan solely being lenders to the ABF. In a noteworthy next step, the ABF 2 (second stage of the ABF) was established in December 2004. The quantum of funds involved was doubled in magnitude (US$ 2 billion), and its mandate is to invest in selected domestic currency sovereign and quasi-sovereign bonds in the eight countries.

More specifically, the ABF 2 comprises two components (US$ 1 billion each): (a) a Pan-Asian Bond Index Fund (PAIF) and (b) a Fund of Bond Funds (FoBF). The PAIF is a single bond fund, while the FoBF is a two-layered structure with a parent fund investing in eight single market subfunds. The International Index Company (IIC), a joint venture between ABN Amro, JP Morgan and Morgan Stanley (iBoxx ABF), has created the benchmark indices for all nine funds. The funds will be passively managed to match the benchmark index. The seed money for single bond funds has been divided on predetermined criteria and local fund managers have been appointed to manage the respective funds (see Ma and Remolona 2005, p. 86).

The specific criteria for market weights in each subfund (and distribution within PAIF) are based on: (a) the size of the local market; (b) the turnover ratio in that market; (c) the sovereign credit rating; and (d) a market openness factor. The market weights will be reviewed annually, with market openness being a particularly important factor in the allocation of weights (Ma and Remolona 2005). The parent fund is limited to investments by EMEAP member central banks only. While the initial phase of PAIF was confined to investments by EMEAP central banks only (US$ 1 billion), it was opened up to investments by other retail investors in Phase 2.

In broad terms, the objectives of the ABF are four-fold. First, to diversify debt financing from bank lending to bond financing by developing regional financial/capital markets by reducing supply side constraints and introducing low cost products and by raising investor awareness and broadening investor base on the demand side. Second, to encourage a convergence in financial and capital market policies and accelerate improvements in financial market infrastructures. Third, to recycle regional funds intraregionaly and also reduce the region's vulnerability to "fickle" international investors. Fourth, to lessen the extent of currency and maturity mismatches (i.e. "double mismatches"). Since we have already discussed the first two objectives (also see Ma and Remolona 2005 and Hamada et al. 2004), we elaborate on the latter two objectives below.

As is commonly noted, Asia as a whole holds the bulk of the world's savings. The excess of savings over investment along with quasi-managed exchange rates has given rise to large current account and overall balance of payments surpluses. Historically, the lack of sufficiently liquid financial instruments has led to much of Asia's savings being rechanneled outside the region, especially to the US. In relation to this, it is often noted that one of the reasons for the intensification of the regional financial crisis of 1997–1998 was the fickleness of international investors, many of whom were extraregional investors who did not have much knowledge about regional economies or differences in economic fundamentals between the economies. There was significant "panic herding" during that period as international creditors and investors chose to reduce exposures to all regional economies *en masse* once they were spooked by the crisis in Thailand and Indonesia, leading to a massive international bank run. Insofar as the ABF proposal promotes greater intraregional financing, this might make the region somewhat less susceptible to extraregional "investor ignorance," which is said to have contributed to an indiscriminate and disorderly withdrawal of funds from regional markets in 1997–1998.

Another source of vulnerability made apparent by the 1997–1998 financial debacle arose due to large-scale accumulation of uncovered external debt. To the extent that a relatively larger proportion of a country's liabilities is denominated in foreign currency vis-à-vis its assets (so-called "liability dollarization"), a currency devaluation could lead to sharp declines in the country's net worth, with calamitous effects on the financial and real sectors (so-called "balance sheet" effects).[13] On the part of the developing Asia-Pacific economies, the ability to issue bonds in domestic currencies mitigates the concerns about currency mismatches (i.e. borrowing and interest payments in foreign currency but assets and revenue streams in local currency), which in turn could negatively impact the project's solvency in the event of a currency devaluation.[14] Thus, while the ABF 1 was solely focused on foreign currency bonds, the ABF 2 is notable in that it involves transacting solely in local currency bonds.

While the ABF is a welcome move for regional financial cooperation, it is important not to oversell the initiative. Why? First and foremost is the quantum of funding available. The current US$ 2 billion funding of ABF 2 is a drop in the bucket relative to the region's aggregate reserve holdings or infrastructural financing requirements. Second, if the supply of good quality sovereigns and quasi-sovereign paper is limited (which appears to be the case), it could merely crowd out private bond purchases, hence leading to no new net financing.[15] This in turn implies the need to support "public providers of infrastructure services in achieving commercial standards of creditworthiness to access capital markets on a sustainable basis over the long term" (World Bank 2004, p. 161). Third, as noted, the ABF to date is limited to only eight countries in the region (as potential debtors). We return to this important issue of membership in the next section.

10.4 Conclusion

Moving forward, the Asian countries need to persist with attempts to develop well-functioning financial markets and institutions. In particular, countries need to deepen and upgrade national and regional government and corporate bond markets as a means of reducing the region's heavy reliance on banks. Greater attention needs to be given to lowering transactions costs in regional financial markets. In this regard it is important to note that discussions have been underway in the region about the possible creation of regional financial infrastructure (clearing and settlements systems, credit agency) as well as harmonization of withholding tax policies and capital account policies. While the ABF initiatives are modest steps in the right direction, it is important that it be expanded in size and membership. With regard to the latter, not all the ASEAN countries nor India are part of EMEAP, and these are therefore not part of the ABF. Expansion of financial (and monetary) regionalism in this manner is justified by the fact that the APT countries as well as India, Australia and New Zealand are founding members of the East Asia Summit (EAS).[16]

While the ABF initiatives are modest steps in the right direction, a recent suggestion has been floated for an Asia Basket Currency (ABC) (Ito, 2003) Initiative. The basic idea is that, while the ABF merely purchases and holds on to sovereign and quasi-sovereign bonds, the ABC corporation would also create and issue basket currency bonds (weighted combination of regional currencies of the underlying national bonds) backed by regional sovereign bonds. If successful, the ABC could provide a fillip for the eventual creation of an Asian Currency Unit (ACU). The ACU is the specific focus of Chapter 11 of this volume.

Notes

1. This chapter draws on an article originally published in *International Relations of the Asia-Pacific*, 8 (1), 2008, 31–45 (Oxford University Press). Reprinted with permission.
2. While steps towards trade/investment and monetary/financial regionalism have been taking place simultaneously in Asia, hence rendering the issue of sequencing somewhat less relevant from a policy perspective, there remain some important analytical issues surrounding the issue of sequencing of regionalism that are explored by Bird and Rajan (2006).
3. As noted by Henning (2005):

   Dissatisfaction with the multilateral regime is not likely to be sufficient to produce substantial movement toward financial regionalism. Convergence of preferences with partners, the ability to come to agreement, the physical or financial capacity to launch common projects, and a degree of economic interdependence are also likely to bear on regionalism. Thus, regions are likely to respond in different ways to a common multilateral environment. Nonetheless, dissatisfaction with the systemic context is a necessary requirement for investment of energy and political resources in regional projects; if the multilateral regime satisfies governments, regional projects would be superfluous. (p. 5)

4. See Rajan (2003) for a discussion of the definitions, types and channels of contagion.
5. The ten ASEAN countries are Indonesia, Malaysia, Philippines, Singapore, Thailand and Brunei Darussalam, as well as the newer/transition members, viz. Cambodia, Laos, Myanmar, Vietnam, Timor-Leste (formerly East Timor).
6. There are a whole host of issues that go into determining the optimal combination of expenditure changing and expenditure switching policies. See Chapter 7 of this volume.
7. See Henning (2005) and Park (2004) for more details on the CMI and monetary regionalism in Asia more generally.
8. See "The Joint Ministerial Statement of the 8th ASEAN+3 Finance Ministers' Meeting" (Istanbul, May 4, 2005) (http://www.aseansec.org/17448.htm).
9. For instance, see Ito and Park, eds. (2004) and Eichengreen and Luengnaruemitchai (2005). See Hamada et al. (2004) for an overview of Asian bond markets.
10. Arteta (2005) finds that bank-based financial systems tend to be relatively more crisis-prone, and financial systems that are more bond financed-based tend to be associated with higher growth whether or not there is a crisis.
11. The EMEAP "is a cooperative organization of central banks and monetary authorities (hereinafter simply referred to as central banks) in the East Asia and Pacific region. Its primary objective is to strengthen the cooperative relationship among its members. It comprises the central banks of eleven economies: Reserve Bank of Australia, People's Bank of China, Hong Kong Monetary Authority, Bank Indonesia, Bank of Japan, Bank of Korea, Bank Negara Malaysia, Reserve Bank of New Zealand, Bangko Sentral ng Pilipinas, Monetary Authority of Singapore, and Bank of Thailand." See http://www.emeap.org/.
12. More information on all these and other initiatives is available on the portal created and maintained by the Asian Development Bank (ADB) http://asianbondsonline.adb.org/.
13. The macroeconomic implications of these balance sheet effects have been explored by Bird and Rajan (2004) and Chapter 7 of this volume.
14. It is important to ask the question as to why some countries are not able to borrow overseas in domestic currencies (so called "Original Sin" hypothesis *a la* Hausmann et al. 2000). Logically, if there is a significant risk premium imposed on a certain currency and if interest rates are "sufficiently" high, there will always be some potential borrowers. While this is true, the concern is that a potential solvency risk will merely be converted to a liquidity risk (to the extent that revenues in the event of a negative shock are not sufficiently high to meet the high interest payments) (see Jeanne 2000).
15. For a more detailed and forceful critique of such regional bond initiatives see Eichengreen (2004) and Eichengreen and Luengnaruemitchai (2005).
16. See Kumar (2005) for a discussion of the East Asia Summit (EAS). The inaugural meeting was held in Kuala Lumpur, Malaysia in November 2005.

References

Aizenman, J. and N. Marion (2003). "The High Demand for International Reserves in the Far East: What's Going On?," *Journal of the Japanese and International Economies*, 17, 370–400.

Arteta, C.O. (2005). "Does Bond Market Development Help Reduce the Cost of Crises? Evidence from Developing Countries," mimeo (April).

Bird, G and R.S. Rajan (2002). "The Evolving Asian Financial Architecture," *Essays in International Economics No. 26* (February), Princeton University.

Bird, G. and R.S. Rajan (2003). "Too Good to be True?: The Adequacy of International Reserve Holdings in an Era of Capital Account Crises," *The World Economy*, 26, 873–891.

Bird, G. and R.S. Rajan (2004). "Does Devaluation Lead to Economic Recovery or Economic Contraction?: Examining the Analytical Issues with Reference to Thailand," *Journal of International Development*, 16, 141–156.

Bird, G. and R.S. Rajan (2006). "The Political Economy of Sequencing: The Trade and Monetary Components of Regional Integration," *North American Journal of Economics and Finance*, 17, 335–341.

Bussiere, M. and C. Mulder (1999). "External Vulnerability in Emerging Market Economies: How High Liquidity can Offset Weak Fundamentals and the Effects of Contagion," Working Paper No. 99/88, IMF.

Disyatat, P. (2001). "Currency Crises and Foreign Reserves—A Simple Model," Working Paper No. 01/18, IMF.

Eichengreen, B. (2004). "Financial Development in Asia: The Way Forward," mimeo (January).

Eichengreen, B. and A. Rose (2001). "To Defend or Not to Defend? That is the Question," mimeo (February).

Eichengreen, B. and P. Luengnaruemitchai (2005). "Why Doesn't Asia Have Bigger Bond Markets?," Working Paper No. 10576, NBER.

Hamada, K., S.C. Jeon, and J.W. Ryou (2004). "Asian Bonds Markets: Issues, Prospects and Tasks for Cooperation," paper prepared for the "Korea and the World Economy III" Conference, July 3–4.

Haque, N., M. Kumar, M. Nelson, and D. Mathieson (1996). "The Economic Content of Indicators of Developing Country Creditworthiness," Working Paper No. 96/9, IMF.

Hausmann, R., U. Panizza, and E. Stein (2000). "Why do Countries Float the Way They Float?," Working Paper No. 418, Inter-American Development Bank.

Henning, R. (2005). "Systemic Contextualism and Financial Regionalism: The Case of East Asia," mimeo (August).

IMF (2001). *Annual Report 2001*, Washington, DC: IMF (September).

Ito, T. (2003). "The ABC of Asian Bonds," paper presented at the Second PECC Finance Forum Conference (Hua Hin, Thailand, July 8–9).

Ito, T. and Y.C. Park, eds (2004). Developing Asian Bond Markets, Canberra: Asia Pacific Press.

Jeanne, O. (2000). "Foreign Currency Debt and the Global Financial Architecture," *European Economic Review*, 44, 719–727.

Kim, J.S., J. Li, O. Sula, R.S. Rajan and T.D. Willett (2005). "Reserve Adequacy in Asia Revisited: New Benchmarks Base on the Size and Composition of Capital

Flows," in *Monetary and Exchange Rate Arrangement in East Asia,* Seoul: Korea Institute for Economic Policy.

Kumar, N. (2005). "Towards a Broader Asian Community: Agenda for the East Asia Summit," Discussion Paper No. 100, Research and Information System for Developing Countries, New Delhi.

Kuroda, H. (2005). "Towards a Borderless Asia: A Perspective on Asian Economic Integration," speech by Asian Development Bank (ADB) President at the Emerging Markets Forum (December 10, Oxford).

Ma, G. and E.M. Remolona (2005). "Opening Markets Through a Regional Bond Fund: Lessons from ABF2," *BIS Quarterly Review*, June, 81–92.

Park, Y.C. (2004). "Beyond the Chiang Mai Initiative: Prospects for Regional Financial and Monetary Integration in East Asia," paper prepared for meeting on G-24, September.

Rajan, R.S. (2003). "Safeguarding Against Capital Account Crises: Unilateral, Regional and Multilateral Options for East Asia," in G. de Brouwer (ed.), Financial Governance in East Asia, London: Routledge.

Rajan, R.S. and R. Siregar (2001). "Private Capital Flows in East Asia: Boom, Bust and Beyond," in G. de Brouwer (ed.), *Financial Markets and Policies in East Asia*, London: Routledge.

Rajan, R.S. and R. Siregar (2004). "Centralized Reserve Pooling for the ASEAN Plus Three (APT) Countries," in *Monetary and Financial Cooperation in East Asia*, Palgrave-McMillan Press for the Asian Development Bank.

World Bank (2004). *Global Development Finance*, Washington, DC: The World Bank.

11

Is There a Role for an Asian Currency Unit?[1]

(Co-authored with Victor Pontines)

11.1 Introduction

While most observers concur that the time is not ripe for Asia to consider a common currency, there has been some discussion about the possible creation of an Asian Currency Unit (ACU).[2] This chapter examines the specific issue of the ACU which, in a general sense, is a weighted average of regional currencies *a la* the European Currency Unit (ECU) which was created in March 1979 under the European Monetary System (EMS) and remained in operation until the launch of the euro in January 1999.[3] The remainder of the chapter is as follows. Section 11.2 provides a critical overview of and rationale for the ACU proposal. Section 11.3 offers an initial attempt at computing optimal currency compositions of the ACU based on the methodology developed by Hovanov, Kolari and Sokolov (2004). This methodology develops basket weights in the context of a minimized basket or portfolio of assets expressed in terms of national currencies. The final section offers a few concluding remarks.

11.2 Rationale for the ACU

At the micro-level the rationale for an ACU is to afford the opportunity for regional economic agents to invoice regional financial and trade transactions in the ACU, hence reducing the region's dependence on the US dollar and other external currencies. If successful, intraregional intermediation of savings may be promoted, in the process possibly reducing the region's exposure to external shocks as discussed previously. However, in reality, it is unlikely that the ACU will be used on a widespread basis for some time to come.

The experience of Europe is instructive in this regard. The initial creation of the ECU did not lead to a widespread use of the unit. Even in the

1990s, until the actual creation of the euro, the vast majority of intra-European financial and trade transactions were not in ECUs but in US dollar, primarily, and other sovereign national European currencies. So it is not just the creation that is important; there has to be a coordinated agreement by regional bodies to start transacting in the new unit, failing which no one will want to take the first step.[4] The ACU has a better chance for success (in terms of becoming a significant regional vehicle currency) if a larger set of countries is included in the basket. In this regard it is imperative that the ACU be broadened from the proposed ASEAN plus Three (APT) countries to also include India, Australia and New Zealand (the other members of the EAS), all of which have significant financial market depth.[5]

It has been suggested that the ACU could be used as a means of enhancing *internal* exchange rate stability if the regional central banks begin to stabilize their respective currencies to the regional unit (i.e. helping reduce the possibility of regional competitive devaluations). The notion of stabilization vis-à-vis an internal basket *a la* Europe's Exchange Rate Mechanism (ERM) is distinct from stabilization vis-à-vis an external unit which would require that the ACU in turn be pegged in some way to external currencies such as the US dollar or euro, or some weighted average thereof.

Of course, internal stability does not require the latter, and in fact may exacerbate external currency stability. This may happen if regional countries substitute the use of external currencies for the ACU, hence being less concerned about fluctuations of their currencies relative to the external currencies. Conversely, effective external stability requires internal stability in the sense that, if regional central banks do not explicitly or implicitly manage their currencies to the ACU, it is irrelevant whether the ACU *per se* is managed against the external currencies, as the proposed ACU will remain purely a theoretical construct. Indeed, the stated aim of the ADB at this stage is for the ACU to serve mainly as a means of benchmarking the extent of currency movements/deviations. As the ADB president, Haruhiko Kuroda, noted:

> The ACU...could be used to monitor the stability of participating currencies and would tangibly demonstrate the need for greater exchange rate coordination. What Asia needs here is basically an exchange rate that is flexible toward the rest of the world but relatively stable within the region. (Kuroda 2005, p. 5)

Focusing on the notion of stabilization vis-à-vis an internal basket (i.e. regional currencies benchmarking movements to the ACU), while the potential microeconomic benefits noted above do not require internal stabilization, the latter could promote the more widespread use of the ACU. This is because the regional central banks will automatically begin to use the ACU more extensively as a reserve and possibly even intervention currency, thus providing an additional inducement for private agents to intensify use of the unit in invoicing and transactions.

It is needless to say that the long-term viability of internal stabilization in an era of open capital markets requires that there be an enhancement of regional surveillance, a degree of policy coordination, and an augmentation of regional liquidity arrangements. Nonetheless, given the divergence in economic and institutional structures in the region, absent macroeconomic policy coordination and mechanisms for automatic intraregional fiscal transfers, any attempt at formal exchange rate coordination—let alone a full-fledged monetary union—is far too risky and premature and will likely be a failure, setting back prospects for other forms of economic integration.

11.3 Computation of the ACU

While the ACU cannot be viewed as an attractive nominal anchor for Asian currencies in the near-term, it could potentially have a role to play in Asian monetary cooperation in the future.[6] Given its potential usefulness, it would be useful to explore the issues surrounding its construction.

Broadly speaking, there are two issues that must be addressed in the construction of a regional currency unit based on currency baskets. First, a decision has to be made as to which national currencies should be included in the currency basket. Second, a decision has to be made as to the weights that are to be accorded to the national currencies included in the currency basket.

With regard to the first issue, while there is good reason to start with a subset of countries in Asia, it is unclear why it should be restricted to the APT. For instance, Dayaratna-Banda and Whalley (2007) note:

> (W)here..(do)..India, Australia, and New Zealand (the latter two are in the Asia-Pacific grouping) stand in this? ASEAN has already entered into a framework agreement with India on a comprehensive economic partnership. China has entered into arrangements with India, New Zealand and Australia, and Japan also has regional arrangements with these countries. Some initial negotiations for a free trade area between ASEAN, Australia, and New Zealand have also begun.

> These three countries have increasingly more open economies, and their links with East Asia are likely to expand over time. These economies have been increasingly integrating with East Asia. Including them in East Asian regional forums and arrangements expands the set of developed and fast growing economies with well-functioning economic and financial systems and markets...The possibility of ASEAN+6 monetary cooperation can thus not be ruled out. (p. 41)[7]

This said, we consider alternative country configurations of the ACU—from the narrow (ASEAN) to broad (ASEAN+6). The principal interest of this study is the application of a technique that determines the optimal weights in a regional currency basket.

11.3.1 The technique

Initial estimates of the ACU currency weights have been based on some economic indicators across countries. For instance, in a widely cited paper, Ogawa and Shimizu (2006, 2007) proposed the construction of an Asian regional currency basket as a weighted average of regional currencies *a la* the European Currency Unit (ECU). They calculate the weights of the national currencies included in the currency basket as an arithmetic average of the country's respective shares of PPP-based GDP and foreign trade.

Hovanov, Kolari and Sokolov (2004) showed that the values of any given currency (e.g., British pound) depend on the base currency chosen (e.g., US dollar, euros, Japanese yen), which creates ambiguity in the valuation of a currency and makes it difficult to examine the dynamics of the time series of currency values. As a matter of caveat, the choice of base currency is critical to obtain a stable exchange rate. For example, using the US dollar as a base currency as opposed to the Japanese yen changes the relationship between the euro and the British pound. To overcome this base currency problem they proposed a *reduced* (to the moment t_0) *normalized value in exchange* of ith currency:

$$\text{RNVAL}_i(t/t_0) = \frac{c_{ij}(t)}{\sqrt[n]{\prod_{k=1}^{n} c_{kj}(t)}} \Bigg/ \frac{c_{ij}(t_0)}{\sqrt[n]{\prod_{k=1}^{n} c_{kj}(t_0)}} = \sqrt[n]{\prod_{k=1}^{n} \frac{c_{ik}(t)}{c_{ik}(t_0)}} \qquad (1)$$

where $c_{ij}(t)$, $i,j = 1, \ldots, n$, are cross-currencies of exchange rates of n currencies at the moment t. By dividing through by the geometric mean of a basket of currencies, the value of any currency is the same regardless of the base currency chosen.

This *reduced normalized value in exchange* ($\text{RNVAL}_i(t/t_0)$) of a currency is useful in comparing the movements of individual currencies and basket currencies. Why? Typically, one makes statements like "the US dollar appreciates against the yen but depreciates against the euro". In contrast, if the *reduced normalized value in exchange* of the US dollar rises, it means that the value of the US dollar rises on average against the national currencies used in the computation of the geometric mean of the basket of national currencies (Hovanov, Sokolov and Kolari 2004).

Furthermore, it also allows the computation of a unique optimal, minimum-variance currency basket regardless of base currency choice. The derivation of this minimum variance currency basket is calculated by searching the optimal weight vector w^* that solves the following optimal control problem:

$$\text{Min}\left(S^2(w) = \sum_{i,j=1}^{n} w_i w_j \text{cov}(i,j) = \sum_{i=1}^{n} w_i^2 s_i^2 + 2\sum_{\substack{i,j=1\\ i<j}}^{n} w_i w_j \text{cov}(i,j) \right) \tag{2}$$

under the constraints, $w_i \geq 0$, for all $i = 1,\ldots, n$, $w_1 + \ldots + w_n = 1$, where $\text{cov}(i,j)$ is the covariance between $\text{RNVAL}_i(t/t_0)$ and $\text{RNVAL}_j(t/t_0)$, and s_i^2 is the variance of $\text{RNVAL}_i(t/t_0)$ for all $i,j = 1,\ldots, n$ and all $t = 1,\ldots, T$.[8] The optimal weights can also be transformed into optimal currencies' amounts $q_1^*, q_2^*,\ldots, q_n^*$ as follows:

$$q_i^* = \frac{w_i^* \sum_{r=1}^{n} q_r c_{rj}(t)}{c_{ij}(t)}, \qquad \text{Let } \mu = \sum_{r=1}^{n} q_r c_{rj}(t), \qquad \text{thus } q_i^* = \frac{w_i^* \mu}{c_{ij}(t)} \tag{3}$$

Here the positive factor μ can be easily solved from knowledge of the optimal weights $w_1^*, w_2^*,\ldots, w_n^*$ derived from the minimization of the variance in eq. (2), and $c_{1j}(t), c_{2j}(t),\ldots, c_{nj}(t)$. Substituting μ into eq. (3) we obtain the optimal currencies' amounts $q_1^*, q_2^*,\ldots, q_n^*$, which constitute the minimum variance currency basket.

What does the technique presented above have to say regarding the current orthodoxy? For one, a key problem here is that the optimal currency basket weights are dependent on the base currency chosen by the researcher (Hovanov, Kolari and Sokolov 2004).

The use of the concept of the *reduced normalized value in exchange* ($\text{RNVAL}_i(t/t_0)$) of the national currencies included in the regional currency basket avoids the problem of the nonuniqueness of the computed optimal basket weights, since their respective *reduced normalized value in exchange* ($\text{RNVAL}_i(t/t_0)$) should be the same irrespective of the choice of base currency. Accordingly, it follows that the calculation of the optimal weights in a currency basket as determined on the basis of either trade flows, or any arbitrary choice of economic indicators for that matter, invariance to the choice of base currency is not guaranteed to hold. As a result, different optimal weights will be generated for the national currencies included in the currency basket when the US dollar, for instance, is chosen as the base currency, as opposed to when instead the euro is used as the base currency.

Since we are minimizing a basket or portfolio of assets expressed in terms of national currencies, the currency weights are primarily determined by two main factors, viz. the variance of the *reduced normalized value in exchange* ($\mathrm{RNVAL}_i(t/t_0)$) of the national currencies included in the currency basket; and the covariance of the *reduced normalized value in exchange* ($\mathrm{RNVAL}_i(t/t_0)$) of the national currencies included in the currency basket, and, hence, their correlations.

11.3.2 Empirics

The data are sourced from the Pacific Exchange Rate Service website (fx.sauder.ubc.ca) and monthly cross rates of Asian and Pacific currencies are generated for the period January 2000 to June 2007. We consider alternative sets of Asian and Pacific national currencies to be included in a regional currency basket—ranging from a smaller core of ASEAN 5 countries (Indonesia, Malaysia, Philippines, Singapore, Thailand) all the way to a much broader set of coverage of national currencies that include the ASEAN 5 + 3 (China, Korea, Japan) + India + Australia + New Zealand. We also consider a regional currency basket that excludes Japan from the set of countries, as it is unclear whether the Japanese yen should be treated as an "insider" or as an "outsider" (external) currency in a future regional currency basket arrangement (Kriz and Thai 2006 and Ogawa and Kawasaki 2006).

The detailed list of all national currencies that comprise a particular currency basket as well as their respective calculated optimal basket weights (w^*) is shown in Table 11.1. The reported optimal basket weights arise from the optimization method with eq. (2) above as the objective function. In other words, we are minimizing the variance of any alternative set of national currencies that comprise a certain regional currency basket (such as those listed in Table 11.1), wherein the values of this same alternative set of national currencies are cast in terms of their *reduced normalized value in exchange*. A careful examination of the results suggests four discernible patterns.

First, when the core consists of ASEAN 5 only, there is a high degree of uniformity in weights, with each of the currencies constituting around 20 percent of the regional currency basket.

Table 11.1 Optimal basket weights for various groupings of regional basket currencies, January 2000–June 2007 (in percent)

ASEAN 5	Indonesian Rupiah	Philippines Peso	Malaysian Ringgit	Singapore dollar	Thai Baht						
	17.4	18.3	21.8	20.9	21.6						
ASEAN 5 + 2	Indonesian Rupiah	Philippines Peso	Malaysian Ringgit	Singapore dollar	Thai Baht	Korean Won	Chinese Renminbi				
	11.9	12.6	11.4	19.3	13.0	15.0	16.8				
ASEAN 5 + 2 + India	Indonesian Rupiah	Philippines Peso	Malaysian Ringgit	Singapore dollar	Thai Baht	Korean Won	Chinese Renminbi	Indian Rupee			
	10.0	11.2	10.9	15.1	13.2	12.6	13.5	13.5			
ASEAN 5 + 2 + India + Australia + New Zealand	Indonesian Rupiah	Philippines Peso	Malaysian Ringgit	Singapore dollar	Thai Baht	Korean Won	Chinese Renminbi	Indian Rupee	Australian Dollar	New Zealand Dollar	
	7.6	6.8	5.2	13.4	11.7	10.4	11.0	14.2	10.3	9.5	
ASEAN 5 + 3	Indonesian Rupiah	Philippines Peso	Malaysian Ringgit	Singapore dollar	Thai Baht	Korean Won	Chinese Renminbi	Japanese Yen			
	10.0	11.2	11.5	15.3	13.7	12.6	13.3	12.3			
ASEAN 5 + 3 + India	Indonesian Rupiah	Philippines Peso	Malaysian Ringgit	Singapore dollar	Thai Baht	Korean Won	Chinese Renminbi	Japanese Yen	Indian Rupee		
	9.0	9.9	9.8	14.0	11.7	11.1	11.3	10.3	13.0		
ASEAN 5+3+India–Australia+New Zealand	Indonesian Rupiah	Philippines Peso	Malaysian Ringgit	Singapore dollar	Thai Baht	Korean Won	Chinese Renminbi	Japanese Yen	Indian Rupee	Australian Dollar	New Zealand Dollar
	7.0	6.0	4.5	12.6	10.9	9.6	9.6	8.3	13.7	9.3	8.4

Source: Authors.

Second, when the currency basket is made up of the core ASEAN 5 + 2 (China + Korea), the Singapore dollar is assigned the highest weight of 19.3 percent, while the Malaysian ringgit has the lowest weight of 11.4 percent. China and Korea together constitute about 30 percent of the currency basket. However, once the Japanese yen is treated as an insider in the basket (ASEAN 5 + 3), the Singapore dollar is still accorded the highest weight of 15.3 percent, though this time the Indonesian rupiah is accorded the lowest weight of 10 percent. China, Korea and Japan now constitute around 40 percent of the currency basket.

Third, irrespective of whether the Japanese yen is treated as an insider or as an external currency, when the currency basket is enlarged to include the Indian rupee, the highest and lowest weights go to the Singapore dollar and Indonesian rupiah, respectively, once again. When Japan is excluded, China, Korea and India constitute around 40 percent of the currency basket. When Japan is included, these four countries constitute about 55 percent of the regional basket.

Fourth, in a broader currency basket that includes ASEAN plus China, Korea, India, Australia and New Zealand, the Indian rupee is accorded the highest weight while the Malaysian ringgit gets the lowest weight (again, this is the case regardless of whether the Japanese yen is included or excluded from these currency baskets). Australia and New Zealand constitute between 15 and 20 percent of the regional basket.

Finally, regarding the issue of the frequency of revision of the currency basket weights, due to the nature of the technique we applied here, the regional currency baskets constructed from alternative configurations of Asian and Pacific national currencies are both stable over time and have little or no correlations with the individual currencies in the basket. This implies that an appreciation (depreciation) of any national currency in a given basket would not raise (lower) the value of the regional currency basket (Hovanov, Kolari and Sokolov 2004). In view of this stability, official regional bodies or agencies do not need to recompute the currency basket intermittently. This is in contrast to the proposal by Kawai (2006) of revising the currency weights every two to three years. The only time revisions would be needed in the near term is if and when the membership of the ACU changes.

11.4 Conclusion

Empirical evidence reveals that there appears to be a general trend towards somewhat greater exchange rate flexibility in Asia, though not complete flexibility. Unease clearly persists about allowing a completely free float. This is further apparent from the massive stockpiling of reserves in China (see Ouyang, Rajan and Willett 2007) and many other Asian economies (see Chapter 1 of this volume).[9] Many observers have pointed out that the export-oriented nature of the Asian economies—especially those in East Asia—has given rise to a collective action problem (the so-called "prisoner's dilemma") whereby the fear of losing competitiveness leads each of them to heavily manage its respective currency, particularly in view of the limited flexibility of the Chinese currency.[10]

In view of the above there have been growing calls for greater exchange rate and monetary coordination among Asian economies. It is in this context that there has been active discussion in the region—more specifically the East Asian subregion—about the possibility of an Asian Currency Unit (ACU) as a means of promoting a degree of explicit exchange rate stability. Clearly it would be premature to consider harmonization of Asian exchange rate and monetary policies to a common currency basket at this stage (let alone a currency union based on the ACU) when neither the economic nor the political preconditions exist to do so.[11] Attempting rigid policy coordination before the necessary preconditions are met would be like putting the cart before the horse; it is doomed to fail.[12]

This said, there remains much interest in the region on examining the role of an ACU and its possible uses, including circulation as a parallel currency cite (Eichengreen, 2006). Accordingly, much work needs to be done on developing alternative methodologies to determine appropriate basket weights.[13] This chapter has used the methodology of Hovanov, Kolari and Sokolov (2004) to compute the optimal weights. In essence the optimal basket weights computed are aimed at ensuring a regional currency basket that has minimal variance. Hence it will deliver stability in intraregional exchange rates for alternative configurations of currency baskets in the Asian and Pacific region.

According to the technique applied in this chapter the optimal solution to a regional currency basket in the Asian and Pacific region is an almost symmetric or similar currency weighting scheme between ASEAN and non-ASEAN currencies. This can be seen easily from Table 11.1, as the +2 (China and Korea) non-ASEAN national currencies and the +3 (China, Japan, Korea) non-ASEAN national currencies are effectively assigned total weights of only around 30 to 40 percent, respectively.[14] This finding is in sharp contrast to what previous studies have proposed. For instance, Ogawa and Shimizu (2006, 2007) effectively assigned a total weight of over 70 percent for the three non-ASEAN national currencies in a regional currency basket consisting of the ASEAN 10 + 3 (China, Japan and Korea). This symmetry of weighting may make the regional currency unit somewhat more politically feasible for smaller economies in ASEAN.

Notes

1. This chapter draws on an article originally published in *Macroeconomics and Finance in Emerging Market Economies*, 1 (2), 2008, 21–39 (Taylor & Francis Ltd). Reprinted with permission.
2. The acronym ACU is actually already used in Asia—the "Asian Clearing Union" has been in existence since December 1974 and is based in Tehran, Iran. This ACU was an initiative of the Bangkok-based UN-ESCAP aimed at developing a region-wide system for clearing payments among members. The current members are Bangladesh, Bhutan, India, Iran, Nepal, Pakistan, Sri Lanka and Myanmar.
3. The weights in the ECU were determined primarily by each member's shares in EC-wide GDP, intraregional trade and total quota of EMS financial support system.
4. This inertial effect of existing currencies (i.e. advantage of incumbency) is based on the concept of "network externalities" or "lock in" effects, whereby there are limited incentives for economic agents to unilaterally take on a new currency (particularly for invoicing transactions). The network aspects of the internal currency status have been analyzed theoretically by Matsuyama et al. (1993).
5. The membership issue is discussed further in Section 11.3.
6. For instance, Moon, Rhee and Yoon (2007) have argued in favour of the creation of an Asian Exchange Stabilization Fund (AESF). As they observe:

   > The objective of the AESF is more comprehensive in that it includes exchange rate stability in addition to liquidity support. In fact, the case of the EMS suggests that three pillars be combined into one institution: ECU, Provision of liquidity, and ERM. Thus, in Asia, once the (A)CU is created and once the provision of emergency liquidity can be strengthened through the CMI, then the next natural step will be to set up an appropriate exchange rate system. This could be carried out with the establishment of the AESF. (p. 20)
7. Also see Rajan (2005). India, Australia and New Zealand have joined the APT economies to be founding members of the East Asia Summit (EAS). The inaugural meeting was held in Kuala Lumpur, Malaysia in November 2005 (Kumar 2005).
8. The optimal weights that minimize the variance of a currency basket can be easily computed using familiar optimization methods for diversifying a portfolio of assets. See Hovanov, Kolari and Sokolov (2004) for details.
9. We do not broach the much-debated issue of the reasons behind the reserve buildup (i.e. insurance versus export-stimulus), except to note the following—quite reasonable—observation by the World Bank (2005):

   > Intervention was initially motivated by a desire to build up a buffer stock after the Asian crisis had depleted levels of reserves.... (H)owever (r)apid

reserve accumulation continued through late 2004, as countries sought to limit the impact of heavy capital inflows on external competitiveness, at a time when domestic demand generally remained subdued. (p. 29)

10. This in turn is contributing partly to large and growing global macroeconomic imbalances and global liquidity.
11. For a recent discussion of how well Asia fits the Optimum Currency Area (OCA) criteria, see Moneta and Rüffer (2006) and Watanabe and Ogura (2006).
12. It is possible—though unlikely—that OCA criteria may be at least partly endogenous, suggesting that some unions may be more justifiable *ex post* rather than *ex ante* (Frankel and Rose 1998).
13. Also see Moon et al. (2007) and Watanabe and Ogura (2006) for alternative computations of ACU weights.
14. If India is also included, the non-ASEAN share is still significant at around 45 percent.

References

Dayaratna-Banda, O.G. and J. Whalley (2007). "Regional Monetary Arrangements in ASEAN+3 as Insurance through Reserve Accumulation and Swaps," Working Paper No. 22, The Centre for International Governance Innovation.

Eichengreen, B. (2006). "The Parallel-Currency Approach to Asian Monetary Integration," *American Economic Review*, 96, 432–436.

Frankel, J. and A. Rose (1998). "The Endogeneity of the Optimum Currency Area Criteria," *Economic Journal*, 108, 1009–1025.

Kawai, M. (2006). "Creating an Asian Currency Unit," *The Japan Journal*, 3, September.

Hovanov, N.K., J. Kolari, and M. Sokolov (2004). "Computing currency invariant indices with an application to minimum variance currency baskets," *Journal of Economic Dynamics and Control*, 28, 1481–1504.

Kriz, P.N. and Q.T. Thai (2006). "Alternative Monetary Arrangements for Asia: A Perspective from a Multi-Country Model," mimeo, July.

Kumar, N. (2005). "Towards a Broader Asian Community: Agenda for the East Asia Summit", Discussion Paper No. 100, Research and Information System for Developing Countries (RIS), New Delhi.

Kuroda, H. (2005). "Towards a Borderless Asia: A Perspective on Asian Economic Integration," speech by Asian Development Bank (ADB) President at the Emerging Markets Forum (December 10, Oxford).

Matsuyama, K., N. Kiyotaki , and A. Matsui (1993). "Toward a Theory of International Currency," *Review of Economic Studies*, 60, 283–307.

Moneta, F. and R. Rüffer (2006). "Business Cycle Synchronisation in East Asia," Working Paper Series No. 671, European Central Bank (ECB).

Moon, W., Y. Rhee, and D. Yoon (2007). "Regional Currency Unit in Asia: Property and Perspective," mimeo, Korea Institute for International Economic Policy.

Ogawa, E. and K. Kawasaki (2006). "Adopting a Common Currency Basket Arrangement into the ASEAN plus three," Discussion Paper No. 06-E-028, REITI, Japan.

Ogawa, E. and J. Shimizu (2006). "Stabilization of Effective Exchange Rates under Common Currency Basket Systems," Working Paper No. W12198, NBER, April.

Ogawa, E. and J. Shimizu (2007). "Progress toward a Common Currency Basket System in East Asia," Discussion Paper No. 07-E-002, REITI, Japan.

Ouyang, A.Y., R.S. Rajan, and T.D. Willett (2007). "China as a Reserve Sink: The Evidence from Offset and Sterilization Coefficients," WP No. 10/2007, Hong Kong Institute for Monetary Research.

Rajan, R.S. (2005). "Asian Economic Cooperation and Integration: Sequencing of Financial, Trade and Monetary Regionalism," in *Asian Economic Cooperation and Integration: Progress, Prospects and Challenges*, Manila: Asian Development Bank.

Watanabe, S. and M. Ogura (2006). "How Far Apart Are Two ACUs from Each Other?: Asian Currency Unit and Asian Currency Union," Working Paper No. 06-E-20, Bank of Japan.

World Bank (2005). *Global Development Finance*, Washington, DC: The World Bank.

Index